CREEPY CRAWLS
A HORROR FIEND'S TRAVEL GUIDE

LEON MARCELO

FOREWORD BY HERSCHELL GORDON LEWIS

Includes the Ghastly and Ghoulish Haunts of:

Stephen King + *Halloween* + *The Exorcist* + H.P. Lovecraft + Hollywood Gravesites + Washington Irving + *Friday the 13th* + Edgar Allan Poe + *The Texas Chainsaw Massacre* + *The Amityville Horror* + George Romero's *Dead* Films + Paris, London, and Dario Argento's Rome + And More!

CREEPY CRAWLS

A HORROR FIEND'S TRAVEL GUIDE

LEON MARCELO

FOREWORD BY
HERSCHELL GORDON LEWIS

SANTA
MONICA
PRESS

Published by: Santa Monica Press LLC
P.O. Box 1076
Santa Monica, CA 90406-1076
1-800-784-9553
www.santamonicapress.com
books@santamonicapress.com

SANTA
MONICA
PRESS

Printed in the United States

Santa Monica Press books are available at special quantity discounts when purchased in bulk
by corporations, organizations, or groups. Please call our Special Sales department at 1-800-
784-9553.

ISBN 1-59580-013-1

Library of Congress Cataloging-in-Publication Data

Marcelo, Leon, 1974–
        Creepy crawls : a horror fiend's travel guide / Leon Marcelo ; foreword by Herschell
Gordon Lewis.
        p. cm.
        Includes bibliographical references.
        ISBN 1-59580-013-1
        1. Travel—Guidebooks. 2. Horror tales—Geography—Guidebooks. 3. Horror
films—Geography—Guidebooks. 4. Literary landmarks—Guidebooks. 5. Motion picture
locations—Guidebooks. 6. Cemeteries—Guidebooks. I. Title.
G153.4.M24 2006
791.43'6164—dc22
                                                                        2006008374

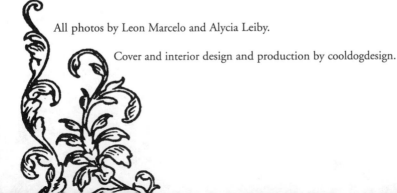

All photos by Leon Marcelo and Alycia Leiby.

    Cover and interior design and production by cooldogdesign.

Contents

"Searchers after horror
haunt strange, far
places . . ."

— H. P. Lovecraft
"The Picture in the House" (1920)

CREEPY CRAWLS

A HORROR FIEND'S TRAVEL GUIDE

is sponsored by:

Charnel House Press
Miskatonic University
Gateman, Goodbury, & Graves Funeral Parlour
The Bates Motel
Ramses Exotic Catering
Thorn Industries
Tanz Akademie (Germany)
WGON Television (Philadelphia)
Smith's Grove Sanitarium
Morningside Cemetery
Camp Crystal Lake
The Seven Doors Hotel
Farmer Vincent's Smoked Meats
WKAB Radio (Antonio Bay)
The Slaughtered Lamb Pub
S-Mart
Silver Shamrock Novelties
Civic-TV (Toronto)
Westin Hills Psychiatric Hospital
Uneeda Medical Supply
Last Round-Up Rolling Grill
Tenafly Viper Wine
Crumb's Crunchy Delights
Shoggoth's Old Peculiar Beers

Acknowledgments

FROM THE WORM-GOOEYEST
BOTTOM OF MY BLACK HEART,
THE FOULEST OF FRIGHT-FIENDING
"FANGS!" TO THE FOLLOWING
BOILS AND GHOULS . . .

lycia: my cadaverously crepuscular creepy-crawling cohort, my dreadfully bloodshot-eyed dead-itor, and my blackly unspeakable bride; my mother & father and all of my family; "UnKle" Eric Pigors; Deady Blagman; my Grimm Brother Killjoy & Necrophagia, The Ravenous, et al.; Grave Fthagner & the black goats of Abazagorath; Moribundy Sheldon & the In Memorium doom-meisters; Morgue-Ghoul Kahan & the kryptic Funebrarum brutalians; Vic-auteur-ia Timpanaro & Keith Salamunia; Cadavertis Schmitt; Herr Stevus Burp; Susin Crane; my appreciators amidst Academia: Professors Isaacs, Whitney, Belanoff, Denny, Videbaek, & Pizarro; Billy Grossera, Jill Ghoulardi, & Razorback Rex; Ryan Gore-ensen & the mad, mad, mad monster-mongers of Engorged; Maniac Neil & the stalk-and-thrash-aholics of Frightmare; the deliriously demented drive-in dread-debauchery that is Blood Freak; Bloodbath McGrath, Ross Sewage, & the Impaled Grand Guignolian grue-garglers; Gurge & the grotesquerie-gross-ers of Lord Gore; Digestor & the howlingly horrid hooded horror-horde that is Ghoul; The Horror Hive Brotherhood; Roy Sleazer & Necroharmonic Records; Joseph Gervasi & Exhumed Films/Diabolik DVD; Lou-natic Rusconi; Dennis Dread & *Destroying Angels* 'Zine; Chas Balun & the Deep Red slaughtercult; Kevin Clement

& the Chiller Theatre Foetid Family of Fiends; Ted Bohus; Dave Baumuller & *Horror Biz* Magazine; O'Neal & Kreepsville Industries; Scott Gabbey & *Ultra Violent* Magazine; Rod Gudino, Jovanka Vukovic, & *Rue Morgue* Magazine; Anthony Timpone & *Fangoria* Magazine.

If the names of any good fiends have escaped my distempered gray matter . . . SORRY!

And, last but far from least, for their endless inspiration throughout the years . . . Edgar Allan Poe; Howard Phillips Lovecraft; Vincent Price; "Uncle Forry" Ackerman & *Famous Monsters of Filmland*; William M. Gaines & E.C. Horror; Zacherley the Cool Ghoul; "Uncle Creepy," "Cousin Eerie," & Warren Horror; Herschell Gordon Lewis; Doctor Morgus the Magnificent; Elvira, Mistress of the Dark; Stephen King; Alan Moore; Chas Balun; Joe Bob Briggs; Glenn Danzig & The Misfits, Samhain, and Danzig; Chris Reifert & Autopsy; Jeff Walker & Carcass; Stevo & Impetigo; Rob Zombie.

—Leon Marcelo

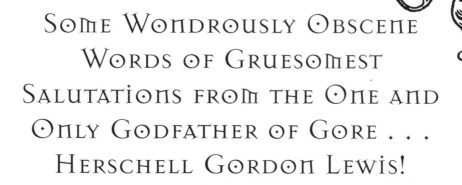

SOME WONDROUSLY OBSCENE WORDS OF GRUESOMEST SALUTATIONS FROM THE ONE AND ONLY GODFATHER OF GORE . . . HERSCHELL GORDON LEWIS!

Where is Bela Lugosi now that we need him? What? You say you don't know nor care where Bela's bones are rattling uneasily? Then what the %$#@ are you doing with this book? We both know what you're doing with this book: You realize that you've finally found the path linking horror fantasy with horror reality. And what a fascinating path it is!

Leon Marcelo's incredible blending of scholarship, dedication, and far-out sense of humor combine right here to offer the most comprehensive compendium of horror-related trivia I've ever encountered. Is *Creepy Crawls* a guidebook? Well, yes, in a way. A tribute to the ghoul and specter that lurks in all of us? Well, yes, with high good humor. The definitive and authoritative nailing-down of the 'haunts' of authors ranging from Edgar Allan Poe to Stephen King? Well, yes, absolutely. Pinpointer of locations where so many horror/cult movies were filmed? Well, yes, in greater detail and specificity than any of us ever have had such exposure before.

I salute Leon Marcelo for a genuine horror aficionado achievement. You will too. Enjoy!

—Herschell Gordon Lewis, Director of *Blood Feast, Two Thousand Maniacs!, Color Me Blood Red, The Gruesome Twosome, The Wizard of Gore, The Gore-Gore Girls*, etc.

Introduction

THE FUNERAL IS
ABOUT TO BEGIN . . .

Creepy: *Of or producing a sensation of uneasiness or fear, as of things crawling on one's skin. Annoyingly unpleasant; repulsive.*

Crawl: *The action of moving slowly on the hands or knees or dragging the body along the ground.*

But what is a. . . "Creepy Crawl"?

G hastliest grue-gargling greetings and shuddersome spook-spewing salutations, Creepy Reader, and welcome to *Creepy Crawls,* yours cruelly's ghoulish and ghastly terror-touring travel guide to the most dreadfully Horror-ed of travel destinations!

But perchance you are asking yourself, "What exactly *is* a 'creepy crawl'?!?"

Well, when I was but a wee fiend—and, verily, *still!*—I was utterly affeared of worms, centipedes, maggots, and the loathsomely wriggling like. By less than formal definitions, such an execrable thing is known as a "creepy-crawly." And anything that rouses a skin-crawling sense of sheer revulsion, as of them squirming upon your flesh, is similarly known: "creepy-crawly." While the sentiment of such a disgusting sensation—or, deeply more so, a disturbing sensibility for such unwholesomeness!—defines the hideous and heinous soul of my horror-fiending *Creepy Crawls,* it does not reveal the travel guide's unspeakable raison d'etre. To do so, I would refer to the terrors of one of America's most infamous "true crimes," from whence *Creepy Crawls'* name came.

During that sultry and shocking summer of 1969, monstrously maniacal would-be messiah Charles "No Name Maddox" Manson bid his brain-fried hippie "Family" to sneak into homes under the veil of deepest midnight darkness and sow terror in the hearts of the unsuspecting slumberers within by displacing their furniture and, deeply more dreadful, dangling knives atop or about their beds. These most morbid roadtrip "missions" were meant to be threats against those whom Manson deemed "pig"-ish members of the "Establishment" and, in the end, would herald the horrors of those infamously horrendous Tate and Labianca Murders, the disturbingly demented death-trips that are said to have killed the '60s. And Manson had called his followers' shocking night-stalkings . . . "creepy crawls."

Indeed, Manson's odiously grim little gloom-obscured outings are *Creepy Crawls'* noisomely notorious namesake and, while they and my horror fiend's travel guide do not share, in the end, so very much, the two same-named strains of spookiest strangeness do have something wicked in common: the frightfully unseemly fusion of the "crawl" and the "creepy": on the one hand, travel, and on the other—the black left hand!—terror. But there is, verily, a crucial difference, because the travel possibilities put before you on *Creepy Crawls'* putrescence-blotted chopping block—from short trips to sprawling tours—would not spread that terror without but . . . *within!*

To experience a true creepy crawl, Creepy Reader, is to embark on an expedition to the most extraordinarily eerie of exotic locations and to explore—to exhume!—all that is morbid, moribund, and macabre therein! To undertake a creepy crawl is not simply to shamble and to lurk and to scuttle but to do so—egads!—within the brutally black worm-befouled belly of . . . HORROR! The Horror, Creepy Reader! That is what *Creepy Crawls* is all about: to creep and to crawl amidst all that is creepy-crawly. Yours cruelly's *Creepy Crawls* was begotten from not only a lifelong love of traveling but a unhealthy hunger for Horror of all sordidly sickening species: the horrors of drive-in bloodbaths, grindhouse chunkblowers, and video nasties; the horrors of shudder pulps and weird tales; and even the horrors of all-too-real social and cultural relics.

Because of this, *Creepy Crawls* is a travel guide for horror fan-addicts, gorehounds, monster-mongers, splatterheads, and all species of ghouls, finks, and misfits—"horror fiends" like yours cruelly. But *Creepy Crawls* is also for travelers who, while perhaps less "Horror!"-fied, do, however, have a thirst for the odd and the obscure, the strange and the unusual . . . the creepy and the crawly!

But perchance, Creepy Reader, you are now asking yourself, "How was that most unnatural marriage of tourism and terror, sightseeing and shudders, begotten?!?"

Yours cruelly's taste for travel—particularly that of an off-beat persuasion—and for Horror were born from the same influence: my dear olde mother. With the former, it very well may have begun on a trans-America summer trip I undertook with my parents when I was, again, but a wee fiend, aged seven or eight years, during which my mother insisted that we explore each and every roadside curiosity.

But with the latter, whilst my mother forbade me from feeding upon those Horrors new to cable television and video cassette in the early and mid-'80s—for fear of such shockingly shudder some stuff, as I have heard many, many, many times since, "rotting my brain"—such disheartening matriarchal disallowance made my thirst for the abominable, the atrocious, and the abhorrent—for HORROR!—into, verily, an obsession. And it was from out of that hunger that *Creepy Crawls* was born! For with the sorrowfully cureless sickness that is what yours cruelly calls "Horror-philia," there are three degrees. Of the first, the symptoms are distinguished by a compulsion to devour all primary specimens: literature, films, magazines, comic books, and so on. Of the second, there is a desire for extremely more rare and unexpurgated delicacies, the disease thus becoming more refined yet, at the same time, more rabid. And of the third and final degree, there is utter addiction. No longer will the simple exposure to the dreadful and the disturbing, the morbid and the macabre, appease the sufferer's appetites.

No, for such individuals, there rises the cruelly insatiable compulsion to consume ("collect" in the parlance of the diseased) sundry related curiosities. And if the case is truly shocking in its severity, there may be an unnameably unnatural urge to travel to and tour the very same localities, often obscure and outlandish, where those very same Horrors—of film, of literature, of history—were birthed, such communion having the same effect upon the horror fiend as that of a reliquary upon the most pious and passionate of pilgrims.

And yours cruelly's horror fiend's travel guide, Creepy Reader, is a testimonial to this. *Creepy Crawls* is as much the appallingly repulsive and reeking annals of the creepy crawls my unspeakable wife and I have undertaken as an aid and advisory for others—be they fellow horror fiends or travelers with a taste for the untypical—who would undertake their very own creepy crawls. It is not an encyclopedia with aspirations of exhaustiveness but, in such a laundry list's stead, an extremely encomiastic exhumation of Horror's most unhallowedly eerie and eldritch haunts.

And so you must ask yourself, Creepy Reader: are you prepared for a good ghastly and gruesome olde . . . creepy crawl?!?

CREEPY CRAWLS' 13 RULES FOR THE REVOLTINGLY REPULSIVE WOULD-BE ILL-RUMOR-RESURRECTIONING CREEPY CRAWLER!

1) Do your research. Where are you going, why are you going there, and what EXACTLY are you going there for?!?

2) Investigate different sources of travel literature. It is always better to have more, instead of less, on your creepy crawl's chopping block.

3) While it is good to have an itinerary so that your creepy crawl isn't an utterly helter-skelter undertaking, don't be a slave to it!

4) If you will be doing your creepy crawl by meatwagon, be sure that it is in good motoring condition!

5) Be sure to have some good—new and detailed!—maps and, perhaps, rudimentary directions between locations.

6) Don't forget to bring a good camera—dependable and easy to use—and lots of film for your Horror-ed crime scene photography. And remember: coverage is key!

7) And don't forget to bring a "souvenir kit" with you on your creepy crawl—at the very least some plastic bags—so that you can collect some of the locations' Horror-ed charnel earth for your crypt's curio cabinet!

8) If you are bringing a fiend (or two or three . . .) along with you on your creepy crawl, be sure that they won't be a drag. If they don't have

ANY interest in where you're going and what you're going there for—and won't respect YOUR interests—they'll become "dead weight" VERY fast!

9) Whilst you are upon your creepy crawl, be a truly horrid ambassador of Horror by respecting the location and the locals but . . .

10) BE CAREFUL! Remember: You are a stranger in a very strange land—and some inhabited by those who utterly hate their Horror-ed infamy—so watch out!

11) Sometimes, you will find nothing but the inhuman remains of a location or, if there is indeed some good meat upon its bones, you won't be able to feast upon any of it for various reasons. Unfortunately, so goes a creepy crawl now and again. So try to make the most out of what you do indeed drag onto your creepy crawl's chopping block!

12) And whilst you are upon your creepy crawl, try to see what else those unknown parts have to offer. You never know WHAT you'll find . . . !

13) And lastly but not leastly . . . HAVE FUN! It isn't truly a creepy crawl if you are not having a foully foetid coffin-full of frightfully fiendish fun!

And so, Creepy Reader, for those about to ROT . . . *Creepy Crawls* salutes you!

PART ONE

Creepy Crawls of Horror in Culture & Society:
In Search of Monstrously
Man-Made Murder,
Madness, and the
Macabre

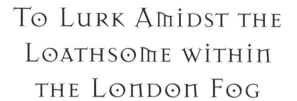

Chapter One

To Lurk Amidst the Loathsome within the London Fog

"There's a hole in the world
Like a great black pit
And the vermin of the world
Inhabit it
And its morals aren't worth
What a pig could spit
And it goes by the name of . . . London"

—Stephen Sondheim
Sweeney Todd: The Demon Barber of Fleet Street (1979)

C an you *see* it, Creepy Crawls Reader? The soot-darkened faces of gloriously architectured churches and monuments that have stood as somber witnesses to the births and deaths of the kings and queens of that empire on which, for some centuries, the sun never set? Can you *smell* it? The pungent odour of ceaselessly churning industry and enterprise and an endless offering of curiosities, domestic or foreign—palatable or not? Can you *feel* it? A suffocating dankness enshrouding you as you journey down some eldritch street through dusk's fog as a blood-red moon rises before you?

Yes . . . *London*, a city begotten about the Roman-constructed progenitor of the present day London Bridge at the very dawn of the Common Era and called "Londinium" (a name with Celtic, not Latin, roots), burgeoning ever forward throughout the sprawling centuries, its cultural identity and language—its very nature—influenced by the Saxons and the Normans from without and the Tudor, Stuart, and Georgian monarchies from within.

But there is *another* London, a shadow-drenched underbelly, a horror-darkened underworld where corruption and chaos, death and decay, await the all-too-unsuspecting, and about which the dusty pages of common history books can tell us but little. And it is this "London"— the veritable horridly wicked Mr. Hyde to the thoroughly more decent, and *safe*, Dr. Jekyll of the British Mecca where tourists the world over search for Buckingham Palace, and, yes, Big Ben and Parliament—that Horror-worshippers, olde and young alike, know and love, a portrait rendered in celluloid by such creepshow classicks as *The Demon Barber of Fleet Street* (1936) and *Corridors of Blood* (1962*)*, a delightfully dreadful drove of Hammer and Amicus shockers throughout the '60s and '70s, and, most recently, *Mary Reilly* (1996) and *From Hell* (2001).

But such romantically rotted realizations of a remarkably repugnant London are truly not the products of sinema but of popular Victorian literature. Authors such as Robert Louis Stevenson, Oscar Wilde, and Bram Stoker, in *The Strange Case of Dr. Jekyll and Mr. Hyde, The Picture of Dorian Gray*, and *Dracula* respectively, transported the "Gothic" heinousness, hideosities, and horrors of the archetypal late-eighteenth/early-nineteenth-century "terrorist" works of Anne Radcliffe, "Monk" Lewis, and the beguilingly reverent Reverend Charles Maturin from the foreign soils of Italy and Spain to the fog-shrouded streets of London.

Along with the blood-and-guts charnel house spooks of "penny dreadfuls," these post-Gothic progenitors of what would come to be modern horror literature helped to make London the black heart of horror itself, repulsively stirring with the worms of iniquity and revoltingly seeping with the black blood of even blacker infamy.

However, such fictional simulacra would seem to pale, utterly, before the all-too-real ghastly and grim *fact* of Victorian London. As portrayed vividly through the non-Horror, yet not horrorless, novels of Charles Dickens such as *Oliver Twist* (1837–39) and *Our Mutual Friend* (1865), the nineteenth century, particularly as defined by "The Victorian Era," that, while verily an age of industrial, commercial, scientific, medical, artistic, and, most significantly, *imperial* flourishings, saw England—London—awash with poverty, disease, crime, perversion, and murder most foul. Olde ways and even older orders were dying and it would seem that, in London, the birth of the new century and, with it, modernity, was heralded by deliriously dread-ridden devotions of derangement, depravity, and death. In such a way, the lascivious and lurid reality of Victorian London is a profoundly more shuddersome source of the most horrendously horrid of Horror than the pages of any book: Highgate Cemetery, the Tyburn Tree, The Tower of London, Bedlam, anatomists and resurrectionists, Jack the Ripper, Sweeney Todd, etc.

And so, when my necrotically fragrant bride and I took leave of our rotten Rot Island abode to journey across that so-called "Pond" for the fog-choked streets of London, our less than wholesome appetites wanted nothing of the traditional temptations of the typical London tourist: the gaudy garishness of the Crown Jewels; the disgusting diseasedness of Trafalgar Square's pigeons; or—dare I say it?—the heart-attacking hardiness of the seemingly countless "authentic" fish-and-chip shoppes.

No. We hungered, like two grave robbers of a ghoulishly ghastly yore for a freshly interred corpse, to dig up coffinfuls of curiosities of a most curiously cadaverous sort, those very same monstrously macabre and morbid mementos of the woefully wicked past of the "City on the Thames." So won't you grab your favorite shovel, Creepy Crawls Reader, and join me as yours cruelly begins this exhumation of the all-too-real Horrors of London!

☉F DEATH & THE DEAD

My unspeakable wife and I would make our crypt-away-from-krypt whilst in London amidst the city's quarter known as Bloomsbury, mere blocks from Russell Square. In days gone by, Bloomsbury was not only the traditional home of London's book publishing trade but also the home of some of literature's most renowned authors, witnessing the production of such litterateurs as that embodiment of Victoriana, Charles Dickens, and belletristic American expatriate T. S. Eliot.

While many a bookseller, whether of rare editions or the most current printings, can still be found amongst its streets, Bloomsbury's superfluity of hotels, restaurants, travel bureaus, currency exchangers, and souvenir shoppes selling such classy sundries as "Mind the Gap" Underground panties and a dubious assortment of nudie postcards attest to its present state as a popular tourist way station.

What made our adopted Bloomsbury charnel house for our week in London so very befitting the infamously incessant nature of our ill-rumoredly ichorous itinerary was the seeming accessibility of Russell Square's Underground station. Put simply, we two most tenebrous of thanatologists would need to become very, very familiar with London's subway system—known variously as the "Underground" or the "Tube"—if we wanted to truly glut our grim and grisly gruehound gullets as heartily as the all-too-hungry East Enders did upon a steamingly Horror-splattered platter of Mrs. Lovett's all-too-human meat pies.

And so, descending deep down into the dark belly of the London Underground by way of one of Russell Square's three cattle car-like lifts, my black bride and I could conceive of no better way to begin our ungentle exhumation of London's most egregiously exquisite of execrable eeriness than with a leisurely lurch through the very archetype of Victorian necropoli: Highgate Cemetery.

HIGHGATE CEMETERY
Swain's Lane N6
(44) 020 8340 1834
(Friends of Highgate)

Rising from out of the Archway Tube Station, we beheld the Highgate quarter of London in all its gray drabness. North of London proper—or "London Town" as it is called—the area began in the Middle Ages as a hilltop staging post (thus the "high" and thus the "gate") and, because of its untainted serenity, became a popular location for the country manors of the rich and the noble seeking escape from the continually swelling—and sordid—limits of the city.

But such exclusivity fell away to the suburban sprawl of the eighteenth and nineteenth centuries, which perhaps explains why, as we gruesome twosome wormed our woeful way up Highgate Hill, we walked past, on one side of the street, a row of fine Georgian and Victorian homes while there stood, on the other, the hulking concrete and brick edifices of more simple housing.

Up through the middle-class neighborhood that is now Highgate we shambled until we came to Waterlow Park at the welcome end of Highgate Hill and the beginning of Highgate High Street. And it was but a few minutes more about Waterlow's winding walking paths before we saw it looming before us: Highgate Cemetery.

Highgate's almost 170-year-old cemetery is actually hewn into two unequal lots: one east of Swain's Lane and another west of that narrow, house-lined road. The former, which abuts the back of Waterlow Park, was installed but 20 years after the latter, but, perhaps because of the regularity of its rows of simply ornamented plots and its general wide openness, it appears much, much newer.

Somewhat modest in size, this eastern allotment of the cemetery actually seems to draw more visitors than its adjacent brethren in the burial business, not only because it houses the earthly remains of Highgate's most famous subterranean inhabitant, Karl Marx (whose devotees can be identified by their "radical" adornments of red communist stars and tassled, black-and-white Arabian scarves), but because, simply, a guided tour is not needed to traipse about its orderly and sun-lit (at least for London!) grounds. But unless a dog-eared edition of *Das Kapital* never leaves your nightstand, this portion of Highgate is all but dispensable, offering nothing, truly, which other, and less renowned, burial grounds do not already offer.

But such is not the case with the latter of Highgate's two allotments. No. For it is this older, western portion that has made Highgate's name deeply notorious. It is this greatly sprawling and profoundly eldritch face of Highgate festering upon the opposite side of Swain's Lane that for true, and truly fiendish, aficionados of all that is funereal, offers moldering cemeterial wonders that can be rivaled only by the likes of Paris's Père-Lachaise—and, even then, only arguably so. And it was here, to ill-reputed

Highgate Cemetery, that we were called like black-winged crows to even blacker carrion.

With its forbidding castle-like façade, Highgate Cemetery's gatehouse broods gloomily upon the western aspect of Swain's Lane and only hints at the grand, and grandly Victorian, grimness that lurks behind its sepulchral austerity. While this gatehouse had once held the cemetery's chapel and the spiritual like, its space is now used for less theistic purposes, namely the housing of the place's administrative offices and a humble (and very tasteful) gift shoppe.

After waiting outside its blackly bleak wrought iron gates for the very first of the day's handful of guided tours, we were beckoned within the cemetery's open-air foyer and, after a few words from our senior yet spry chaperone, were ushered beneath a memorial arch and then up a short set of stairs. When we came to the head of that flight, it was as if yours cruelly had entered an utterly foreign land which knew nothing—*wanted* to know nothing—of the London we had left behind: a shadow-drenched land weltering in a heavy miasma of inexorable mortality and seething with a disturbingly deep sense of inexplicable mortal dread—a true and utter land of the dead.

Before us lay a simple dirt path hacked out of the thick foliage which enshrouded the whole cemetery and, as we followed our aged tour guide down this, creeping further and further into the ghastly belly of this oft-esteemed "most 'evil' place in London," we slowly espied the wondrous wealth of woe-begotten funerary monuments that moldered on either side of us, an estimation of their sheer number being an impossibility as they were eventually swallowed by the vegetation beyond. We made our

way past row upon row (upon row!) of Celtic crosses of varying size and form, sepulchers both modest and ostentatious, and a copious congregation of simple tombstones, such an already plentifully begloomed cemeterial vista made all the more thrillingly shuddersome by a profoundly

eerie patina of green moss and their generally deformed posture, some leaning this way and others that.

Upon, atop, and even within these somber tributes to the dearly departed were memento mori of a particularly Victorian species, among them: empty Chairs representing the absence of the once-living, the shawl laid over their arms as Death; eternally beatific angels, their stone wings in different stages of unfurling; little lambs and cherubs representing the loss of the all-too young; and an obscure host of Freemason iconography as well as symbolism of a similarly cryptic nature, testimonials to the nineteenth-century's obsession with all things to do with mysticism.

Some graves were honored by an immortally loyal bestiary, such as the effigy of "Nero the Lion" who sleeps docilely upon the tomb of nineteenth-century "menagerist" George Wombwell, founder of what was, for a time, England's largest and most popular animal amusement, or that of "Lion the Hound" whose mourning for his master, Victorian bare-knuckle boxing champion Thomas Sayers, knows no end.

While that dirt path and the funeral statuary that lay just to either side of it were well-kept and in a general state of orderliness, thus testifying to an ongoing—and doubtlessly exhausting—renovation, this was, unfortunately, the exception and not the rule, as, throughout our expedition through the eldritch boneyard, we beheld chaos reigning within the corpse-heavy necropolis that is Highgate Cemetery.

With vines as thick as men's arms winding about headstones and obelisks, fully-grown sycamores growing up through sundered tombs, and suffocating brambles enshrouding distant acreage and the plots therein, it was obvious that, for some time, Nature had held sway here and, despite recent attempts at wholesale landscaping, verily did so still. But we also found funerary angels who had suffered different acts of dismemberment at the hands of vandals and tombs and vaults that looked as if they had been wholly violated, their charnel holdings, part or whole, perhaps long-since absconded.

While the cemetery, perhaps not unlike any of its ilk, is rumored to be the location of a host of supernatural phenomena—such as the ghostly appearance of a madwoman who is said to creep frantically amongst the graves for the children who died under her very own hands or the tall, top-hatted revenant who has been seen dissipating through the cemetery's Swain's Lane walls—Highgate's *true* infamy is the product of something all-too-natural, all-too-*human*: black masses, animal sacrifices, graverobbings, vampyric predation, and murder that plagued the necropolis during the acid-mad occult heyday of the '60s and '70s.

The most infamous of all those guilty of conducting such unlawful acts within Highgate was Allan Farrant, who, despite calling himself a vampire hunter and, thus, Highgate's would-be watchdog, was charged with and convicted of, in 1974, various counts of grave desecration and—

egads, Creepy Reader!—corpse molestation. But such dastardly dread-ridden doings were not always Highgate's defining nature.

The very first cadavers were interred within Highgate Cemetery's virgin earth in 1839, when those gates on Swain's Lane opened for "business." Before then, death— better yet, the decomposing left- overs of death—was a matter of no little distress in good grim and ghastly olde London.

After spreading throughout Asia and Europe during the fourteenth century, a bacterium called *Yersinia pestis*, began passing to humans from both fleas and rats. Calamitously, *both* species, came to an already overpopulated London by way of seafaring tradeships in the year 1348. Having already laid waste, historians say, to a quarter of Europe's medieval population (a jaw-dropping sum of 25 million), what became known as "The Black Plague" killed so very many Londoners (anywhere from 17,000 to 50,000 by different late-fourteenth-century records) that there were too few living-and-breathing residents left to bury them, at the very least not properly. Because of this, plague pits were dug and the black-skinned, pus-dripping, buboes-ridden corpses were cast, helter-skelter, into their yawning maws—the rich and the poor, the young and the old, herein finally tasting a cruelest flavour of the equality life had denied them.

After disappearing, inexplicably, the bubonic plague returned to London in the summer of 1665. Throughout that woe-begotten season, the sweltering heat allowed a swarm of pestilence-bearing fleas to swell unfetteredly and to infect, unknowingly, that generation of London's inhabitants with the dreadful bacillus, the "distemper," as Daniel Defoe called it in his *Journal of the Plague Year*, which snuffed out the lives of some 70,000 by official records. As three centuries before, so too were

mass graves the only practical solution for disposing of those contagion-stewing cadavers.

A year after the black dawn of the Great Plague, on the mourning of Sunday, September 2, to be exact, a simple kitchen fire in the Pudding Lane bakery of Thomas Farryner, King Charles II's very own baker, spread throughout the plastered, timber-skeletoned buildings and "wattle-and-daub" shanties that crowded the city's already narrow and labyrinthine streets.

By the time this seething inferno was finally stifled three days later, it is said that four-fifths of London had been devoured by its flames: more than 13,000 dwellings and 87 churches were consumed by the conflagration, leaving 200,000 Londoners homeless and indigent. Amidst such wholesale destruction, only five deaths were recorded.

In the end, the Great Fire of 1666 did indeed have some "positive" results. Perhaps most fortunate of all, the fire saw an end to the previous year's Great Plague. But it also burned a way towards the modernization of that hitherto medievally-cast city. Because of the Great Fire, London had been freed for replanning and redesigning. This wholesale reconstruction not only made London better, it made London bigger—*much* bigger.

By the end of the eighteenth century, London had become the largest city in the world, its population swelling from approximately 600,000 to over a million in the course of only a century. At the end of the Great Fire, London's churchyards had already been choked with year after year of corpses. With the dawn of the nineteenth century, they were very literally—and very loathsomely—*overflowing* with them. Cadavers had been buried upon cadavers buried upon cadavers, the natural (or *un*natural) product of which was the foetid earth of these oh-so-modest boneyards bulging like a grotesque belly that has gobbled too many dead-meat pies.

As outside them, inhumations within London's churches were no better. It was tradition that only the very rich and the very powerful were buried inside the churches themselves, either within the vaults and crypts beneath the churches or within the churches' very floors. However, their eminence did not spare their corpses the same gruesome and ghastly fate of the poor and the feebles. Because of the inevitably decreasing quality of even these interments due to their inexorable demand, the flagstones that lay atop the churches' dirt floors—and on the church pews atop them—are said to have faltered or fallen through.

But such a morbid mortal muddle was, seemingly, the least of London's worries when it came to the grave matter of death. By the beginning of the 1800s, the poor state of tombyards within London had given way to some less than wholesome commercial ventures: the theft of coffin planks for fire wood; the exhumation of paupers' bones for use as fertilizer; and, most unspeakable of all, the robbing of whole—and, most important of all, *fresh*—corpses by the ghoulish hands of body snatchers, also known, variously, as "resurrectionists" or "resurrection men," for use by anatomists and medical students.

In *Our Mutual Friend*, the last novel ever completed by Charles Dickens, the author wrote of the "healthy" adjacency of the mobbed neighborhood to the revoltingly more populated graveyard, such a portrait making the grim realities of death and decomposition—corporal corruption most foetidly factual—an inescapable part of London life. And because of such felonious charnel foulness continuously infaming London's ubiquitous churchyards, something was needed to contend with such "unhealthiness." Parliament's answer came in the form of mammoth private cemeteries skirting London's periphery. And, yes, Highgate was one of these.

Highgate was opened for the cemetery business in 1839. And because of its picturesque remoteness, its beautifully landscape grounds, and, more than anything else, its astonishingly grand array of funereal artistry—gravestones, tombs, monuments, and so on—Highgate became *the* London necropolis. It became a popular, if not wholly fashionable, place for Londoners to while away a mourning or afternoon, strolling, in wonder, in the shadow of its Gothic, Romanesque, and Arabesque ostentation.

Perhaps the height of Highgate's Victorian grandeur was and, for sarcophagic spook-hounds of a shockingly sinister sort such as we, still *is* the allotment of the cemetery opened up to Egyptian Avenue. The façade of Egyptian Avenue's imposing vestibule, with its twin pairs of towering Pharaonic pillars and fancifully carved mantle, looked like something out of the adventure pulp-y pages of H. Rider Haggard's *She.*

As we lurched beneath this ingress and down the mausoleum-ranked throat of Egyptian Avenue, it was with no small rise of goosebumps. The heavily vegetation-canopied open roof of the passage left us drenched in shadows as we trudged up past the vaulted remains of London's most prominent families. When we left such darkness, it was to step out into what is called the "Circle of Lebanon," its very name testifying yet again to Victorian England's obsession with the Arabesque. And as this name suggests, the Circle was an outer ring of wall-tombs circumscribing an interior turn of the same.

Walking about the pathway that split the two charnel house circles filled yours cruelly with an inexplicable tinge of the alien, not only because of the continuously rounded flow of the tombs' faces but the overall sensation of being *entombed* between them. While creeping within the Circle of Lebanon is an utterly thrilling experience, we had to climb the steps out and over that outer wall to behold its true sublimity. Because from such a vantage point, we were finally able to perceive that, atop the Circle's interior hub was not yet more masonry but a green-grassed lawn and, in the middle of this, the Circle's namesake: a majestic Lebanon Cedar, or "Cedar of Lebanon" as it is known Biblically, that is said to be three centuries old.

Witnessing Highgate's Circle of Lebanon thusly and drinking in all its gloriously grim grandiosity, it is no wonder that the Friends of Highgate, a crew of voluntary custodians who took over the responsibility of the eldritch cemetery's management and maintenance a few years after its unfortunate closure on financial grounds in 1975, was recognized with a Europa Nostra Award in 2000 for the restoration of this most extraordinary of Highgate's cemeterial offerings. And from what we saw with our very own bloodshot eyes—eyes that have espied an *unhealthy* slew of boneyards—of the Circle of Lebanon and the rest of Highgate's funereal wonders, its Friends deserve much, much more than an award for their restoration and conservation of such a gorgeously grand necropolis as this!

CAFÉ-IN-THE-CRYPT
St. Martin-in-the-Fields
Trafalgar Square
020 7766 1129

After lurking amongst the doom-wrought and dread-worthy properties of ill-renowned Highgate Cemetery, my black bride and I were taken by a hunger of a more dietary sort. So as we came down from Highgate, what did our gray matter come to as a culinary establishment where we could "tuck in" to some delectable gastronomic delicacies of a thoroughly *English* sort? A traditional pub for some fish and chips with malted vinegar? The grocers for a prepackaged triangle-cut sandwich? Any one of the too, too many American fast food slop-houses that plague London like the pest-bearing rats of yore?

No, Creepy Reader. After a long mourning's shamble amongst the cemetery's molderingly morbid mysteries, we gruesome twosome could think of no more appropriate a way to fill our horrors-hollowed bellies than with visit to a *crypt*, of corpse! And so we took the Tube to Trafalgar Square, weaving in and out of the tourists who flock there like the pigeons they come to throw crumbs of stale bread at before the square's twin granite fountains, and wound our way to St. Martin-in-the-Fields and its Café-in-the-Crypt!

While the building of the present church at St. Martin-in-the-Fields, conceived by James Gibbs whose design went on as the blueprint for the Colonial style in the United States, was finished in 1726, a church of some kind or another has stood upon the very same lot since the very early thirteenth century. And beneath this historic temple is its aged crypt, which, with its vaulted brick ceiling, its pillar and archway embellishments, its dusky lighted expanse, and, most gloom-effusing of all, its gravestone-inlaid floor, makes for an utterly spine-tingling experience.

While the crypt's use for the deposition of London's dead ended in 1774 due to those already described dangers born of the desperate premium on burial space (by this time St. Martin's simple—and small—graveyard, it is said, had already swallowed some 60,000 corpses), this did not mean that its overall use had ended.

Following World War I, St. Martin's crypt was used as a harbor for not only down-and-out veterans but for all of London's displaced and destitute. Some years later, it was used as an air-raid shelter when the Third Reich's Blitzkrieg struck London. While this sort of altruism still defines St. Martin's, as the church continues to help the homeless through a regular soup kitchen, its crypt also houses both the London Brass Rubbing Centre and the Café-in-the-Crypt.

Walking through the crafts market that is erected within St. Martin's perpetually open gates, my unspeakable wife and I found the front of St. Martin's and, within the vestibule there, the way downstairs to the eerily aromatic belly of the Café-in-the-Crypt. The simple wooden sign that we passed beneath, which welcomed hungry patrons such as us with the promise, in gold letters, of "fresh food prepared on the premises daily and licensed beverages" did little to ready yours cruelly for the prospect of a stomach-grumbling drove of midday diners standing in wait upon the eldritch headstones of the centuries-long dead for a little morsel of lunch.

The respectably wholesome repast dished out, cafeteria-style, by the eatery's servers varied from differing kinds salads and pastas to hot entrées such as a chicken-and-sausage goulash of some nameless sort and was sufficiently appetizing to appeal to common Londoners and not simply tourists with a taste for the weird.

However, the true reason to descend upon the dread-delicacy that was the Café-in-the-Crypt was not a meal but to savor its surroundings—the odd and olden stuff of that titular crypt. After our meal was eaten, we two ghastly grotesquerie gore-mands *truly* feasted, as we lurked about espying the floor, for it was here where the death-begotten beating of the crypt's black heart rang out amongst the chattering of the clientele and the clattering of their silverware.

The gravestones were arranged across the floor like a sort of marvelously morbid mosaic and their faces had been rubbed to a high sheen by the passage of innumerable shod feet. Because of this, sadly, their inscriptions, with all

but a few exceptions, were seemingly in various states of erasure. That said, though, despite such gravely unfortunate disengraving and those most proverbial of time's ravages, many of them still displayed the most exquisite of memento mori: skulls and crossbones, gravediggers' shovels, lilies, and so on. And for ghouls such as we, Creepy Reader, is there a finer ambience with which to digest our humble lunch whilst deep down in the darkness of a crypt?

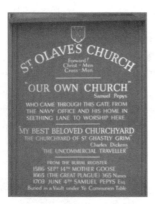

"SAINT GHASTLY GRIM"
(St. Olave's Church)
8 Hart Street
020 7488 4318

Our day's dread-worshipping dwellings amidst London's dead-delicacies was coming to an end. But there was indeed time enough for a last nasty taste of the necrosed—small but oh-so-wormily sweet! And so, leaving St. Martin's Café-in-the-Crypt behind us, my black bride and yours cruelly took the Tube to the Tower Hill Station, overlooking the abominable imperial austerity of the Tower of London, and crept towards Hart Street.

After all of the death in which we had already weltered so revelingly, what, Creepy Reader, could have possibly summoned us to such a seemingly unassuming stretch of London? The answer stood grimly—perhaps the very *definition* of the word, in stone and iron—at the corner of Hart Street and Seething Lane: St. Olave's Church.

There are many, many churches in London, but there are *none* like St. Olave's. Because of its bleakly gray walls with their abundant (and abundantly barbed) spikes and its stone-and-black-wrought-iron churchyard gate with its triumverate-of-death's-heads-adorned cornice, its spike-impaled-skull corners, and its motto, in Latin, reading "Death Is a Light to Me," the simple church (spatially speaking, not structurally!) has become known more commonly, and infamously, as "Saint Ghastly Grim"!

St. Olave's is named after King Olaf of Norway who, in 1014, pulled down the primeval, wood-thewed London Bridge in his efforts to bring down England's Saxon reign, namely that of the Dane Sweyn Forkbeard, and, in doing so, became the unattributed inspiration for that traditional children's rhyme of the bridge's "falling down." It is not at all surprising, then, that the small church is but blocks east of its steely modern incarnation built in the 1970s.

St. Olave's lacks the utter enormity, in size and shape both, of either of those neighboring landmarks, the Tower of London or the London Bridge. Medievally built (circa 1450), St. Olave's proper is a completely modest edifice that is perhaps best defined by its seeming resiliency: the church is but one of 14 that escaped that Great Fire of 1666 and, in spite of renovation and some wholesale rebuilding following wartime demolition by way of German bombs, much of its original self remains.

As the blue wooden sign affixed next to that churchyard gate attests, such a thusly defined construction is further distinguished by its historic postmortem parishioners. While St. Olave's—or at least its churchyard—does indeed lay its claim to the earthly remains of "Mother Goose," buried "1586 Sept. fourteenth," the church is most famous for the dutiful Sunday attending of Samuel Pepys, the seventeenth-century Seething Lane diarist in whose journals are recorded his firsthand experiences of not only the

Great Plague but the Great Fire as well. Pepys was interred beneath St. Olave's altar in 1703 beside his wife who preceded him to this final resting place by a little more than 30 years.

But even given all this, though, St. Olave's would simply be yet another of London's aged churches. But this is, again, Saint Ghastly Grim. How, Creepy Reader? It is said that the churchyard of St. Olave's—no, Saint Ghastly Grim!—which would, more than likely, be deemed small by even small churchyard standards, swallowed the putrefacted and pestilentially pustulant corpses of 365 of the Great Plague's unfortunate victims. The very earth of Saint Ghastly Grim's simple tomb-yard was thusly swollen, so much so that, in the years thereafter, stairs were built to get to its hitherto equal-heighted olde south entrance.

Its gate on Seething Lane, what with its verily ghastly and grim char-nel house aesthetic, exemplified that very same ethos dripping off the works of other post-plague artists such as those morbidly macabre Flemings, Peter Breughel, and Hans Memling. And even though it, by its very own inscription, dates from 1658 and, thus, predates the Great Plague by, at the very most, seven years, Saint Ghastly Grim's churchyard gate would seem to testify to the all-consuming morbid colouring of life embraced by that life-weary epoch, still so very scarred, seemingly, by the Black Death of 300 years previous.

All in all, as my crepuscular wife and I wormed our way about St. Ghastly Grim's humbly-sized boneyard and gaped, without end, at its grotesquely gorgeous death-glorifying gate outside, yours cruelly could only pay respects to Charles Dickens for thusly naming St. Olave's so very properly in 1860's *The Uncommercial Traveler.*

Although not at St. Olave's Sunday mass, we two appalled explorers of the nethermost limits of blackest moribundity did indeed worship before this awe-fillingly atrocious altar of Death that is Saint Ghastly Grim as Dickens had himself done more than a century before. And as Dickens wrote, "[T]here is attraction of repulsion for me in Saint Ghastly Grim." Indeed!

Of Anatomists & Resurrection Men

Having buried London's harrowing hoard of hideously horrid death-and-burial-holdings, we sank down into a deep sleep, that little sweet taste of oblivion, and dreamed of the wickedly wretched wonders that the city had still to retch forth for us, like the morgue-mysteries of a fresh cadaver.

While our previous day's exploration amidst London's eerily deadest ends was dreadfully delightful, this next chapter of our exploration of its macabre and morbid underbelly would be flavoured by an ill-repute-investigating itinerary of a different sort. Whereas we had seen the different final resting places of generation after generation of London's dead, we would be bearing droolingly dread-devouring witness to a far different—and less restful—fate for slab after slab of Londoners' corpses. For this new day would see us stepping out of the cemetery and the crypt into the hallowedly healthful—and no less horror-choked because of it!—halls of the Victorian hospital.

And so we two gruesome twosome pulled on our grue-encrusted operating coats, pulled together the tools of the thanatological trade, and left for our rounds of London's most monstrously morbid medical mal-practices. And the first, Creepy Reader, was London's only surviving nineteenth-century surgical setting: the Old Operating Theatre!

THE OLD OPERATING THEATRE MUSEUM & HERB GARRET
St. Thomas's Church
9a St. Thomas Street
020 7955 4791

When the Tube got to the London Bridge Station, we walked out into the mourning's sun thawing the south bank of the River Thames and then, mourning the day's absence of London's familiar fancy-feeding foggery, lurched up Duke Street Hill to Borough High Street. From there, we turned onto St. Thomas Street and saw the seventeenth-century tower of St. Thomas's Church looming before us in all its red-and-white-bricked antiquity. The exact date of St. Thomas's construction is not known and it is believed to have begun as the chapel of a medieval hospital—St. Thomas's Hospital—that had stood upon that tract of land amidst the shadow of the London Bridge—what is now Borough High Street—since 1215.

An even *older* incarnation of St. Thomas's had been founded more than 100 years before by Bishop Giffard of Winchester as part of the priory of St. Mary Overie (Southwark Cathedral, just across Borough High Street); however, this ancestor was destroyed in a massive fire that had escaped from the London Bridge and, later, was rebuilt here, self-sufficient in its secularity yet still handled by monks and nuns. While initially founded as a place offering hospitality to the pious, such as to journeying pilgrims (such an archaic function thus giving "hospitals" their name), St. Thomas's nature was defined by medical healing and surgery.

In the centuries following its inception, St. Thomas's Hospital earned a less than commendable repute. In the sixteenth century, its administration was accused of theft, extortion, and wholesale immorality and, thus, the already aged hospital was esteemed "bawdy" and closed in 1540. The place was left to dereliction and deterioration for some years until the mid-1550s, when Edward VI brought together an assortment of London's older hospitals (such as St. Bartholomew's and St. Mary at Bethlehem, known more infamously as "Bedlam"!) as a royally-sponsored assemblage to provide for the poor and, thus, St. Thomas's experienced its resurrection. It was rebuilt and expanded over the seventeenth and very early eighteenth centuries. Sometime during the 1720s, Guy's Hospital arose beside St. Thomas's (at first intended to treat the so-called "incurables" that its elder refused to see) and, together, the two saw to the education, both academically and practically, of class after class of London's future physicians.

However, London's Victorian zenith brought with it a slew of substantial changes for the then more than 600-year-old hospital. Most severely, a Parliamentary resolution to restructure railway thoroughfares would put a new line within feet of St. Thomas's newly built northern surgical block. Because of this, St. Thomas's directors, their protests unheard by Parliament, made the decision, supported by none other than Florence Nightengale, to move St. Thomas's to the London suburb of Lambeth and, thus, the hospital's olden doors closed, for good, in June of 1862.

Thereafter, much of St. Thomas's structures were pulled down, all except for its southern surgical block and, of corpse, St. Thomas's Church, which adjoins it. The former came under the supervision of London's Post Office. During their renovation of these properties for their own, thoroughly different, purposes, a doorway that had fed into the garret of St. Thomas's Church was walled up. Another entranceway to this very same garret was similarly blocked up with bricks.

In 1956, research on the history of St. Thomas's Hospital was begun by Raymond Russell and an investigation of what lay behind those bricked-over doorways undertaken. And what was found, Creepy Reader? St. Thomas's Old Operating Theatre, England's oldest, its once moan-echoing walls and blood-weltered floor unseen for almost a century. And it was here that yours cruelly was climbing up through that very same tower of St. Thomas's Church.

When my unspeakable wife and I got to the landing of the Old Operating Theatre Museum, we were relieved to put behind us the tower's entombingly narrow, twisting staircase, a length of rope hanging down through its throat, from top to bottom, to help its veritable climbers. From it, we stepped out into, naturally, the museum's small gift shoppe, which was stuffed with a smorgasbord of medically-themed sundries: various games and kits, such as diminutive see-through models of the human corpus; books on all matters of medical history—curiosity, anomaly, and, most dreadfully, criminality; and a whole host of smaller souvenirs like post cards, pamphlets, and so on. Saving such consumption for our exit, we paid our entrance fee and made our way, up a smaller set of stairs heading behind and then atop the shoppe's counter, to St. Thomas's hoary herb garret.

With its oak-framed ceiling and wonderfully creaky wooden floor, the herb garret—basically, the liberally-sized attic of St. Thomas's Church—looked as it must have when it was still used, this simulacrum furthered by the adornment everywhere of herbs, such as liquorice,

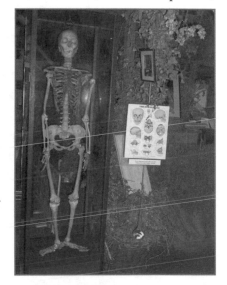

pennyroyal, marshmallow, and that most malefically mysterious "cure-all," wormwood, all of them either hung up as if being dried or stored in baskets and bowls of all sizes as well as glass vessels.

While the garret's use as such is believed to have begun with the very beginnings of the church itself, the first recorded use of the garret's herbs for the medicinal purposes of St. Thomas's Hospital dates back to Elizabethan times. The maintenance of the garret's herbs, as well as their dispensation, was headed by St. Thomas's official apothecary, who was traditionally the hospital's chief resident. He would also oversee the herbs preparation for various ailments and surgeries, an example of which, "Snailwater"—dating back to the very early eighteenth century and used for the treatment of venereal disease of a ubiquitous sort—was displayed amidst those herbal displays.

Given the less than palatably named remedy, which called for condensing "garden-snails" and "6 Gallons Earthworms washed and bruised"—yes, six GALLONS of worms!—with wormwood, cloves, and other herbs, and the fact that such "social disease" was an all-too-common ailment of St. Thomas's patients (the thusly ill-treated within the hospital's out-of-sight "Fowle" wards), it makes you *truly* appreciate the advent of antibiotics, does it not, Creepy Reader?

As we gruesome twosome walked about the St. Thomas's garret, inhaling the head-spinningly heady odour of all those very real herbs mixed with the attic's very own eldritch mustiness, we explored the museum's other, non-apothecarical displays, which detailed the history of St. Thomas's Hospital in its various incarnations, the famous tenure of Florence Nightengale, and its dedication to pediatrics.

But for morbidly grue-gargling malpractitioners of the macabre such as we, it was the museum's woe-inspiring exhibition of atrociously weird apparatuses, all within olden, glass-topped wooden display cases about the garret-space, that called to our foulest attentions. There were razor-edged lancets used for the opening of patients' flesh, abscesses, pustules, and so on; various disgusting accoutrements for the act of leachery, all of it used

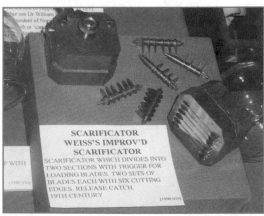

SCARIFICATOR
WEISS'S IMPROV'D
SCARIFICATOR
SCARIFICATOR WHICH DIVIDES INTO
TWO SECTIONS WITH TRIGGER FOR
LOADING BLADES. TWO SETS OF
BLADES EACH WITH SIX CUTTING
EDGES. RELEASE CATCH
19TH CENTURY

for the letting of patients' blood; finely blown glass "cupping jars" used for pumping blood; and the engineering wonders that were the mechanical "scarificators," which were used for the mass letting of, yes, blood! All of this hemophilic instrumentation stood as a testimonial to the fact that medicine of the past was a thoroughly ensanguined practice.

But all of this medical paraphernalia was not thusly invented with the raison d'etre of life's preservation but, rather, its termination. Thus even *we* shuddered as we espied the grave *smallness* of the decapitating hooks, with their oh-so-tiny serrated metal hoops meant to hem in—and *hew through*—the necks of birthing infants. Even if meant to sacrifice a child in order to save its mother's life, these tools painted for us the most disturbingly dreadful of delivery room horrors.

Such a portrait of the grim, and at times ghastly, realities of surgery's past was continued as we made our way from that herb garret to St. Thomas's nineteenth-century Operating Theatre! When it was rediscovered in the mid-1950s, the operating theatre was in a very sad state of utter and thorough disrepair: its skylight's glass had been removed and replaced by slate, its floorboards were missing in places, and, most significantly, the five rows of "standings," upon which medical students and other physicians both had stood to observe the surgical goings-ons below them, had been dismantled long before.

After years of meticulous renovation, with painstaking detail paid to achieve historical accuracy, St. Thomas's Operating Theatre and its herb garret were opened to the general public as a museum. And besides what was on display in the herb garret, the museum's steely sundry of sharply sinister surgical stock was furthered as we lurked within the Operating Theatre. While this continuation of the museum's artifactual exhibit was meant to attest to surgery's progress at St. Thomas, it was very easy for yours cruelly to dwell upon surgery's roots: roots nurtured by the hot blood gushing forth from patients' flesh as if from a slashed wine skin; roots harmonized to the pain-glutted pitch of patients' cries and moans.

Behind the glass of display case after display case we espied a delightfully dreadful deluge of amputation instruments: bone shears that looked much more like tin snips, bone saws with thick or thin blades, and either long and narrow amputation knives or a shorter and skewed sort. All of them, some in fancily lacquered boxes, looked like a higher end variety of carpenter's tools or, more macabrely apropos, more like carving knives than surgical instruments. And knowing

that, at least at St. Thomas's, these knives and saws cut off arm after arm, leg after leg, in a time before the common use of anesthesia (a thing done first by surgeon Robert Liston in 1846), gave their immaculately clean and mirror-polished metal a gleam of grimmest irony.

The museum's exhibition of these disarmingly high-toned tools of human butchery, as well as other surgical oddities such as trepanning instruments and a cringe-eruptive array of urethral sounds (long and thin steel probes meant for dialation!) having ended, we came to what we had risen up through that tower stairwell to behold with our very own bloodshot eyes: the Old Operating Theatre!

Because of the painstaking research that went into its restoration, the Operating Theatre looked veritably as it would have before it was closed back in 1862. The theatre was smaller than yours cruelly had thought it would be, but, then again, it was built within the roof of an olde church. It was also much more adequately illumined, this owing to those refitted skylight-windows above. The Operating Theatre was tenanted by five tiers of horseshoe-shaped standings and, at its middle, the operating table and its "stage." Made of wood and sitting upon four rugged legs, this operating table, while not authentic to St. Thomas's, incorporates all the same features its contemporary would have, most oddly of all a retractable plank at its foot which was used for amputations!

As my black bride and I wormed our way about the Operating Theatre, we studied the row of pegs to its right, upon which would hang the surgeons' operating coats—primeval, and seemingly putrescently so, ancestors of the present day's bleached-and-starched variety, as they, in this time before Joseph Lister's antiseptic surgery, were communally worn and never washed and have been described as out-and-out butchers' aprons, "stiff and stinking with pus and blood"! Beneath the operating table was the sawdust-box: a rectangular box made of wood and filled to the brim with sawdust that was used to absorb the rivulets of a patient's red blood as it flowed forth into, and then out of, the table's carved side-gutters, making it a "bloody porridge."

It was hard for yours cruelly to invoke the place's grimly ghastly spirit of gruesomest surgery because of how, well, *clean* it all was now. To have been there *before* 1862, with those standings packed with obstrusively ogling onlookers, with those doctors, adorned in their once-white coats and their well-manicured hands unwashed, wading through the woe of their surgical work, with those patients, either held down or strapped down upon a gore-encrusted operating table, not simply awake but very much *aware*, and with that stomach-churningly sickening smell of human seepage filling the already stale air . . . would that not be *something*, Creepy Reader?

It is no wonder, then, that this abominable age of Victorian surgery—an age when the surgical mortality rate was *gravely* high, an age before Liston's anesthetics and Lister's antiseptics, an age whose knowledge of human anatomy, at times, came from the work of unscrupulous physicians with twisted investigative thirsts and their dreadfully dubious dealings with less than reputable underworld resurrectionists—has become the gloriously gruesome and grisly stuff of celluloid horror. From 1959's *The Flesh and the Fiends*, a pseudo-docudrama about the questionably arrived at advances in the knowledge of human anatomy acquired by Edinburgh physician Dr. Robert Knox (Peter Cushing) through his unspeakable associations with "true crime" forefathers, Burke and Hare, the latter played by Donald Pleasence, to 1962's *Corridors of Blood*, a history of anesthesia's birth, with Boris Karloff as its self-medicating inventor, Dr. Thomas Bolton, and a truly nasty (and young) Christopher Lee as the horrid means to Bolton's ends, Resurrection Joe, the all-too-grim reality of medicine has always been stranger and more severely shuddersome than *any* fiction!

Our noisomely nastiest of necropsies of the nightmare that was surgery's past having ended, we two profoundly perverse postmortem-pilgrims scraped the thus-corrupted cadaver of the Old Operating Theatre from our slab. Having had but the most foully foetid, yet far too fleeting taste of that skeleton in the closet of many a nineteenth-century anatomist and surgeon—the grave-robbing and body-snatching resurrectionist—my unspeakable wife and I would glut ourselves upon his legendarily loathsome like. And so we took the Tube back west across the Thames towards Oxford Street for our lovingly loathsome lunch with London's very own ghastly, shovel-mad, graveyard-creeping ghoul, Ben Crouch!

BEN CROUCH'S TAVERN
77a Wells Street
020 7636 0717

London's Eerie Pub Co. chain seems very reminiscent of New York City's Eerie Entertainment, Inc. (whether or not the two fun-filled fright-franchises are indeed one and the same is unfortunately not known to yours cruelly) with its very own offering of horror-themed (and extremely anglophilic) restaurant bars, such as the extant likes of The Slaughtered Lamb Pub, the Jekyll and Hyde Club, and the Jekyll and Hyde Pub. Eerie's pubs in London were in the same jugular vein. All rooted in some hauntingly horrid chapter in London's fact-or-fiction history, there is The Black Widow, The Bell, Book, & Candle, The London Stone, Bram Stoker's Tavern, The Marlborough Head, and Ben Crouch's Tavern.

But perhaps, Creepy Reader, I should have said "There *was . . .* " as, sadly, none but the last two are still in the horror business of serving pints of stygian-coloured stout and grease-pounding pub-grub. While the terror-fraught theme of The Marlborough Head is based upon London's very own infamous triple-faced gallows, the Tyburn Tree, which had festered for almost 600 years next to where the Marble Arch stands today (fittingly, but blocks from the Eerie pub), Ben Crouch's Tavern is based upon the unspeakably underhanded undertakings of its name's nefarious ne'er-do-well, and it was here that we gruesome twosome were heading when we rose out of the Oxford Circus Station.

With its numerously windowed classic-stylized façade painted blood red, its faux gas-lamp fixtures, and its name in wrought iron letters, Ben Crouch's Tavern did not look all that different from any of London's other traditional pubs. But such a customary "old school" character was dropped like a stiff into a vacant grave as we lurked into the shadow-choked belly of Ben Crouch's.

As the pub's namesake is London's very own, and very vile, version of Edinburgh's Burke and Hare—to whom the term "resurrectionist" was first applied—its deliciously Death-dealt decor, amidst the pub's overall dourly and drearily Gothic furniture and fixtures, is a ghoulish and ghastly homage to all things *grave-robbing*. A blackly humorous painting of two sneering body snatchers pulling a cadaver from its all-too-fresh grave hangs upon one of the tavern's sanguinolently-stained back walls. In a glass case above the basement stairs was a graveyard tableau in which a shrouded Death lurked behind an open casket, a body snatcher's shovel and pick ax resting against its defiled side.

And behind a somewhat beaten-up wooden banister at the front of the tavern stood an eerily execrable effigy of bald-pated Ben Crouch himself—that frightfully fearful father of London's post-funeral fouling—a bloody knife in his right hand, a tool of his terrible trade in his left hand, and an utterly horrid grimace upon his notoriously pock-scarred mug. This was Ben Crouch: former bare-knuckle prizefighter; former poor hospital porter, very likely at St. Thomas's; and former riotously retrograde ringleader of London's Borough Gang. From 1802 to 1825, this truly transgressive thug, along with his cohort in criminality, Joseph Naples—who was actually a head grave digger at a London cemetery—and their contemptible Borough Gang cronies, were ill-renowned practioners of resurrectioning, that most repulsively repugnant of practices.

As the number of medical schools and teaching hospitals grew throughout the eighteenth century, so too did the very practical need for cadavers. Such was the utter desperation—and unnatural and unrestrainable curiosities—of the anatomists and surgeons, whose work itself depended upon that of their anatomizing colleagues, that many, if not most, of them, in both England and Scotland, saw it utterly necessary to do business, of the most bloodcurdling sort, with the cruelly corpse-corrupting likes of body snatchers and, thus, resurrectioning was born, the first recorded instance being in 1742.

Through an almost iniquitously ingenious assortment of methods (such as the surreptitious burial of corpses above their empty coffins; the digging of a tunnel beneath a coffin-filled grave so that the plot was left, seemingly, undisturbed; the fraudulent claiming of paupers' corpses from workhouses; and even, in some cases, the theft of dead bodies from their very own homes as their wake-holding families wept over them), these body snatchers sold cadaver after cadaver to respected and seemingly reputable physicians in the blackness of night at the back of these medical institutions.

But as this want for fresh corpses, the coldly carneous stuff of scientific exploration and experiment, deepened, so did the utter *horror* of these body snatchers' transgressions, as they began to procure the freshest of corpses by means of *murder*! The most infamous of this hideous breed of homicidal resurrectionists were Scotland's very own William Burke and Bill Hare, who are said to have snuffed out anywhere from 13 to 30 innocent victims in order to sell their cadavers to morally questionable medical schools.

The body-snatching trade having become a bigger business in England, Burke and Hare left Scotland to continue their murder-for-money-spree to the south but, in 1829, their dread-riddenly despicable misdeeds having been revealed, Burke's neck was stretched at a London gallows—and his hanged corpse then publicly dissected, his defleshed skeleton put on permanent display, ironically, at the University of Edinburgh's Anatomical Museum, and, as the story goes, a wallet was made from tanned flesh skinned from the back of his neck—while Hare was rumored to have lived out the end of his wretched days as a blind beggar in the squalid London streets.

While the most ugly unlawfulness of Ben Crouch and his boogeyman bunch of Borough Gang boils may not compare to the utter and ultimate ghoulishness of those archetypes of anatomical atrocity, Burke and Hare, it does not signify by any means that the infamy of these felony-lousy London lowlifes was not well-earned. They were London's most creepsworthy corpse-selling cartel, supplying the freshest of dissection-ready human meat to none other than our recently autopsied St. Thomas's Hospital, among others. According to Naples's diary, which was later published as a "penny dreadful," the profusion and sheer pace of the Borough Gang's body-snatching was prodigious, digging up and dealing out several cadavers in a single night.

Their woeful work was so seemingly fundamental to that of some of London's physicians, such as St. Thomas's Sir Astley Cooper, that great sums of money were doled out of their very own pockets to keep these ghouls out of prison and to feed their families when such a thing was unavoidable. But resurrectionists such as Crouch were put out of that boogeyman's body-snatching business in 1832 after Parliament passed the Anatomy Act, which allowed medical schools to use the workhouse-poor's unclaimed bodies to meet their dissective needs, thus eliminating the necessity for grave-robbing. Sad but true!

Yours cruelly does not know what happened to ugly olde Ben Crouch after 1832, but, apparently, the ex-resurrectionist became a restauranteur, at least according to Eerie Pubs' deviously "Horror!"-fied designs. Had grave-robbing Ben Crouch indeed laid down his shovel and crowbar for a spatula and ladle, Creepy Reader, would he have cooked the same class of "comfort food" slop to be had at Ben Crouch's Tavern? Would the pub's "peppered mushrooms" have roused his unwholesome appetites? Would he have hungered to sink his black, rotten teeth into the "home-made potato wedges with cheddar cheese"? And would he have known what to even make of "nachos with beef chili"?

While Eerie Pubs has attempted to extend the dreadfulness of the tavern's historical derivation and resultant decor to its menus, with their alliteratively apportioned allotments of "Food To Die For," "Sadistic Sandwiches," and "Devilish Deserts," such cadaverously becreeped creativity unfortunately ended there. Where were dishes that *truly* incarnated Crouch's ghastily ghoulish graveyard-goings-on, like a "Body Snatcher's Unburried Human Beef Burger" ("Bloody" or "Belly-Up"—rare or well-done—and with or without "Cadaverous Cavity-Cheese")?

But the Ben Crouch's Tavern's food, albeit thusly less than horrid, was indeed rather *good*. And, in the end, we had not gone there for an extremely choice culinary experience but to have a simple meal at a pub that the resurrectioning likes of Boris Karloff's John Gray from 1945's *The Body Snatcher* would have called home! And for loathsome charnel house lurkers such as we, that it was, at least for a time between our ichor-dripping itinerary's rounds. But once our humble repast was devoured, we were on the Tube yet again and headed towards the next of London's gloriously grave wonders to exhume.

Of Madness & Manslaughter

With our reprobatively repulsive rounds amongst some less wholesome chapters in London's medical history, we two hideously inhospitable Horror-vores washed the grue and gore of the operating table and the plundered coffin from our hands so that we could have a night's taste of the sweet oblivion that is sleep and, like corpses interred into the wormy bosom of the grave, rest our dread-gorged brains for our next day's terror-mongery.

And what, pray tell, would be at the severed head of our spook-schedule's hideous singularities, Creepy Reader? Well, another *hospital*, of corpse! However, this London hospital is not known for either the severe scalpel-skills of its surgeons or for the profoundly perverted physique of its patients. No. My black bride and I would be exploring the eldritch and execrable thirteenth-century hospital that has become the very archetype of insane asylum infamies and iniquities and whose *name* has become the very definition of a dreadfully deranged extremity of discord and disorder: *Bedlam*!

Although Bedlam—a commoner's Cockney corruption of "Bethlem," which is itself a bastardization of "Bethlehem," as in "Old Bethlehem Hospital"—no longer festers within London's East End, having been removed to the London suburb of Bromley in 1930 where it, as the present-day Bethlehem Royal Hospital and a part of the South London and Maudsley NHS Trust, not only offers mental health but also substance abuse treatment, where the final rotting place and butchered remains of that aged madhouse can still be savoured by the likes of loathsomeness-lunatics such as we two headshrinkers. So pull down your straightjacket's straps, Creepy Reader, and let us commit ourselves to the frightful madness of the one, the only . . . Bedlam!

"BEDLAM"
(BETHLEHEM HOSPITAL FOR THE INSANE)
Former Location
London Wall at Moorgate

Squirming through the big pecuniary hustle and bustle of the Liverpool Street Station, but blocks from the Bank of England and London's Stock Exchange, my unspeakable wife and I walked amongst London's banking and stock-bartering set until we came to London Wall. While it is named after the 2nd-century bulwark that Roman legions had raised about Londinium to separate London Town from the rest of London, the eighteenth/nineteenth-century-born thoroughfare that spans from Aldersgate to Bishopsgate, London Wall, with its higher-end boutiques and coffee shoppes, was no different than any of the other streets we had traversed throughout our sojourn amongst London's most spookfully sanguinolent stretches.

When we came to where London Wall met Moorgate, which is named after one of that aged London Wall's lesser gates, things were none too different. And as we stood there, utterly lost amidst that capitalist sea of corporate raincoats and briefcases, it was with a true sense of stupefaction that we espied that particular stretch of the London Wall because it was there, beyond that Moorgate of yore and upon what was once the greatest parcels of open land in London Town, known as the Moorfields, that, until almost 200 years ago, Bedlam had festered as not simply London's—if not *all of England's*—biggest insane asylum but, odiously, its most *infamous*.

But Bedlam was not indeed born into the unhallowed halls of history's horrors here at the junction of these modern incarnations of London Wall and Moorgate, but some 500 yards further east along the former outside of what was the primeval Roman egress of Bishopsgate, whose spiked namesake had once, infamously, been ornamented with the hacked-off and crow-picked heads of a host of social and political transgressors.

Before it was "Bedlam," it began, in 1247, as the Priory of St. Mary of Bethlehem and, almost a century later, became a hospice—not a mad-house—for the poor overseen by the sisters of the Order of St. Mary of Bethlehem. It was not until the very dawn of the fifteenth century that this small and simple, and by now royally-distinguished, hospital was redefined to see to the treatment of the mentally ill, "lunatics" as they were then called: from the simply distracted to, worse, the downright disturbed.

While historical records show evidence that, by the mid-fifteenth century, the hospital was already being called "Bedlam," that slang-slung name would not come to truly evidence its profoundly infamous present-day purport, a thing born out of not simply the helter-skelter nature of its patients' hospitalization but, more so, the hideous and horrid nature of their "treatment," until, seemingly, 1547. It was then that Bedlam, that early priory already having seen its end, was grandly sanctioned, by none other than Henry VIII himself, as a state insane asylum and, but 10 years thereafter, was put under the atrociously austere authority of the governors of Bridewell Hospital, which, although called a "hospital" and initially founded as a workhouse and a place of vocational schooling, was truly nothing but a *prison*.

Before this dread-portending redefinition of Bedlam's raison d'etre and rule, the "treatment" received by its mad internees was by no means humane, mostly, if the benefit of proverbial doubt is given to Bedlam's earlier management, from sheer ignorance of mental illness, as it was all too commonly held as the natural product of some inherent criminality, moral weakness, or, least offensive of the three, simple brain damage. Because from such unlearned perceptions—not all that removed from ancestral beliefs in the influence of evil spirits and faeries upon the human brain—the most common way of "curing" lunatics, when they weren't simply left to meander about the asylum and mutter to their own mad selves, was to chain them to walls or the floor, or, for the most incorrigible amongst them, to teach them constraint by lacerating them with cudgels or whips.

But this sort of treatment experienced by Bedlam's "patients" would *pale* in comparison to the bloodcurdlingly unspeakable brutality that would befall them, so very appallingly, when the madhouse came under Bridewell's penal-consumed rule. Those old methods remained but were twisted further into the chilling depths of cruelty. The restraining of lunatics—done not simply by chains but, now, the harsh ingenuities of straightjackets, or "straight-waistcoats" as they are called in England, and "restraining chairs"—not only became commonplace but continuous. It is said that one poor wretch was chain-fettered to Bedlam's squalid floor, without abeyance, for *14 years*! And the battery of the insane . . . well, remained *battery*, plain and simple—little more than mugging with no true end other than a grim expression of inexorable might and mastery.

To Bedlam's old and already heinous stock of hospitalized sufferings was brought a new morbidly deplorable menu of monstrous "treatments" with the asylum's superintendence by the wardens of Bridewell. Under such a dreadfully distress-defined dominion, Bedlam's patients—those archetypal "bedlamites"—were left unfed and, thus, to starve, perhaps in an attempt to urge unhealthy passions from their now-wasting and weakened flesh. Patients who did indeed have swollen bellies, perhaps filled from ladle after ladle of grubby gruel crammed down their gullets, were made to fully purge its steaming contents, whether manually or medicinally, such involuntary emesis meant to very literally vomit the madness from within them. Patients, stripped to their unwashed skin, were plunged, brutishly, into tubs of bitterly cold water with the deeply misguided hypothesis—

seemingly rising more out of simple cruelty—that the thusly produced shock would reorder a disordered mind.

Maybe most curious—and least cruel—of all Bedlam's "cures," patients were made to look upon their own photographed portraits because it was believed that such looking upon their own mad selves would dispel delusions and lull their lunacy. As a whole, such troublingly torturous "treatment" prescribed by Bedlam's macabrely misery-meting, mad doctors, even if from the "best" of ill-fatedly ignorant intentions, had the inevitable effect of making its lot of "lunatics" even *more* deranged and disturbed than they had been—*if* they actually had been to begin with!—when they were committed to the mental asylum.

What made Bedlam a true, and truly grotesque, wellspring of ghastliest terror, Creepy Reader, was that, from this "hospital" which was, unquestionably, nothing but a prison and whose "therapeutic" regimen would seem to have actually *bred* insanity, it was common procedure that, after 12 months, "patients"—tellingly, a designation not used until the eighteenth century—were discharged and released to walk amongst an unsuspecting London populous, "cured" or not!

This repulsively rabid retrograde reality of Bedlam Hospital—a wickedly shuddersome wedding of gibbering madness and gruesomest malpractice—made it, by the late seventeenth century, a truly gawk-worthy grotesquerie: a humorously hideous and, because of it, a "happening" spot for the high-born, that plunged the insanity and inhumanity of Bedlam into unknown depths of absurdity. Such a thing would seem to have begun with the madhouse's relocation outside the Moorfields in 1675.

An inspection of Bedlam, still England's *only* insane asylum, by Bridewell's governors at the very end of the 1500s revealed that the hospital was in a wretched state of disrepair and disregard. In spite of this, it was not until almost a century later that Bedlam, by this time having become irreparably squalid, seedy, and simply lunatic-stuffed, was moved from its original Bishopsgate location of some 400 years to a newly founded edifice along the London Wall, across from which yours cruelly stood that sadly fogless day in London. Bedlam's new quarters were not only the first in all of England to be built wholly for the purposes of an insane asylum but, based upon the architectural conceptions of Robert Hooke, were esteemed to be one of London's pre-eminent constructions.

Again, it was about this time when Bedlam and its bedlamites entered upon their inhabitance of this very, and seemingly very fine, London Wall ward that the visitors began to come. At first, only Londoners paid the penny fee to gape and guffaw at the rantings and ravings of the madhouse's lunatics, but then, as the years went on and Bedlam's insanity-induced infamy deepened and dispersed, they were followed by travelers from not only other English parts but foreign commonwealths as well. Poets, artists, and even travel-writers—yours cruelly's ancestral stock—flocked to Bedlam to behold its scintillatingly scurrilous and shocking spectacle and bear witness to its compellingly cacophonous and convulsive chaos in wood, paint, or pencil.

As portrayed perhaps most famously in the eighth and last painting of William Hogarth's *A Rake's Progress*—an early eighteenth-century serial portraiture that tells the cautionary tale of Tom Rakewell and his moral and mental corruption after a descent into the belly of purest hedonism—the Bedlam of the late seventeenth century and most of the next was nothing but muddled madness writhing upon muddled madness.

Handsomely accoutered gentlemen and ladies would walk through the madhouse's grimly forbidding gates as if to the theatre—a notion perhaps reified by the Hellenic Comedy and Tragedy mask-like statuary sculpted by Caius Cibber that ornamented those very gates, of a pair of pitiful lunatic patients, one with a maniacal and unhinged mien the other with a bleak and begloomed cast, each representing the hospital's two observed kinds of lunacy: "Raving and Melancholy Madness."

Once within the most monstrously ill-renowned belly of Bedlam, they would go through it whilst cruelly galling the masses of manacled "mad" as the asylum's orderlies greedily fingered their shiny pence. Although this practice was put to an end in 1770 because such a thing, in the laughably understated, and unhurried, words of Bedlam's chairmen, "tended to disturb the tranquillity of the patients," what an exquisitely nightmarish experience it would have been to lurk through the burblingly loathsome bowels of Bedlam's lurid lunacy, would it not, Creepy Reader?

As we gruesome twosome stood in reminiscence of Bedlam Hospital's ill-rumored repugnance of yore, it was like communing at a vacant grave, as it has not been found at that address, only past London Wall and Moorgate, since 1815 when that eldritch insane asylum was moved yet again, this time to St. George's Field in the London suburb of Lambeth.

But it was to our surprise that there was nary a historic marker or ubiquitous blue plaque to tell the unknowing passersby that they were indeed walking in the shadow of what had once been, all those years before, the still-memorialized shuddersome madness of Bedlam. To espy such a thing, my black bride and I would have to return to the Liverpool Street Station and take the Tube to Lambeth and, therein, the Imperial War Museum, which was actually housed within the hollowed out carcass of Bedlam Hospital.

IMPERIAL WAR MUSEUM
Present Location of
Bedlam's Edifice
Lambeth Road
0171-416 5000

When the Tube came to the Elephant and Castle Station, we two abominably atrocious alienists made our way to the street above and found the surpassingly residential sprawl that is Lambeth. After a rather leisurely stroll down St. George's Road, we came to what had once been St. George's Fields, now known as Geraldine Mary Harmsworth Park, and found, amidst its blossoming vernal splendor, the Imperial War Museum, two 50-foot-long cannons planted before it attesting, in many twin tons of metal, to the place's martial purpose.

Such a bellicose theme was further promoted when we stepped out into the museum's sunny and spacious main gallery. Festooned, from floor to ceiling, with a truly wide array of modern weapons of war—tanks, biplanes, jets, field cannons, and even a reproduction of nuclear armaments—the museum, as its name foretells, is a tribute to England's wartime engrossments, with seeming emphasis put upon World War II.

The beginnings of the museum date back to 1917 when it was decided that artifacts from the Great War should be collected and exhibited, and this very endeavor was undertaken when the Imperial War Museum opened to the public three years later. It was first housed within New Hyde Park's Crystal Palace—that relic from the Great Exhibition of 1851 during which Victorian England's multifarious supremacy was declared to the world—but then in 1936, after some seemingly problematic relocations, one of which to this very Lambeth structure, that dreadfully delirious dwelling of Bedlam's disturbed and deranged denizens.

But not to worry, Creepy Reader, about why English officials would house ordnance of such proportions as those at which yours cruelly stared with, well, "lunatics." By the time the very first war machines were towed to these Lambeth parts, Bedlam Hospital had already vacated the edifice some six years before. Bedlam had putrefied in ill-famed prominence at those once so very grand and great Moorsfield digs until 1807 when, after the madhouse had come to an utterly disheveled and defiled state no different than that in which its original Bishopsgate incarnation had fallen, it was judged that the hospital needed to be moved yet again.

The newly built structure at St. George's Fields, finished in 1815, had space to house some 200 patients and, as the years went by, was expanded and made more extravagant, at least externally. But, within Bedlam, it was, naturally, bedlam as usual: shackling, dragooning, and, through it all, experimental "treatments" and "cures" seemingly more fit for a prison, if not a torture chamber.

But, with the coming of the Victorian epoch and the medical and scientific headway made therein, such things began to change following routine and rigorous inspections. Wards—veritable "jailers," apathetic at best and abusive at the very worst—were eventually replaced by nurses and attendants trained specifically for the treatment, not torture, of the mentally ill. Those olde, mad doctors were replaced by those representing more progressive knowledge of mental illness.

For the poor and pitiable "lunatics" of Bedlam, the asylum's very nature had changed; however, Bedlam's notoriety, a thing born out of hundreds of years of heinously unhealthy hospital-horrors, was unforgettable—it's very name had, by the Victorian Age, come to signify anarchy and abnormality, even outside of England. Perhaps this is why, in 1930, the mental hospital, despite those appreciable rectifications, left London for the lesser known and more "healthy" locality of Bromley. And there Bedlam is still, now known as the Bethlem Royal Hospital, the world's oldest psychiatric hospital, governed now not by Bridewell but the National Health Service.

Fortunately for the truly mentally ill, if not so very sadly for morbid macabre-meisters such as we, it is not the Bedlam of yore; that Bedlam behind the Val Lewton-scripted 1946 shocker starring monsterman Boris Karloff as mad doctor Master George Sims, and which has since inspired almost every sinematic madhouse, such as the one at the heart of, most recently, William Malone's remake of William Castle's *House on Haunted Hill*, which, its ample deficiencies aside, offered a "Lunatic Holocaust" opening that is truly a wonder to behold.

As yours cruelly walked about the Imperial War Museum's war machines with my ghastliness-distempered gray matter crawling with such fiendish fancies of Bedlam's past foulness, it was truly hard to see any traces of the hospital's eldritch essence within the museum's renovated insides. This was made difficult because of the fact that, while the hospital's domed portico remains, its east and west wings, where its patients were eventually housed, were torn down just after Bedlam left the premises, that space then used to make the park that surrounds the museum.

The part of the museum, though, that did indeed seem to hearken back to those disturbed Bedlam days, at least to my bloodshot eyes, was the red-brick façade that constituted that main gallery's front wall. Perhaps it was not a coincidence, then, that a commemorative royally-stamped Lucite plaque hung just beyond that wall, within the museum's foyer, that testified that the museum was indeed "housed in this building, the former Bethlem Royal Hospital, since 1936."

How many of the Imperial War Museum's visitors, who come to take in its educationally worthwhile social and culturally-contexted displays, know of the very building's insane past is unknown. But had they indeed come to such knowledge and wanted more of Bedlam, they could have made the journey to that London suburb of Bromley to spend some hours eyeballing the historical documents and works of art that comprise the Bethlem Royal Hospital Archives and Museum, which was founded in 1967 to record "the lives and experience, and [celebrate] the achievements, of people with mental health problems."

No matter how we two bloodfreaks relished the thought of reveling amidst those relics of Reason's repellent ruination from ill-rumored Bedlam—in particular Cibber's stone-hewn seventeenth-century "Raving and Melancholy Madness"—our itinerary had no room for such extra-London explorations, so, most unfortunately, we had to forgo such a thing. But perchance, Creepy Reader, should you find yourself Bedlam-bound, and with more time than we, you will allow yourself to become adrift amidst those abysmal annals of Bedlam's ancient aberrance?

DONALD RUMBELOW'S "JACK THE RIPPER HAUNTS"
WALKING TOUR
Tower Hill Tube Station
020-7624-3978
(The Original London Walks)

MARY ANNE NICHOLS MURDER SCENE
Durward Street (formerly Buck's Row)

ANNIE CHAPMAN MURDER SCENE
Hanbury Street (between Wilkes Street & Brick Lane)

ELIZABETH STRIDE MURDER SCENE
Henriques Street (formerly Berner Street, off Commercial Road)

KATHERINE EDDOWES MURDER SCENE
Mitre Square (Junction of Mitre Street, Duke Street via Church Passage, and St James's Place)

MARY KELLY MURDER SCENE
Miller's Court off Dorset Street (off Commercial Street, between White's Row & Brushfield Street)

ST. BOTOLPH'S ALDGATE
("Prostitutes' Church")
Aldgate High Street
020 7283 1670

THE TEN BELLS PUB
84 Commercial Street,
020 7366 1721

"JUWES . . ." GRAFFITI
108–119 Wentworth Model Dwellings
Goulston Street

Leaving the Imperial War Museum and Lambeth, we two morbidly murderous macabre-maniacs discharged our delightfully dreadful selves from Bedlam and took the Tube back into the wormy black heart of London. With that macabrely quintessential madhouse, we had weltered in the horrors of madness chain-trussed and "cure"-tortured within the confines of a "hospital." But what awaited us next on our terrifyingly ghastly gore-tour of London would be an offensively outraging offering, as if upon a guts-and-grue-splattered platter, of madness at its most maniacally manslaughterous—and stalking the fog-smothered streets of London! And we would only have to kill but a few hours until darkness fell upon those now-familiar harrowing haunts of Whitechapel for our one-night stand with the one and only *Jack the Ripper*!

June of 1887 heralded Queen Victoria's 50th year of sovereignty— her Golden Jubilee. It was the glorious cusp of that magnificent crown of Britannia: the Victorian Age, when, truly, the sun did not set upon the British Empire. Culturally, scientifically, technologically, imperially: Victorian England was held as the ultimate evolution of human "civilization"—perhaps "humanity" itself.

A little over a year later, during the sanguine and sultry dusk of August, this culmination, this zenith, would meet its utter antithesis, its negative, its veritable nasty and noisome Mr. Hyde. It was the antisocial, anti-*human*, zeitgeist of London's "other half," a dread-oozing symbol of Victoriana's all-but-ignored bankruptcy and brutality slashed and hacked—*ripped*—from the abject flesh of five Whitechapel prostitutes. It was an unexplainable and unsolvable nightmare of benighted backstreet butchery that as imputed upon a mysterious, human-murdering machine known to those affeared late-nineteenth-century Londoners—and, thereafter, generation after ghastly grue-guzzling generation of Horror-worshippers—as "Saucy Jack," "Jack From Hell," or, his most infamous "trade name" of all, "Jack the Ripper."

Between August 31st and November 9th of 1888, Jack the Ripper had his horridly razor-whetted blade—most likely an amputation knife very similar to those we had espied at the Old Operating Theatre—against the quavering throat of all of London, the "low"-born as well as the "high," because of the more and more deeply vicious and vile killings of that ill-fated quintet of trollops. While some so-called "Ripperologists" have attributed other Whitechapel prostitute murders, before and after—as late as 1891—to him, bringing his body count to, variously, six or seven or even, at most, *11*, those five are unquestionably "his": Mary Ann "Polly" Nichols, Annie Chapman, Elizabeth Stride, Catherine Eddowes, and, last but most loathsome of that streetwalking lot, Mary Kelly.

But why, Creepy Reader, has Jack the Ripper become so very *infamous*, so very *frightful*, so very *fascinating*? In the end, his autumnal Whitechapel atrocities are not only small in number but short in duration when scrutinized against the legacy of serialized brutality of latterday human monsters: Richard Ramirez, mid-1980s Los Angeles's "Night Stalker," who killed 13 men and women, old and young alike; Jeffrey Dahmer, the "Wisconsin Cannibal," who killed—and *ate*—16 young homosexual men; Gary Ridgway, "The Green River Killer" of the American Northwest, who, for *16 years*, raped and killed—or killed and *then* raped—*48* young women, many of whom, like the Ripper's very own victims almost a century before, were prostitutes, in what would be, until 1998, America's longest, and largest, unsolved murder investigation.

Again, given such heinous inhumanity as these twentieth-century horrors, *why* is Jack the Ripper's name still uttered with such *disgust*, with such *dread*? It would seem that his interminable, and interminably shuddersome, ill-renown is rooted not in the particulars of his morbidly misogynistic—*misanthropic*—misdeeds but their, and his, crypticness. *Who* was Jack the Ripper? *Why* did he slaughter those five women and in the macabrely peculiar manner he did? And then *why*, after thusly terrorizing Whitechapel and all of London, did he, simply, disappear?

The 100 and more years that have passed since has been rife with postmortem investigations endeavoring to resolve those mysteries and their conclusions have been a proverbially "mixed bag," from the plausible to the preposterous, Jack the Ripper therein identified—"Finally Revealed!"—as anybody from the suicide Montague Druitt and the Victorian painter Walter Sickert to, so very laughably, even the likes of *Alice in Wonderland*'s Lewis Carroll and the "Elephant Man," Joseph Merrick—the artifacts pertaining to whose pitiable and poignant life can actually be found at the Royal London Hospital Archives and Museum alongside some deliciously dreadful documents relating to these madly morbid Whitechapel mass-murders.

Another strain of Ripper scholarship has focused upon a "Royal Conspiracy," wherein those five Whitechapel prostitutes were massacred by a syphilis-deranged Prince Edward or, almost reversely, by an assemblage of Royal assassins tasked with secreting, through savage curb-side surgery,

Prince Edward's forbidden marriage and its infantine evidence, this latter theory fleshed out most gloriously in the fantastic occult fancies of Alan Moore's *From Hell*.

But despite year after year of continued research and speculation, those mysteries still remain and *that* is why, even more than a 100 years after he disappeared from those fog-shrouded London streets, Jack the Ripper has become not simply the atrociously aberrant archetype of the modern-day serial killer but, simply, the Boogeyman: He-Who-Stalks-and-Slashes-by-Night, the Victorian forefather of those fictional celluloid slashers like Michael Myers, Jason Vorhees, or, more realistically, *Maniac*'s Frank Zito, latter-day "rippers," one and all.

This "unknown" quality explains why Jack the Ripper has been Horror's wellspring at the horrible black heart of numberless books, short stories, graphic novels, plays, and, most notably to Horror-mongers such as yours cruelly, films, played by such big screen thespians as Klaus Kinski in Jess Franco's 1976 *Jack the Ripper*, David Warner in 1979's *Time After Time*, Anthony Perkins as a type of Mr. Hyde/Ripper in 1989's *Edge of Sanity*, and, most recently, Ian Holm as Dr. William Gull in 2001's *From Hell* adaptation.

Through it all, after decades and decades of such Ripper portraiture, "fact" has become infected by "fiction" and vice-versa, the consequence of such blurring being, despite the all-too-real tragedy of those 1888 murders, a truly wondrously weird web of wickedest Horror!

And so, Creepy Reader, when my unspeakable wife and yours cruelly wanted to glut our grotesque ghastly ones' fill upon a hideously heaping helping of Jack the Ripper horrors, we concluded to not simply walk amongst his Victorian Aged Whitechapel crime scenes but have a guided tour of them. But something we had come to find out during our short expedition through London's befouled bowels was that there was truly no shortage of "walking tours" to sift through, traversing London territories relating to everything from William Shakespeare and Sherlock Holmes to ghosts and gangsters.

Crucial to the decision about not simply what walking tour to take but *whose* is whether or not you want "theatrics" or "truth." Well, we two terror-touring thanatologists forwent the former and, instead of tour guides accoutered in Victorian top hats and frock coats, armed with dubious leather bags and their more dubious contents, and drawling on so very dramatically in their fanciful diction, took the "Jack the Ripper Haunts" walking tour hosted by well-respected Ripper authority and author and London Tourist Board Blue Badge Guide, Donald Rumbelow.

When yours cruelly was but a teenaged ghoul in 1988, my first foul taste of Jack the Ripper came in the form of a "live" centennial television event, *The Secret Identity of Jack the Ripper*. Although his appearance had escaped my gray matter in the years since, Rumbelow was featured on the special as a Ripper "expert"—his standing as such based upon his 1975 book, *The Complete Jack the Ripper*, which is still recognized as the definitive text in the fiercely fiendish field—and not only shared with the viewing audience his very own Ripper research but offered them a tele-vised tour of the Ripper's slashing grounds.

And, more recently, when Johnny Depp was preparing for his part as *From Hell*'s absinthe-sipping and opium-smoking Inspector Fred Abberline, it was Rumbelow that twentieth Century Fox paid to introduce the American actor to the Ripper's Whitechapel. With this thusly credentialed Ripperologist, we gruesome twosome *knew* that we would be feasting well upon that grim and ghastly authentic grittiness that we had wanted.

But when we rose out of the Tower Hill Tube Station, it was very evi-dent that Rumbelow's reputation had preceded him, as we found ourselves immersed in a true sea of tourist flesh. With no exaggeration, Creepy Reader, well more than 100 would-be tour-goers were awaiting the start of Rumbelow's seemingly much suggested Whitechapel walk. My black bride and I tried to worm our way as close to the front as we could; however, such maneuvers were very difficult as, simply, we did not know exactly where the "front" was, as we did not know what Rumbelow looked like and, even if we *could* espy him from amongst all those strangers' faces, it was truly hard to eyeball things other than that which was in our fiends' cadaverous faces.

But then, after but a little while's wait, we heard a booming English-accented voice cutting through the murmuring of the throng of tourists and, then, from whence it came, the hatted-head and scarfed-shoulders of an older gentleman rose above those gaggles of yearning gore-gawkers.

Yes, this was former London police officer and chairman of the Crime Writers Association, Donald Rumbelow, and, by his very own estimation, that night's was the biggest turnout his walking tour had ever had. To contend with the logistical realities of such a thing, Rumbelow told those gathered there at the Tower Hill Station that he'd be giving the tour of the same blood-sodden Ripper's stretches about three more nights that week and that, that night, he was accompanied by his personally trained assistant who would be giving the same walking tour but in a somewhat different order so that there would not be any unwanted overlapping.

When some took their leave to come back for Rumbelow's other tour that week and some others for his assistant's this night, his "Jack the Ripper Haunts" exploration of Whitechapel's eerie egregiousness began.

While yours cruelly had wondered whether the respected profundity of Rumbelow's Ripper research would be dissipated, what with the still-sizeable pack following him from the Tower Hill Station to the tour's first location, such dubiety was all but eviscerated like a Whitechapel gutter-tramp. London Walks had promised us a tour during which what unfolded would be the bloodcurdling and stomach-churning tale of Jack the Ripper: "Watching. Stalking. Butchering raddled, drink-sodden East End prostitutes. Leaving a trail of blood that led . . . *nowhere.*" And I am *very* pleased, Creepy Reader, that it was in such a verily mephitic morass of murder so monstrously morbid that Rumbelow indeed dragged us through that, yet again, fogless London night.

While Rumbelow's tour of the Ripper's 1888 reign of terror stretched, chronologically, from the vicious killing of "Polly" Nichols—her throat, from ear to ear, hacked through to the spine, a blade-born smile still burbling black blood when a night-patrolling constable examined her corpse—on the 31st of that August to the profoundly more painstaking butchery of Mary Kelly—her consumately dehumanized carcass having been unspeakably defaced, disemboweled, defleshed, and dismembered over the lapse of hours—on the 9ᵗʰ of that November, his tour's route did not follow such a historic course. To do so, particularly with a tourist-troop of that night's size, would be a simple impossibility, taking him, and us with him, back and forth and back again through Whitechapel's somewhat labyrinthine side streets.

Furthermore, Nichols's place of death was actually along Buck's Row, now Durward Street, almost a kilometer from the horridly hideous heart of the Ripper's woman-hunting ground, only but a block across Whitechapel Road from the Royal London Hospital. To avoid such logistic convolutions, Rumbelow's two-hour walking tour stalked a more simple path through the East End quarter, now settled with office buildings, businesses, and low-income housing, in no way reminiscent of the raunchy and ruinous slum it had once so very infamously been.

Thusly, Rumbelow's "Jack the Ripper Haunts" tour ushered us morbidly murder-mad Whitechapel-migrants from one loathsomely cutthroat locale to

the next. There was the late-eighteenth-century St. Botolph's Aldgate
Church on Aldgate High Street,
which, in 1888, was known so very
notoriously as "The Prostitutes'
Church" not because of the still-
inclusive nature of its congregation
but because its titular streetwalkers
would walk around the church again
and again for a little rest between,
well, streetwalking, lest they be
arrested for solicitation whilst
stopping elsewhere for the same.

There was Ripper's Corner: the shadowed and still-cobblestoned solitude of Mitre Square, formed between Mitre Street and the merger of Beavis
Marks and Duke's Place, where, in the very early hours of September 30th,
in what Ripperologists call the "Double Event," Kate Eddowes would
become not only the Ripper's fourth victim—her throat slit from ear to ear,
her nose cut off with a slash across her face, and her abdomen sundered,
hideously, from breastbone to, *literally*, bottom, her rain-wet corpse
disemboweled and also missing a kidney, which would later, at least *most*
of it, accompany that infamous "From Hell" letter—but his *second* of that
very same night, as, in a courtyard, Dutfield's Yard, off what was then
Berner Street (now known as Henriques Street, off Commercial Road),
that Elizabeth "Long Liz" Stride's throat had been, signaturedly, slashed
but her corpse saved from postmortem mutilations by the arrival of
"costermonger" Louis Diemschutz, this interruption, sadly all-too-late
for Stride, fouling the Ripper's human-butchery habits and stirring him
to seek out a second, and more secreted, victim in the form of Eddowes.

There was the small and simple Goulston Street dwelling upon whose
doorway's jamb was scrawled, in chalk, a "clue," indubitably left by the
Ripper because a blood-soaked bit of Eddowe's frock was found close-by,
that read "The Juwes are not/The men that/Will be/Blamed for nothing,"
this much-deciphered message, more specifically its peculiar misspelling,
being proof in that Royally Freemasonic Conspiracy explanation of the
Ripper's identity and intentions.

Lastly, after these, and other, tour-stops and after our originally swollen herd had thinned with each of them, there was the relatively empty but extensive alley, between a towering row of tasteful apartments and a similarly tall  parking garage off Commercial Street—and only just across from that infamously prostitute-patronized Ten Bells Pub, which, while it was, for years and years, a dingy and dismal dive that catered to the all-too-curious Ripper-combing crowd, is today the home of bohemian hipsters—which had been, in 1888, Dorset Street.

It was here, Creepy Reader, in the post-midnight blackness of November 9th, at what had been 26 Dorset Street, that Jack the Ripper found his fifth and final victim: Mary Kelly. In the closed-door seclusion of that residence's rented-out rear room which had opened into a bygone courtyard off Dorset known then as Miller's Court, that wickedly woe-sewing Whitechapel woman-slaughterer had not simply the space but the time to *truly* satisfy his unspeakably unwholesome and unknown Ripper raison d'etre and, therein, so very revoltingly reap his unceasingly dread-veiled name and its bloodcurdling notoriety.

Poor Mary Kelly's would not only be Jack the Ripper's last murder (at least by Rumbelow's sum) but his most deeply horrid and hideous display of homicidal dissection: in her Miller's Court room, the Ripper, as with that exterminated quartet of her sister prostitutes, had hacked her throat through, almost decapitating her; likewise, he had very nearly amputated her left arm, but a little sinew and flesh keeping it on the torso; he had laboriously peeled the skin from her forehead and, worse, had *defleshed* both of her thighs all the way down to the feet; he had cut off her breasts, as well as, here too, her nose; he had torn open her belly and then pulled out her bowels and abdominal organs, piling them between her feet.

When Kelly's thusly ruined corpse was found that mourning of November 9th, by the landlord's helper, who had been sent to collect her back rent, her room—ill-omenedly, Room 13—was like an abattoir, as streaks of sprayed blood had painted anew its dingy walls and soddened her bed and her body's carved-off *meat*—breasts, nose, and the flesh from her legs—had been arranged upon the room's table like so much slaughterhouse offal. Mary Kelly's heart, however, was not found, nor has it ever been.

And just as shockingly as he had fallen upon these very same Whitechapel locales that "Autumn of Terror" like the most deeply disgusting, penny dreadful fiend, Jack the Ripper seemingly faded, like a phantom, into the London fog, leaving Mary Kelly's most brutal and bloodthirsty butchery as his sickening farewell. And with it, Donald Rumbelow's walking tour was done.

Throughout its two hours, Rumbelow's narration was truly a thing of blood-weltered beauty, verily something he had recited many, *many* times before. His booming delivery was dry but never dead and, as he disseminated the facts and the fictions of the Jack the Ripper murder mystery, his deeply knowledgeable expertise on—and even deeper engagement with—the case shined through like the ghastly gleam of that Whitechapel butcher's knife cutting through the darkness.

Because of this, Creepy Reader, should you want to walk amongst those East End back alleys that Jack the Ripper himself once stalked, you can either buy one of the sundry "Jack the Ripper Walk" maps that we gruesome twosome saw being sold like newspapers all about London and do it yourself or, as yours cruelly did, be guided about those horrendous homicide-horrid haunts by that famously foremost Ripperologist, Donald Rumbelow. The option is yours, but if you do settle for the former, know that you'll be missing out on a truly *killer* night!

Upon returning to our crypt-away-from-krypt from our sickeningly seedy and savage one-night stand with the one and only Jack the Ripper that was Donald Rumbelow's walking terror-tour of Whitechapel, we gruesome twosome sank into a well-deserved sleep, but, at least for yours cruelly, this slumber would be all but glutted with the most macabrely gruesome and grotesquely mad glimpses of murder, perhaps—very well, Creepy Reader!—even more so than those "From Hell": the execrably man-exterminating and man-eating exploits of that "Demon Barber of Fleet Street" . . . Sweeney Todd!

Behind "Saucy Jack," Sweeney Todd is the most fiendishly infamous of London's foully fatality-ferocious felons and, thusly, the atrociously unspeakable acts for which he—and his accomplice in awfully anthropophagic alimentation, the shocking pie-shoppe shoppe, Mrs. Lovett—has been a veritable, and venerable, boogeyman for almost 200 years have become immortalized, time and time again, in almost every medium.

Within the world of the printed word, Sweeney Todd was first introduced to London's repugnantly "penny dreadful" reading populace in the 1846-published pages of Thomas Peckett Prest's *A String of Pearls: A Romance*—that other notoriously noisome nineteenth century "penny blood" narrative, *Varney the Vampire; or, The Feast of Blood,* is also, variously, attributed to Prest—which told the terribly sordid tale of that "bloodthirsty wretch" and "human ghoul" known as "The Demon Barber of Fleet Street," who waited, like a spider for a fly, behind his ingeniously engineered barber's chair for "any victims presumably possessed of valuables who might present themselves at his shop for a shave or what-not" so that he could, instead, offer them a—egads!—"polishing off."

The detestable "dreadful"-disseminated disgusts of Prest's seminal Sweeney Todd-shuddersome shocker would be dramatized so very disquietingly but a year later by playwright George Dibdin Pitt into *A String of Pearls, or The Fiend of Fleet Street*—although some would, indeed, have Pitt's play be the progenitor of the Demon Barber's portraiture rather than Prest's "penny."

Throughout the remainder of the 1800s, begotten by Sweeney's many would-be biographers were various, and variously worthwhile, serialized short stories, dramas, and even novels, each of them—feeding, at times plagiarizingly, upon the fabrications of Prest or Pitt or both—further fleshing out that Fleet Street barber's fiendishness. With the birth of the motion picture at the dawn of the twentieth century, so too would begin Sweeney's sinister celluloid simulacra, the very first of which was 1936's *Sweeney Todd: The Demon Barber of Fleet Street,* with the appropriately named sneering and churlish scenery-chewer Todd Slaughter "polishing off" all those all-too-unsuspectingly seating themselves within Sweeney's Fleet Street barber shoppe.

While other features, for sinema and television both, would take a swing at Sweeney Todd's straight razor, that Demon Barber did not become, truly, a nefariously horrid household name—his hideous homicidal and homovorous horrors whispered with the same sense of worry and woe, Creepy Reader, as those of Jack the Ripper's—until, on March 1st, 1979, Steven Sondheim's "musical thriller" opened in New York.

Based upon Christopher Bond's early-'70s stage play, whose treatment of Todd was, verily, tempered by its seedy, sordid, and salacious Victorian London setting, Sondheim's obscenely exquisite "opera"—with Len Cariou as the Demon Barber and Angela Lansbury as Mrs. Lovett, who will always be for yours cruelly, Creepy Reader, that disreputably dread-defining duo—curdled the blood of a whole new audience so very consumingly and, with its chorus of "Swing your razor wide, Sweeney!", transformed Sweeney Todd's simple "penny dreadful" story into an utter saga of profoundly staggering proportions.

And with not only Broadway's recent second revival of Sondheim's magnificently macabre murder-and-meat-musing musical, but the recent news that Tim Burton himself will direct the adaptation of its delectable dreadfulness—with, very possibly, Johnny Depp lullabying Todd's razors with such lyrics as, "My lucky friends./Till now your shine/Was merely silver./Friends,/You shall drip rubies,/You'll soon drip precious rubies . . ."—the tale of Sweeney Todd would seem to know no end.

While all of these versions of that vital story of a voracity for violence most vicious and of victuals most verily vile that was Sweeney Todd's differ in the details of the Demon Barber's raison d'etre—he is either the murderously money-maniacal monster of Prest's or the less than villainously whetted vessel of woefully vengeful wrath who is, in truth, Sondheim's Benjamin Barker—as well as in the particulars of Mrs. Lovett's partnership with Todd—she herself either, so very simply, hates or loves Todd and, thus, her perverse human-meat pies are cooked in the name of avarice or adoration—the bare bones of Todd and Lovett's extremely egregious enterprise remains: carnage and cannibalism, in all their now-classick cold-blooded cruelty.

All of them portray Sweeney Todd appropriate to their particular purposes; however, none of them attend to whether or not there ever truly *was* a Sweeney Todd settled amidst Fleet Street, let alone one who shaved—and slit!—throats, because, Creepy Reader, the answer is deranged in the deepest of debates. The "facts" and "fictions" of Sweeney Todd intermix extraordinarily more enigmatically than was the case with his blood-bathing London-born brother in boogeyman-erisms, Jack the Ripper.

Some would attest that the outright fictional origins of Sweeney's sinister Demon Barber scheme—the murder as well as the meat-pies which hid all-too-hideously the resulting human remains within the all-too-hungry—are found either with the French tale of the petrifying Paris *peruquier*—or barber—a translation of which appeared, as "A Terrible Story of the Rue-de-la-Harpe," in London's very own *The Tell Tale* magazine in 1825 or with repulsive nursery rhymes recited by mean French mothers to affear their recalcitrant and unruly French rug rats as early as the fifteenth century.

On the other hand, others would attest that all of this is but the macabre mythmaking of a very real man verily known as "Sweeney Todd"—a very madly man-slaughterous real man, born in London on October 26, 1756, at 85 Brick Lane and hanged for his homicidal Fleet Street horrors on January 25, 1802, at London's notoriously grotesque Newgate Gaol—and that, as ravening "Demon Barber" researcher Peter Haining has esteemed the "facts" of "the real story of Sweeney Todd is [. . .] far stranger than fiction; and, equally, more interesting and gruesome than any of these alleged prototypes."

But whether or not he is truly "real"—whether he is in league with the all-too-legitimate likes of such monstrous man-eating mass-murderers as fifteenth-century Scotland's very own "Sawney" Beane, who, with his wife and a contemptibly savage clutch of their sickeningly consanguined spawn, killed and cooked almost 1,000 tragically wayward travelers, or if he's the frightful urban legend forefather of those shuddersome celluloid slashers such as *A Nightmare On Elm Street*'s Freddy Krueger, whose very own finger-razors sliced through the tender throats of teenagers—does not matter because, in the end, Creepy Reader, Sweeney Todd simply *is*.

As concluded by godly comic book great Neil Gaiman—whose very own fully-realized chapter in Sweeney Todd's horrendously Horror-fied heritage would have done for the Demon Barber what Alan Moore's *From Hell* did for Jack the Ripper—"Sweeney lived, or he didn't" but that "Whatever his roots [. . .] Sweeney is part of a line that began with the first innkeeper ever to cut the throat of a lonely traveler and feed him to the next party to come that way."

And it was for those very same "roots" that Gaiman's work would have explored—that awfully atrocity-appalled archetype of the shuddersomely smiling, straight razor-stropping slaughterer, the hideously black-hearted human-butchering horror, the Demon Barber himself, Sweeney Todd!—that, the very next mourning, my unspeakable wife and yours cruelly shambled down to that fiendishly infamy-fouled Fleet Street to exhume.

SWEENEY TODD'S BARBERSHOP
186 Fleet Street
(next to St. Dunstan's Church)

ST. DUNSTAN'S CHURCH
("St. Dunstan-in-the-West")
Fleet Street
020 7405 1929

We two most terribly strange Sweeney Todd terror-seekers disembarked the Tube at the Blackfriars Station and, as we rose unto New Bridge Street, found ourselves amidst a somewhat grayly grim setting before the Blackfriars Bridge and, thereunder, the tenebrous waters of the Thames. It was but two blocks more before we came to Fleet Street upon the left-hand side of New Bridge at Ludgate Circus.

In the late fifteenth century, the very first printing press in not simply London but in all of England was founded here upon Fleet Street and, perhaps thusly, it became synonymous with publishing and the press. London's earliest newspaper, *The Daily Courant*—known then as a "one-sheet"—was printed through some Fleet Street press in 1702 and, almost a century later, the "penny dreadfuls," whose job it was to goosebump the skin, curdle the blood, and turn the stomach with horrors heaped upon horrendous horrors, would follow it.

One of these petrifyingly purposed Fleet Street-printed publications was the perhaps poorly titled *The People's Periodical and Family Library*, the seventh issue of which—dated November 21, 1846—witnessed the blood-heralded birth of Sweeney Todd with the serialized "dreadful" slaughter of Thomas Prest's *A String of Pearls*. In his tale of terribly

TO LURK AMIDST THE LOATHSOME WITHIN THE LONDON FOG + 77

xyrophobic terror, Prest ascertained the whereabouts amidst Fleet Street of Sweeney Todd's basely shrouded barbershop by way of two legendary London landmarks: Temple Bar and St. Dunstan's Church.

The griffon-mounted monument known as the Temple Bar Memorial stands, since 1880, where the former had stood between Fleet Street and the Strand. Sculpted in 1672 upon the deeply majestic designs of Sir Christopher Wren, that awesome Portland stone arch of which Prest wrote, upon whose spiked height was once adorned the severed heads of traitors and felons and other such troublesome sorts, was one of the eight aged gateways into the City of London itself—called the "Temple Bar" because it existed alongside the Temple Law Courts, known now as the Royal Courts of Justice, and because it also existed at the very same location where its primeval thirteenth-century progenitor had been fashioned in the form of a "bar," which was, more than likely, simply a chain strung between two posts.

However, in a late-nineteenth-century attempt to contend with Fleet Street's congestion, the arch was removed to Theobalds Park, where it decayed in utter decrepitude, at least until November 10, 2004, when it was returned, reconstructed so very remarkably for the sum of some three million pounds, to the City of London, where it sits within the sacrosanct shadow of St. Paul's Cathedral as the gateway to, now, Paternoster Square.

But while the Temple Bar abides there no longer, St. Dunstan's Church does still and, as we lurked further and further down Fleet Street, we gruesome twosome espied that latter late-twelfth-century building looming before us. Founded as early as 1070—and utterly rebuilt in 1831—and named after the patron saint of blacksmiths, jewelers, and locksmiths, St. Dunstan's—also known as "St. Dunstan-in-the-West"—had, at one time in its history stood, not only at the very heart of Fleet Street but some 30 feet out into it.

But as London rose all about it, that once-toweringly imperious Anglican temple shrank further and further into Fleet Street's bustlingly burgeoning backdrop until that extraordinary Gothic edifice was all but hidden therein. Although its olden eminence has become thusly obscured, St. Dunstan's has remained a curiosity because of two of its peculiar characteristics: its octagonal insides throughout which seven different Christian sects are honored between four different chapels and three different shrines and, most famously, its conspicuous Fleet Street clock—erected there after the Great Fire of 1666 by parishioners in honor of the church's survival—which is rung every quarter of an hour by the clubs of two clockwork giants.

However, it was for none of this, Creepy Reader, that we were beckoned to St. Dunstan's but, in the stead of its antiquity and architecture, its very abutments, for it was indeed next to that church—but a block from where, until 1878, the Temple Bar would have been found—that we came upon 186 Fleet Street: the very address of Sweeney Todd's simple-barbershop-cum-human-slaughterhouse!

But what my black bride and yours cruelly found there was, rather, a horrendously un-Horrible business known as "Kall Kwik," which, from its advertised "Print Copy Design" avocations, was some sort of graphic design service. Kall Kwik inhabited, seemingly, but the first floor of 186 Fleet Street, while its slim and sooty red-brick façade was also adorned with the seemingly defunct signage for the *Sunday Post*, the *People's*

Friend, the *People's Journal*, and the *Dundee Courier*, all of this a rather prodigious reminder of Fleet Street's printing pressed past.

Because of the emphasis upon the "people's" press therein, yours cruelly wondered if that publisher of Prest's *A String of Pearls* was not, in fact, housed here and, thus, Sweeney's address having come from that of his foully perverse fiendishness's very first printing. But regardless of such reasoning, 186 Fleet Street was where Haining had said it would be with the exception that the wee alleyway known as "Hen and Chicken Court"—which he had verging Sweeney's shoppe upon the one side and St. Dunstan's the other—was actually 185 Fleet Street and, therein, a Thomas Leng Publications.

Despite such a small discrepancy, it was here at No. 186, before which we lurked in all of our loathsome bloodlustfulness, that "real-life" Sweeney was said to have set up his barber-turned-human-butcher-shoppe, with a window-hung signboard scrawled with the words "Easy shaving for a penny—As good as you will find any" advertising his services, which also included, at least as his "real" story goes, surgery!

Within that shabby and perhaps even somewhat squalid shoppe of Sweeney's was his otherwise unassuming barber chair, which, "constructed in the most ingenious manner"—despite the minute variations of its exact mechanisms as portrayed throughout the Demon Barber's many, many portraitures—had the primarily perverse purpose of delivering Sweeney's customers, whether alive or dead, into the drippily disgusting darkness of the hideous charnel house that was 186 Fleet Street's basement!

In some of those Sweeney Todd stories, it was the fall unto it alone that "polished off" the barbarously base barber's patrons; in others, it was Sweeney's all-too-savagely close shave that did the dirty dreadful deed. But the Demon Barber's thusly cruelly served clientele all became, in the end, nothing but *meat* and, once Sweeney had cut it from their bones, it was their repulsively rotting remains from which exuded so execrably, Creepy Reader, "those horrid smells" that, as portrayed in Prest's *Pearls*, "came from a cellar under Sweeny Todd's shop here," the "unpleasant odour which threatened to suffocate the congregation" of dismayed neighboring St. Dunstan's.

And as the customer-carrion of Sweeney Todd's cursable carnage foetidly festered so foully, that most shuddersomely manslaughtered mortal-meat was made into the "savoury-smelling and pleasant-looking pies" of that Demon Barber's partner in consummately inhuman crimes, Mrs. Lovett. It was at her "ordinary twopenny pie shop" where these profoundly odious pies of Lovett's were "sold by hundreds to hungry customers who came from far and near, attracted by the reputation which the pastry cook's widow had obtained for [their] succulence and savoury flavour."

While Sondheim's obscenely outstanding operatic ode to the outrages of Sweeney Todd had located Lovett's bakehouse but beneath his barbershop, all of the other versions of the tale of that Demon Barber found it but a block or so further down Fleet Street, upon the other side of St. Dunstan's, amidst what is known as Bell Yard. And it was there that we gruesome twosome, after sniffing about for the smallest scent of the shameful Sweeney Todd-spewed stench that was said to have suffused 186 Fleet Street, went to this very same Bell Yard in search of one of Lovett's meat pies.

MRS. LOVETT'S PIE SHOPPE
Bell Yard (right side, going from
Fleet Street to Carey Street)

THE OLD BANK OF ENGLAND
194 Fleet Street
020 7430 2255

Leaving that supposedly former Fleet Street barbershop of Sweeney Todd's, we lurked beneath the Demon Barber-unblessed shadow of St. Dunstan's Church and then past Chancery Lane, whereupon we found ourselves before the dourly dignified Italianate digs of the Old Bank of England. At 194 Fleet Street, the Old Bank was, as its name alludes, a bygone Fleet Street branch of the Bank of England that was, some time ago, turned into a particularly classy pub, Fuller's Ale & Pie House, by the London-born Fuller's brewery.

Before the Old Bank we espied a simple and small signboard on which was scrawled, in chalk, an advertisement: "a great selection of PIES—what we're famous for." Beneath this somewhat peculiar public praise was a sketch of a steaming specimen of its subject: a meat pie. But this was not, Creepy Reader, some simple self-promotion of a mouthwatering morsel from its menu but, rather—by means of their "succulence and savoury flavour"—some truly terrible territorial ties for which the Fuller's Old Bank of England is not so much "famous" but, verily, *in*famous!

For you see, it was some feet beneath Fleet Street that Sweeney was said to have brought those macabrely meat pie-misfortuned men who were his unknowing customers—whole or cuts—from No. 186's black, butchering bowels to Mrs. Lovett's Bell Yard shoppe, our walk an approximation of his corpse-conducting course. And it was further said, Creepy Reader, that it was, indeed, the viciously tenebrous vaults and tunnels under the Old Bank of England that offered Sweeney the passageway for his dreadfullest dead-dealing deeds.

However, St. Dunstan's is said to have vaults and tunnels of its very own, which, verily, have also been repulsively ill-rumored as Sweeney's route to and fro, something that made me wonder exactly how many vaults and tunnels there were under our feet as we stood there along Fleet Street!

It was but at the next block, after leaving that buried butcher's byway there beneath the Old Bank, that my noctiflorous bride and yours cruelly came upon Bell Yard, before which the Temple Bar would have been had we ourselves been upon Fleet Street sometime in the nineteenth century. Bell Yard was—of corpse!—a dead-end street—formed between the stately spike-gated severity of those Royal Courts of London and a straight stretch of some all-too-signless buildings—with an entrance, or exit, where it struck Carey Street but with neither upon Fleet.

While we crawled up and down it, from Fleet Street to Carey and then back again, our abhorrently atrocious Horror-fiending attentions were called to the lower left-hand side of Bell Yard, for it was there, Creepy Reader, that Prest had established the location of Mrs. Lovett's luridly loathsome pie shoppe! However, unlike Sweeney's barbershop, no exact address has ever been given for Lovett's extremely egregious establishment, other than the fact that, as Prest wrote, upon "the left side of Bell Yard, going down from Carey Street."

Even less is known about the "facts" of this most morbidly mysterious meat pie-maker known to wretched ghastliness-worshippers such as we as Mrs. Lovett, that awfully anthropophagy-abetting accomplice of Sweeney Todd, whose Bell Yard bakehouse was one of "the most celebrated shops for the sale of veal and pork pies that London had ever produced. High and low, rich and poor, resorted to it; its fame had spread far and wide." Who was Mrs. Lovett? How did she come to own that Bell Yard pie shoppe? How was she introduced to Sweeney—and was she his cohort in, simply, carnage and cannibalism, or in carnality as well? The answers to these questions and more offer no ultimate "truth": in the end, there is either a fathomless mess of "facts" or, simply, none at all.

But, yet again, Creepy Reader, yours cruelly had not come to Fleet Street for "truth" but—indeed!—two of Horror's most abysmally horrendous archetypes. Back at 186 Fleet Street, we gruesome twosome had feasted so Horror-fiendishly upon the first of them: the Demon Barber and his shudder-shrouded barbershop. And here—somewhere!—amidst Bell Yard was the second: the house of human meat pie horrors, unto which, through a fake basement wall, Sweeney Todd would deliver the shockingly gruesome stuff with which Mrs. Lovett made them. Therein, she became the gloriously macabre grandmother of other grisly cannibal gore-mets, from *Motel Hell*'s Farmer Vincent and his fritters to *The Untold Story*'s Wong Chi Hang and his human pork buns.

Simply lurking there about Lovett's very own putrid mystery meat pie-loathy Bell Yard made yours cruelly yearn to have but a taste of their "succulence and savoury flavour." Just thinking about them does make the mouth water, though, does it not, Creepy Reader?

Of Punishment & Prison

Having just finished "polishing off" Sweeney Todd's very own 186 Fleet Street as well as his Lovett's Bell Yard from our infamy-disinterring itinerary, we two most horrendously hungry Horror-hounds so ended our journey down amidst the most loathsome madness and mass murder—Bedlam, the

Ripper, the Demon Barber!—of London's utterly macabre underbelly. But in spite of our straight razor-shocked sojourn upon Fleet Street, the mourning was still as fresh upon our trauma-tormented London terror-tour's chopping block as a still-coffined, unmolested corpse, and so my crepuscular bride and yours cruelly headed out hunting for more horrors!

In particular, Creepy Reader, this next hacked-off leg of our exploratory exhumation of London's exceedingly execrable extremities would witness us interrogating its blackest legacy of bloodcurdling legalized brutality. Renowned Russian writer Fyodor Dostoevsky once said that, "the degree of civilization in a society can be judged by entering its prisons." If such an investigation of London's very own profoundly pernicious penal past was undertaken, its portrait thusly produced would be utterly horrifying! And it was indeed for those very same horrifically dark and dreadfully disquieting chapters in "civilized" London's history that we gruesome twosome were in search of as we wormed our wickedly woe-wanting way from Fleet Street towards the Marble Arch.

TYBURN TREE
(Former Location)
Junction of Bayswater Road, Oxford Street, Edgeware Road, and Park Lane (Across from the Marble Arch)

NEWGATE GAOL
(Former Location; Now the Old Bailey Central Criminal Court)
Corner of Newgate Street and Old Bailey
020 7248 3277 (Old Bailey)

After lurking about the Marble Arch Tube Station for some minutes, we two torturously terrible torture-tourers finally found the exit we wanted and then, thusly, found before us the stout and stately stone structure known so very simply as the Marble Arch. The monument was built in 1827 upon the very triumphal vision of John Nash, the Royal Family's very own architect, to be the grand and glorious gateway unto Buckingham Palace— which Nash had also remodeled for King George IV—

but it would seem as if its already decidedly majestic design was simply not majestic enough, as the Court's horse-drawn coaches could not pass through it. Because of that, it was moved, in 1851, to the northeast corner of Hyde Park—Park Lane's distance from Buckingham Palace—and called, of corpse, the Marble Arch.

But before it—for almost 600 years, at least in some form, until 1783—reigning here upon the London landscape, but a little further down Bayswater Road, where it converged upon not only Oxford Street but Edgware Road, was a structure of an utterly singular species, whose existence the monument before us was not simply meant to exchange but—verily, Creepy Reader—exorcise. At its heart was a wooden triangle, each of its three arms some nine feet wide, held off the earth by three 18-foot-tall posts like some huge three-legged stool. It was called the Tyburn Tree and it was upon the capably constructed crossarms of this "triple tree"—not only London's very first gallows but its ghastliest!— that almost 60,000 "criminals" were hanged.

Since ancient times—at least since the Roman colonization, if not before—the territory all about the Marble Arch was known as Tyburn, named after the Tyburn, or "Ty Bourne," Stream, one of the many either extinct or simply eclipsed tributaries of the Thames. Oxford Street and Park Lane were two Roman roads then known, respectively, as Tyburn Road and Tyburn Lane that ventured unto this time-forgotten village of Tyburn and it was at their junction—with, now, Bayswater Road from the west and Edgeware Road from the north—that the Tyburn Tree was founded in 1571.

However, that lot of Tyburn land upon which it stood had been the location of executions at least since 1196—the very first being that of the seditious Saxon-seeded William Fitzosbert, or "William the Long-Beard"—very likely with nooses tied onto the limbs of very real, tall Tyburn trees. In fact, the trees there along the bank of the Tyburn Stream were known as "The King's Gallows." But again, Creepy Reader, it was not until almost 400 years later that that terrible triple tree of Tyburn was first used, with the hanging of Dr. John Story, a Catholic who denied the sovereignty of Queen Elizabeth I.

Although Tyburn had been allotted for the hanging of court-condemned "criminals"—from felons to religious martyrs to traitors, each of them made "a Dreadful and Awful Example to Others, a Sacrifice to his Country's Justice"—it was, verily, upon the revoltingly ill-rumored rooting of that terrifically repugnant Tree, Creepy Reader, that most of the 60,000 who died there in Tyburn were executed. Because of its cruelly ingenious construction, 24 could "dance the Tyburn jig" at the very same time, eight hanged from each of the triple tree's "limbs." However, it was only once—recorded as June 23, 1649—that the Tyburn Tree was the host to such a foully full, horridly neck-hung house.

It was traditionally from noisomely notorious Newgate Gaol, almost three miles to the east—"this gloomy depository of the guilt and misery of London," as Charles Dickens referred to it in 1836's *Sketches by Boz*, founded there in the heinous black heart of the City of London in 1188 upon the decree of King Henry II, where it stood as the deepest disturbingly dread-defined of all of London's already atrocious prisons until 1902 when

it was demolished so that London's Central Criminal Court, the Old Bailey, could be founded there in its savagely primeval stead—that the tragedy-traumatized victims of the Tyburn Tree were brought in tasteless horse-drawn tumbrels.

These hangings were not only public but, in

order to serve their dreadfully deterring raison d'etre, were promoted as hideous public holidays and thousands upon thousands of loathsomely death-lusting Londoners would turn out to watch the profoundly perverse "parade" that was this procession unto the Tree. These monstrously morbid-minded mobs would wish a "Good Dying!" to the condemned but then heckle them so very horridly if they wept. They would then surround the Tyburn Tree in severely savage swarms, even stuffing themselves—for a fee!—into unsteady grandstands erected there for those gruesomely shock-gawking gangs by terribly enterprising Tyburners, and there they would wait that deadly "dance" of the disquietingly Tyburn Tree-doomed.

Those tumbrels would be brought beneath the triple tree, nooses would be affixed about the necks of the viciously condemned victims within, and then—egads!—they would be damned to dangle there so very dreadfully as the carts were drawn out from under them. In those ghastly days of gore, death by hanging was not from a neatly broken neck but, deeply more disturbingly, *strangulation*! It was thus not so very uncommon then, Creepy Reader, for humane relations of the hanged to pull down upon their lamentably shaking legs until they did indeed finally—finally!—decease.

But then after a time, their frightfully black-faced bodies would be cut down from the Tree and the fate that awaited their hanging-ravaged human remains was, typically, as foul as that which had faced them in life. Sometimes, their corpses would be "drawn"—the belly hewn in order to expose, and then extract, the bowels—and then "quartered"—the arms and the legs and, finally, the head cut from the torso—so that the corpses' thusly parceled carneous parts could be displayed throughout London as a wretchedly putrid warning against lawlessness, treason, and the undesirable like, a most "effective" practice if the hanged were of renowned ill-repute.

Other times—and, seemingly, more often—their corpses would be sold to hospitals or medical schools—the creeps-coloured coming of their cadaver-collecting couriers oftentimes inciting the mean Tyburn-assembled masses to riot in utter revulsion—and would be found underneath the tools of the anatomist's trade. Because of the less than exact method of execution that the Tyburn Tree offered, it was not unheard of for the horrible corpse of the hanged—the "half-hanged man"—to revive upon the terrifying realization that the anatomist's knife was cutting into his (or her) frightfully *still-living* flesh!

From 1196, with the hanging of the William Fitzosbert, until November 3, 1783, with that of the malicious highwayman John Austin—and the almost 60,000 others in between—Tyburn was the most shockingly shudder-shrouded location in all of already loathsomeness-lousy London—more than Bedlam, more than Newgate, and more than even the Tower of London—and it was the Tyburn Tree, that ghastly torture-tailored triple-gallows also known as "Tyburn's Deadly Nevergreen," that became the very heinous symbol of such severest horror.

The Tree actually became "the Tree of Life and the Gate of Heaven" for the sisters of London's very own Tyburn Convent—which can be found, still, at 8 Hyde Park Place but paces from where the Tree once stood—who honor, as martyrs, the 105 Catholics who were hanged upon it during the Reformation simply for their treasonous religious tendency.

While such a totally un-terror-ed transformation of the Tyburn Tree was an utter anomaly, it would indeed seem, Creepy Reader, as if the execrable excess of executions there as well as—if not more so!—the sickeningly perverse sideshow-esque public spectacle with which they were so very obscenely and odiously observed—had, finally, become too unwholesomely horrid because, in 1783, the hangings there were stopped and the tremendously terror-told Tree was, so very sadly, torn down.

The demoralized gallows-doomed would do a disturbing new "dance," thereafter, amidst the same but smaller sort of revoltingly repugnant revelry outside Newgate's very own grotesquely hangings-gloomed Debtor's Door until 1868, when they were done inside the gaol and then, in 1902, no more.

But where the Tyburn Tree had once stood—again, at the junction of Bayswater Road, Park Lane, Oxford Street, and Edgware Road—we gruesome twosome found, all but hidden by a heavy flow of cars and trucks, an inconspicuous triangular cobblestone traffic island, at the heart of which was set a modest stone marker inscribed, so very simply, with the words, "The Site of Tyburn Tree." While yours cruelly did not expect to find some marble statue of a cruelly condemned criminal "dancing" at the end of a revoltingly noosed rope, that marker seemed a less than adequate memorial to that grandly dreadfullest gallows unhallowed so very Horror-ifically in London's history.

THE CLINK PRISON MUSEUM
1 Clink Street
0171 403 6515

We gruesome twosome took the Tube, yet again, to the London Bridge Station and then wormed our black woe-begetting way through the small sinuous and singular streets of Southwark and came upon the excavation of what was known as the Winchester House, of which but a still wondrously rose-windowed wall remains. From 1109 until 1642, the Winchester House was the marvelously magnificent manor of the Bishops of Winchester, which was built by the next Bishop of Winchester, Henri de Blois, in 1109.

Almost 20 years later, King Henry I dubbed both the estate and the environs "The Liberty of the See of Winchester in the Clink in the Borough of Southwark"—The Liberty of the Clink. It is said that its "Liberty" referred to either the fact that the Bishop was granted, by the King, absolute autonomy and authority over the vicinity or, simply, that it was a regal residency thusly recognized; however, the referent of its "Clink" is not thus known. While some would say that it was the name commonly held for the Bishop's share of Southwark, others attest that it either alludes to, onomatopoeically, the actual "clinking" of massive metal manacles or, by way of a derivation of the Middle English *clenchen*, the process upon which they were pinioned upon prisoners.

Regardless of which of these is the exact origin of that "Clink," taken together, they both evidence that, verily, the province of the Bishop of Winchester's power extended not only to the imprisonment of all those living under it but—egads!—their punishment as well. And it was but a little further along Clink Street, past the ruins of those very same bishops' Winchester House, that my black bride and yours cruelly found the Liberty of the Clink's very own petrifying primeval penitentiary that would become—indeed, Creepy Reader!—the egregiously notorious eponym for all prisons and pitiless penal perils thereafter!

While the real "Clink Prison," as it would become known, was utterly burned down by those very same ruinous Lord George Gordon rioters of 1780 who had attempted to do the very same to Newgate but across the Thames, the Clink Prison Museum was founded within a portion of what appeared to be, at least to yours cruelly, a hulking warehouse erected where its thusly passed-on punitive predecessor had stood since 1109. The declared raison d'etre of the Clink Prison Museum was to depict the history of—as the placard beneath the cruelly gibbeted corpse that greeted us but before the museum's entrance had proclaimed it—that "prison that gave its name to all others."

Because of this, a good deal of it was indeed devoted to telling the Clink's terribly curious tale: from its very origins out of an olde Saxon-aged ordinance that all religious order residences within England had to set aside some secluded space in which to, more or less, jail any of their

YOU ARE ENTERING THE ORIGINAL SITE OF THE CLINK THE PRISON THAT GAVE ITS NAME TO ALL OTHERS.

mischievously wayward members, to its existence as the very first women's prison in all of London, due to the Bishop of Winchester's renownedly peculiar regulation of a bevy of Thames-banked brothels there in that Medieval "red-light district" of Southwark and his power to punish any "unprofessional" prostitutes thereby.

However, as we gruesome twosome explored that self-sung educational simulacrum of the very first frightfully foul, felon-filled Clink, it became apparent that the museum was not simply fashioned and fancifully dread-festooned for the purposes of rendering a portrait of the notoriously noisome natures of *all* of London's pronouncedly primitive prisons but—indeed, Creepy Reader!—*reveling* in their piteously torturous punishments!

From the very first, with the fore-bodingly black timber-and-brick façade of the museum's entrance, yours cruelly knew that it would be, genuinely, a jailhouse of horrors whose educational essence was but extraneous and, while its displays were indeed immensely informational, their true reason was to repulse—something which they evoked very well.

Found throughout the museum's somewhat modest space—which was made to look, through wonderfully faux-stone walls, distressed wooden décor, and luridly atmospheric lighting, like what that original Clink very well may have—were these delightfully dreadful depictions of loathsomest London prison life: a jailor hammering shut a morose prisoner's manacles; a contemptibly debased convict with his feet in the stocks; a grim prison guard waiting so very wickedly behind a chair of the torture chamber; a foully dehumanized felon playing with his revolting pet rat! Whilst not in bad taste by any means, Creepy Reader, all of the Clink Prison Museum's disgust-designed diorama displays were horrendous enough to thrill even we two hideously felonious Horror-fiends!

The Clink Prison Museum offered my unspeakable wife and yours cruelly perhaps more fiendish-fun—in particular, at least for me, its various tools of that terrible torture trade!—than that profoundly prominent prison should! But exactly why it would be this very same Clink of those Bishops of

Winchester that continues to nickname all other jails almost 200 years after it was actually destroyed is unbeknownst to me, Creepy Reader—especially since a seemingly more shocking penal specimen festered but on the other side of the Thames in the frightfully foul form of Newgate.

Yours cruelly is not a Shakespearean scholar, but perhaps, as his Globe Theatre is not so very distant, that Bard immortalized this iniquitous Southwark institution in one of his dramatic works? Regardless, that "excellent piece of villainy" that was once London's very own Clink Prison was, indeed, a worthy well-Horror-fied chapter of our terror-tour of London's basest prison-and-punishment-boiled underbelly.

THE TOWER OF LONDON
Tower Hill
0171 709 0765

After our deeply disquieting, dread-devouring day amidst the abhorrent penal archetypes of Tyburn, Newgate, and the Clink—egads, Creepy Reader!—we gruesome twosome continued our exploration of London's loathsomest legally Horror-lousy leg-endry with a cruelly creeps-crawling curiosity that was so utterly monstrous that we gruesome twosome had to devote a whole day to exhuming its exquisite terror-execrated treasures: the Tower of London!

Amongst all of London's all-too-in-demand tourist destinations—from the august sacrosanct wonders of Westminster Abbey to the proudly bounteous pomp of Buckingham Palace—the Tower of London is, verily, the only one that is truly of a shuddersomely Horror-fied sort.

It is indeed most commonly known—to the tremendously popular tune of some 2.5 million tourists each year—for the likes of: the regally restored former royal residence that is the Medieval Palace; the Crown Jewels overseen in all their ostentation within the Waterloo Barracks; the olde and original eleventh-century keep known as the White Tower, for which the Tower of London itself was named; the Yeoman Warders, or "Beefeaters," who once guarded England's kings and queens whilst at the Tower, but who now guide visitors about it; and, of corpse, those nine ravens upon whom the fate of all of England is said to be founded.

However, the almost 1,000-year-old Tower of London became so very unfathomably infamous—a shuddersome symbol of sinister sovereign severity, an affearingly agony-atmosphered archetype of the atrocities of absolute authority—not because of any of these but, in their acutely more agreeable stead, the excruciatingly dread-ridden, royally-decreed executions that happened here: almost 125 outside of the Tower of London, within what is now known as Trinity Square, and but seven inside of the Tower upon Tower Green.

For you see, Creepy Reader, for a markedly ghastly many of its most grand Medieval guests, a visit to that tenebrous terror-told Tower of London was a one-way trip! And it was indeed for this very same nause-atingly Horror-natured taste of the Tower that we gruesome twosome hungered for so very hideously—except, of corpse, for the beheadings!—as we came out of the Tower Hill Tube Station and beheld before us what stands as the very heart of England's horrid history: the Tower of London!

We two horrendously fear-feasting Horror-fiends had to wait for almost an hour in one of many lines at the Tower's ticket office before we could pay

for our admission and, once we had, we lurked first through the Middle Tower and then the Byward Tower—between which had once existed, traversing the Tower's moat, one of the Tower's many now-extinct drawbridges—and it was then, Creepy Reader, the we found our sickening shock-savoring selves trapped within that terribly dreaded Tower of London!

The Tower's roots are found amidst the late-eleventh-century reign of William the Conqueror, who, in about 1078, had begun the building of the White Tower, that very eldest medieval edifice at the Tower that defined its raison d'etre as not only a king's home but a hold as well. Thereafter, that truly forbidding Tower was enveloped by further erections throughout the following 300 years: from 1190 until 1285, an inner and then an outer tower-tended "curtain wall," as well as the moat which surrounded them both, and then, during the fourteenth century, the Wharf.

Thusly founded, and then further fortified under the rule of eight different kings—Williams I and II, Richard I, John, Henry III, and Edwards I, II, and III!—it was not until some time after most of the Tower had, in fact, been already built that those egregiously excruciating episodes for which the Tower would become so repulsively ill-rumored occurred.

And as we shambled deeper into that shuddersome Tower down Water Lane, which sat between the Tower's thirteenth-century outer wall and its twelfth-century inner wall, we espied, fashioned into the face of the former, what has become known as Traitor's Gate: a water entrance unto the Tower from the Thames—built with St. Thomas's Tower sometime between 1275 and 1279 by King Edward I—through which many of those petrifyingly ill-fated perfidious prisoners of the Crown and Court were said to have come to the Tower of London, never to leave—at least not alive, Creepy Reader!

But across Water Lane from Traitor's Gate was what is very well the Tower's most commonly creepily-curious construction: the Bloody Tower! Before St. Thomas's Tower—as well as most of that outer wall—it was this that had stood upon the banks of the Thames; however, afterwards, it would become the main egress from the Outer Ward where we gruesome twosome still stood into the Inner Ward of the White Tower, the Tower Green, and so on.

While it was called the Garden Tower after it was built sometime in the early thirteenth century, it was renamed—sometime during the Tudor Dynasty, whose kings and queens ruled England from 1485 until 1603—as the deeply more distressing Bloody Tower because of the dread-commemorated disappearance of the sons of King Edward IV. After his death in 1483, these two princes—"The Princes of the Tower" as they have become known—were brought to the Tower of London by their uncle, Richard, Duke of Gloucester, but, after a time, were seen there no more, their uncle ascending to England's throne, as King Richard III, in their atrocity-veiled absence.

While the gory details of the horrors that befell them under the morbidly murderous ministrations of Richard III are the most macabre of mysteries, they have become the source of spooky and sordid speculation by such "histories" as William Shakespeare's *Richard III* (1597) and Roger Corman's *The Tower of London* (1962), in which Vincent Price starred as the wantonly villainous wretch, King Richard III.

Lurking beneath the Tower of London's legendarily loathsome Bloody Tower, my black bride and yours cruelly entered into the Inner Ward and, there, found ourselves within the supremely stately shadow of that White Tower. Beginning in 1509 with Henry VIII, the White Tower became the home of the Royal Armories and, today, it is similarly occupied with the Tower's collection of some 40,000 works of English weaponry.

But the White Tower was not only used for the accumulation and arrayal of armor and armaments but, horridly, for the tenanting—and torture!—of the terribly Tower of London-terrorized. The very first recorded prisoner of the White Tower was the Bishop of Durham, Ranulf Flambard, who was jailed there upon the obdurate royal orders of King Henry I in 1100. Throughout the following years—particularly during the sixteenth century with the divorce of the Church of England from Rome—its disturbingly dreadful dungeon became utterly infamous for its terrifically tormenting torture tools, the most feared of which was—of corpse!—the Rack!

But for yours cruelly, Creepy Reader, the most hideous torture tool would have to be what was called, variously, "Skeffington's Daughter" or "Scavenger's Daughter," which was invented in the mid-1500s by Sir Leonard Skeffington, an actual lieutenant of the Tower of London, to inflict upon a viciously violated victim an inhuman torture that was, basically, the very reverse of the Rack's: "The prisoner's body is folded into three, with the shins up against the thighs and the thighs against the stomach. The torturer then forces the ends of the two iron bows together and locks the prisoner inside, almost crushing his body with a hellish compression."

We gruesome twosome found a specimen of the curiously simple cruelty-contrivance that was the Tower's "Daughter," thusly placarded,

on display along with a Rack and other iniquity-intended instruments amidst an extraordinary permanent exhibit called "Torture at the Tower" in the basement of that terror-bathed Bloody Tower.

It was upon the left-hand side of that White Tower—at the very head of the Tower Green near the Waterloo Barracks, before which a seemingly interminable queue of tourists wanting to drool upon those Crown Jewels—that we two most traumatizingly terrible Tower-tourers found a somewhat somber stone-set square within which, cordoned off by black chains, was a metal-faced wooden marker inscribed, so very simply, with the words "Site of Scaffold." Yes, Creepy Reader, it was here, upon that small lot of the Tower's land before us, where, at least since the late fifteenth century, the Tower of London's most famous prisoners had been executed.

On this site stood a scaffold on which were executed:

Queen Anne Boleyn Second wife of Henry VIII	19 May 1536
Margaret, Countess of Salisbury Last Plantagenet Princess	28 May 1541
Queen Katherine Howard Fifth wife of Henry VIII	13 Feb 1542
Jane, Viscountess Rochford Wife of Anne Boleyn's brother	13 Feb 1542
Lady Jane Grey Uncrowned Queen of 9 days	12 Feb 1554
Robert Devereux Earl of Essex	25 Feb 1601
Lord Hastings was also beheaded near the spot in 1483	

While London's contemptibly common condemned criminals were, again, hanged upon that terrifying triple tree of Tyburn, some 125 others, found guilty of treason and imprisoned because of it at the Tower, were given a deeply more "honourable" death, because of their eminently estimable entitlements of Earl, Lord, Duke, Bishop, Archbishop, or simply Sir, by being not simply dying upon Tower Hill but by the more "tasteful" means of beheading.

However, their executions—while thusly respectful of the repute of those executed and utterly below the compare of the shockingly savage spectacles that so foully infamied the Tyburn Tree—were still execrable public events. But for seven scandalous sufferers of the Tower of London's shuddersome severities—including two of King Henry VIII's very own woefully unwanted wives, Anne Boleyn and Catherine Howard, both convicted of adultery—their executions were beyond the execrable ogling eyes of lousy everyday Londoners. These seven were ushered out of, very likely, the White Tower and then atop that simple wooden scaffold erected upon Tower Green. After laying their nobly notable necks down upon the headsman's chopping block, the rest, Creepy Reader, is history . . . horrendously horrid history!

As yours cruelly said before, we gruesome twosome spent most of our day at the Tower of London, not only because there was a staggering super-fluity of sovereignly specimens to see there, but because there were, so very simply, hundreds upon hundreds of other less terrorizingly Horror-fied tourists there too, producing lines after lines in which to wait! While the Tower was indeed a true and utter tourist attraction—the very utmost amongst all the chapters of our infamous London terror-tour's itinerary— it was, despite its viscous flood of visitors, an utter pleasure to walk about that legendarily hoary and Horror-loathsome London location.

After sitting for a little while before the venerable violence-vilified vista that was the Tower of London's exquisite expanse there upon the Thames, my unspeakable wife and yours cruelly lurked across Tower Hill Road to Trinity Square where stood the site of the Tower's subordinate second scaffold. There, we found a modest mournful memorial consisting of a stone square, not unlike that within the Tower, within which were founded greening metal plaques listed with the names and death-dates of some of the 125 who were beheaded here some centuries ago. The actual execution block which was used for not only Tower Hill's last beheading but all of England's—that of the seditious Scotsman, Simon Fraser, in 1747—can be found, alongside an actual headsman's axe, on display within the White Tower.

Having taken some crime scene photography of that bygone bed of blue-blooded beheadings, we gruesome twosome returned to the Tower Hill Tube Station and, from there, our London crypt-away-from-krypt so that we could sleep, for the mourning would bring the very last stop of our journey amongst London's delightfully hideous Horror-dreadfulled haunts: The London Dungeon!

THE LONDON DUNGEON
Tooley Street
020 7403 7221

During our execrable extremity-exhuming exploration of London's harrowingly horrendous and horrid historical horrors, my crepuscular bride and yours cruelly feasted so very fiendishly upon the foulest of frightful fare: Highgate Cemetery, the Old Operating Theatre, Bedlam, Mrs. Lovett's Pie Shoppe, the Tyburn Tree, the Clink, and so on. These were some of Horror's most atrociously morbid and macabre archetypes, themselves inspiring some of Horror's most revered masterpieces. Perchance you are asking yourself, Creepy Reader, how we gruesome twosome would be concluding such a tremendously terrifying tour as this? Well, we could find no more fitting end to this infamous Horror-fiend's creepy crawl than with the notorious London Dungeon!

It is almost a tradition for wax museums to have some space set aside for shuddersomely sordid simulacral spectacles—the chamber of horrors!—and it would seem that even the least horrid of visitors enjoy some beguilingly ghastly blood and guts along with their movie stars, athletes, historical figures, and the less lurid wax-like because they prove extremely popular.

And perhaps because the perversest petrification-purveyors of the London Dungeon have hacked off all such futilely wholesome "fat" from their very own waxworks and, instead, transmogrified it so very terrifyingly into one huge chamber of horrors, it is—as it has dubbed itself!—"the world's most chillingly famous horror attraction." And as the London Dungeon has chosen—of corpse!—London's very own history as the grave from which to rob their gloriously ghoulish wax grotesqueries, we knew that we would be experiencing again some of the madness and monstrosities we had already been introduced to whilst journeying through London.

Because the well-known waxworks declared that it "brings more than 2,000 years of gruesomely authentic history vividly back to life . . . and

death" and, furthermore, directed unwary waxen-woe-wanting wayfarers to "remember: everything you experience really happened," yours cruelly was utterly curious how the London Dungeon would compare to those rotted remains of remote London's all-too-real repulsiveness before which we had, until now, worshipped. Let us see, Creepy Reader.

We two most fearfully Horror-hungry fiends took the Tube to—again!—the London Bridge Station and, as we exited it, we immediately espied the London Dungeon but there upon the right-hand side of Tooley Street. From the fright-fanciful façade of its entrance—delightfully dread-décored with artificial Gothic architecture, true gas-burning torches, grimly looming gargoyles and hooded gaunts, and, almost everywhere, the wax-works' luridly sanguinolent logo—there could be, truly, no mistaking the London Dungeon's definedly revolting raison d'etre.

Tortured by Troopsmen

Although it was, in fact, but mourning, there was already a sizable line of shocking-sight-seers out before the Dungeon. But after waiting upon it for some time—during which we gruesome twosome were utterly entertained by witnessing a wretchedly hideous Victorian Aged woman brushing fearsome flecks of fake blood upon the otherwise cherubic faces of three potato crisp-eating children!—we were ushered into the London Dungeon; however, it was to wait upon—yes!—another queue within. But as the all-too-curious shambled, so very slowly, deeper into the Dungeon itself, we began to behold its hideously notorious horrors—and what horrors they were, Creepy Reader!

The basic layout of the London Dungeon's exquisite wax-engrossed loathsomeness was chopped into conspicuously thematic cuts: "Under Siege" and the wanton gruesomeness of medieval war; "The Great Plague" and the pitiable pustule-pocked putridity of that seventeenth-century pestilence; the

"Torture Chamber" and the torturously painful tribulations of London's prisons; "The Ripper" and the strange slaughter of that Whitechapel woman-slayer; and all the brutal and beastly gory bits in between!

The extraordinary, and extraordinarily explicit, wax effigies within each of these were the most macabre of wax masterpieces. Their wound-bubbling red blood looked revoltingly *wet*; their grisly outspread guts looked *stinking*; and all of their murder and mayhem and mutilation looked respectably *real*.

For yours cruelly, the grandest grue-goodly amongst them had to have been either a savagely curring soldier eviscerating a villager hung upside down or Catherine Eddowes's cruelly Ripper-disemboweled corpse. Yes, Creepy Reader: in a chamber of horrors like the London Dungeon, the redder and the wetter the guts, *the better*! And they were all indeed brought to "life" because of not only their marvelously creeps-coloured mise-en-scene but, also, an affective spooks-atmospheric soundtrack that lent screams, shrieks, sobs, squeals, and so on to the still-lifed.

All of the Dungeon's disgust-doused displays were each accompanied by signage that described in explicit—if not edifying!—detail exactly what was being seen. As if to enhance even further the London Dungeon's loathsome Horror-lousy "liveliness," each of its chapters—most memorably those exhibiting the excruciations and execrations of the Great Plague and Jack the Ripper—were, more or less, "hosted" by an awfully costumed actor or actress who not only dramatized the dreadfulness of the displays but played so very provocatively with the appalled chambers of horrors-partaking public.

And whilst their job was to curdle the blood and churn the guts still further, they were also dwelling there in the London Dungeon to usher its visitors such as we two affearing Horror-fiends from one chapter of London's putrescently pernicious past to another. After we had thusly prowled through those "2,000 years of gruesomely authentic history," we gruesome twosome found our severely spooksome selves surviving not only London's seventeenth-century Great Fire and then, thereafter, all of the London Dungeon's heinous wax horrors as well!

As my unspeakable wife and yours cruelly exited the waxworks into—but of corpse!—its very own shuddersome, and shuddersomely expensive, gift shoppe, The Dungeon Shop of Horrors, I must confess, Creepy Reader, that it was not with the least taste of disappointment. While the Dungeon's deliciously gruesome and grotesque displays were, again, masterful examples of chambers of horrors monstrosity, it was very unfortunate, however, that we did not truly have time enough to thor-

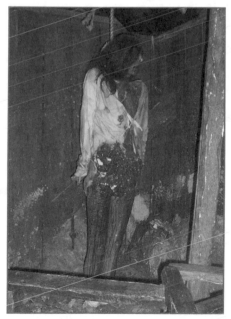

oughly investigate each and every one of them because we were not allowed—due to the supervision our high-spiritedly horrid "hosts" and to the somewhat packed size of the groups in which we toured that grand grotesquest-gallery— to linger throughout the dark bowels of the Dungeon.

Because of this, we experienced a hopeless sense of haste as we passed from one hoard of London's past horrors to another, which was not produced from the less Horror-fied lurkers about us wanting to get away from the Dungeon's ghastliness but—at least so it seemed to yours cruelly—those hosts wanting to get more fright-beset flesh-and-blood bodies through them!

My black bride had visited the London Dungeon when she was still but a truly un-terror-fied teenager and she attested that this had not, then, been the case. But, alas, perhaps because of the Dungeon's repugnantly ill-rumored renown—it has "franchises" in York, Edinburgh, and even Hamburg!—it is more than ever a big horror business and, thus, the more visitors creeping through its gloriously grisliness-glutted guts per hour, the better. Perhaps, in the end, Creepy Reader, we gruesome twosome simply needed an unhealthy stretch of time in order to welter in the London Dungeon's handsomely hideous wax horrors as we wanted to.

London's fantastically infamous London Dungeon was an utter Horror-palled amusement park puking forth history's profoundest anathemas, abominations, and atrocities. What other chamber of horrors has its own water ride—"Traitor! Boat Ride to Hell"—and a disquieting bubonic plague display scurrying with repulsively all-too-real *rats*?

Throughout our tour of that 30-year-old London Dungeon, we had espied yet again the loathsomely Horror-fied likes of Newgate Gaol, Jack the Ripper's Whitechapel, and the Tower of London's Traitor's Gate and it was indeed a terribly traumatizing treat to witness their likeness here. But although they were indeed "factual," the London Dungeon's disturbingly dreadful design for them was frights not facts and, in the end, Creepy Reader, no matter how gruesome, how grisly, how gloriously grotesque its displays may have been, they pale before the heinous historical horrors of the one and only . . . London!

And with the London Dungeon now slashed from our expedition's iniquitously insane itinerary, the wholly unwholesome whole of our loathsomely torment, trauma, and torture-trolling terror-tour of London's terribly aged territories had been—finally!—hung, drawn, and quartered.

Regardless of how deeply my wretched wife and yours cruelly had descended into London's dreadfully disturbing dark past and glutted ourselves so very ghoulishly upon some of the utmost atrociously Horror-fied archetypes, it had been but a taste, no matter how fiendishly foul, of

London's—let alone all of England's!—mammoth morbid and moribund monstrosities. To exhaustively plumb those depths would require much more time—and money!—than we gruesome twosome had at our disposal with this journey here. London has been, for almost a *millennium,* the horrendous black heart of some of Horror's most unhallowed masterpieces and, during our very own exploration of it, Creepy Reader, we saw why.

Chapter Two

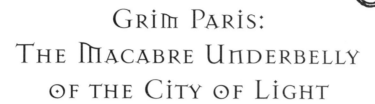

GRIM PARIS:
THE MACABRE UNDERBELLY
OF THE CITY OF LIGHT

h, can you see it, Creepy Reader? *Paris*! I had gazed upon its likeness sundry times throughout my hideous life, from the writings
of that Lost Generation of expatriates like Ernest Hemingway
and Henry James to the celluloid opuses of such *auteurs* as François
Truffaut and Jean-Luc Godard. Its name paints vivid tableaus of sidewalk
bistros filled with tables of diners supping upon the most sumptuous of
haute cuisine; of bohemian *artistes* withdrawn to the smoke-filled recesses
of alleyway cafés talking of nothing but painting and poetry; of lovers
strolling down centuries-old, cobbled streets, stopping for a kiss along the
dark waters of the Seine. Yes, *this,* as they call it, is "Gay Par-ee!"

So when my mortuary wife and I had the opportunity to make the
jaunt across the churning Atlantic to walk these very same Parisian locales,
was it to partake of those time-honored *hors d'oeuvres* that have drawn
endless drooling droves of tourists to the City of Light before us: the Arc
de Triomphe, the Champs Élysées, the Eiffel Tower? *Au contraire, mes
dégoûtant aimes!*

For we are not your *average* travelers and you can rest assured that our
expeditions across this graveyard Earth are always of an awfully *macabre*
sort! We two gore-mets, gormands of all that is ghastly, yearned to gorge
our necrophilous appetites not on some bland tourist's repast of rancid
croissants and dishwater champagne but a foetid buffet of France's foulest
funereal fare! Like coffinyard worms to a festering cadaver, we were lured

to Paris to tour its horrific underbelly, a tenebrous realm unpierced ever by the glitz and glamour of the city's more urbane attractions.

And so, casting aside the traditional tourist garb of tacky berets and draping ourselves instead in funeral shrouds, we set foot on French soil to feast upon all the reeking sepulchral delights that the "City of Blights" had to offer, a pestilential menu of which visitors are seldomly aware and upon which even fewer have the stomachs to nibble! So join us then, won't you, Creepy Reader, as I take you with me through the extricated bowels of the one and only. . . *Grim Paris*!

When my unspeakable bride and I stepped off the plane after a grueling, hours-long flight, all we wanted was the dank comforts of a tomb to sleep off the journey. An RER ("Réseau Express Régional") commuter train from Charles de Gaulle Airport brought us into the black heart of the city and we walked the rest of the way to our crypt-away-from-krypt whilst in Paris. Mere blocks from the tourist Mecca that is the Eiffel Tower, the quaint, alley-cloistered inn would provide us inexpensive, hospitable, and, perhaps most important of all, *clean* lodging during our sordid sojourn in Paris (it had its own bathroom no less, a true luxury). After waiting a few hours in the scenic Champ de Mars gardens that lay at the foot of the Eiffel Tower for our room's modest bed to be made for us, we were finally allowed the pleasure of slumber and sank into our first night in Paris with cobwebbed dreams of coffins and carrion dancing in our weary heads.

NÔTRE-DAME CATHEDRAL
6 Place du Parvis Notre Dame
Île de la Cité
(01) 42 34 56 10

Awaking to the morn with an unwholesomely ravening thirst for all that is dead and dying, we bought a few pallets of Metro tickets (a *carnet* of 10 cost only 52 francs), reckoned just how the century-old subway system worked, and made our way to what is perhaps the city's most famous landmark after the Eiffel Tower, the venerable and looming Nôtre-Dame Cathedral!

Sitting upon a sliver of land amid the Seine known as the Île de la Cité, Nôtre-Dame is at the very wormy heart of not only Paris but all of France. The cathedral's foundation laid in the twelfth century atop the remains of an ancient Roman temple, and taking more than 200 years to complete, it was a truly stunning edifice, utterly massive in size and even more magnificent in design.

No words could better capture the cathedral's beauty than those of French writer Victor Hugo, who described its oh-so-finely sculpted façade as a "symphony of stone" in which is "displayed in a hundred forms the imagination of the craftsman disciplined by the genius of the artist." From this, the broad face of the mammoth church was one vast tribute to Christianity, adorned with ornately carved effigies of saints, apostles, angels, and, naturally, the Nazarene himself. The most eye-catching of them all had to have been that of John the Baptist, who was depicted as holding his severed head in his pious hands!

Although we had arrived early, there was already a vast host of tourists waiting outside Nôtre-Dame for its mammoth doors to open. Rather than immerse ourselves in that veritable sea of flesh for a look at the place's exalted insides, we decided to first surmount one of the cathedral's 225-foot-tall twin square towers, the real reason we had wanted to visit Nôtre-Dame in the first place. After waiting on the short line at the side of the grand church (the tour of the tower being free!), it was our turn to face the spiral staircase that would lead us to our destination high above the courtyard.

Offering only a severely narrow passage beset with a seemingly endless succession of shallow steps, it was a grueling climb that many a tourist opt not undertake; our leg muscles burning with lactic acid in mere minutes, we began to think that decision a wise one! But when we finally took our leave of those claustrophobia-inducing confines, our fatigue was soon forgotten as we stepped out onto the tower's wind-whipped perch. We were in awe before the view of all of Paris spread out beneath us! And we shared this truly breathtaking vista with some sight-seers of a rather dubious nature, as we found ourselves surrounded by gargoyles! A veritable bestiary hewn from white stone had taken up residence upon the corners of the balustrade, giving the perch its moniker: the Chimera Garden.

Designed by Eugène Viollet-Le-Duc, the "Pope of Architects," in the nineteenth century, each of these grimacing beasties was more monstrous than the next! One had the tusked head of an elephant, another that of a baying jackal; some stuck a lascivious tongue out from between fanged jaws, others forever devoured some hapless prey.

The most well-known of all these cathedral lurkers was called the "Stryga," a bird of night or vampire from ancient mythology. It was perhaps the most stoic of its grim brethren, pensively looking out upon Paris as we did with its horned head held in its claws. It was a true pleasure to stand amongst these Gothic monstrosities and share with them such a view of Paris as that to be had from atop Nôtre-Dame.

After consorting with the likes of Nôtre-Dame's infamous gaggle of gargoyles, we made our way to the cathedral's belfry, domain of an even more renowned tower denizen, Victor Hugo's Quasimodo, the tragic

hunchback! Further along the tower's gargoyle-lined balcony, a small door led into the shadowy belfry and a somewhat rickety wooden staircase within brought us face to face with the cathedral's bell, a mammoth thing weighing some *13 tons*! Although Quasimodo was able to move it by the sole strength of his deformed, brutish body the bell apparently requires a crew of eight to do so in reality.

While Quasimodo's contribution to the vermiculosed annals of horrordom has made the poor deaf and deformed hunchback a genre icon on the same moss-covered pedestal as Frankenstein's Monster— attained through unforgettable portrayals by Lon Chaney in 1923 and Claude Raines in 1939—his most profound role would be as Nôtre-Dame's very savior.

For you see, before Hugo's novel saw print in 1831, the cathedral had fallen into a sorry state of neglect and disrepair; forgotten and left to rot, it had at one point even been used to shelter livestock! However, because *The Hunchback of Nôtre-Dame* was *so* popular with French readers, it reawakened interest in this aged structure at the heart of Hugo's novel, inspiring Napoleon III to pour a wealth of time and money into its restoration.

As we stood within the cathedral's belfry and before the great bell, I could almost picture Hugo's ill-fated hunchback swinging madly from it, each crash of the clapper against the bell's thick side but an echo of the mournful pangs of that hulking wretch's heart. All visitors to the cathedral have this most poignant of Hugo's literary offspring to thank for their opportunity to experience the grandeur of Nôtre-Dame.

Having our fill of Nôtre-Dame's tower-haunts, we made our descent through yet another narrow spiral staircase, which let us out into the cathedral's picturesque gardens along the Seine. Nôtre-Dame was a true wonder to behold and dripped with more Gothic atmosphere than a dozen Hammer films!

PÈRE-LACHAISE CEMETERY
6 Rue du Repos
(01) 43 70 70 33

Climbing the stairs out of the Metro station to Rue du Repos, we saw Père-Lachaise Cemetery before us, the first worm-ridden offering of our grue-soaked buffet of Paris's dreadfully dark Death-devoted delights. From outside those tall and unassuming soot-stained walls, it was difficult to fully grasp the breadth of funereal wonders that awaited us within them. And so, after buying a map of the cemetery for a few francs at  a neighboring florist, we ventured inside and were immediately taken by the sheer, grim majesty that was Père-Lachaise!

This mammoth cemetery is the most renowned in not only Paris or France but perhaps all of Europe and, as we began to walk about its grave-adorned grounds, it was not difficult to see why. Creepy Reader, my black bride and yours cruelly have been to many, many cemeteries throughout our morbid travels across this graveyard Earth, but this had to be the grandest of them all. It was not the cemetery's sheer size that rendered us so very awe-filled but rather its moribund potpourri of sarcophagi. This was no mere coffinyard, bedecked with row upon row of modest headstones.

The ornateness displayed amongst the grave decor here was simply astonishing. Tombs were watched over by shrouded stone mourners or slept upon by never-aging children. Burial monuments were carved with elaborate memento mori or religious symbols. Vaults stood literally stories tall while others resembled diminutive cathedrals. The morose aura of these tributes utterly *reeked* of the Gothic era during which they were erected. A true and utter city of the dead if there ever was one, Père-Lachaise was a sprawling necropolis the likes of which we had never seen before. Basking in the shadow of all that death, we set out on our tour of Père-Lachaise's funerary abundance.

Spread out over more than 110 acres, Père-Lachaise was built by Napoleon's government in 1804 to relieve the burden placed upon Paris's other, closer, cemeteries. However, because it was so far from the heart of the city, families were reluctant to bury their dead within its newly broken soil. To contend with this dilemma, Napoleon ordered the remains of a handful of France's most famous inhabitants, such as star-crossed twelfth-century lovers Abélard and Héloïse, be exhumed and reinterred at *Père-Lachaise*. Napoleon's strategy seems to have been a successful one, as the graveyard has become known as "the grandest address in Paris" because of the plethora of noteworthy personages buried here, such as Honoré de Balzac, Oscar Wilde, and Gustave Doré, one of this fiend's favorite artists.

The most famous of Père-Lachaise's holdings, however, has to be that of the Dionysian frontman of The Doors—Jim Morrison. Throngs of Morrison's admirers congregate about his rather modest plot, paying tribute to their "Lizard King" with alcohol, marijuana, and graffiti, the latter unfortunately straying onto the beautiful vaults that find themselves alongside his grave. There had been a bust of the rocker's famous countenance upon his gravestone; however, because it had become so worn over the years at the hands of his overzealous followers, it was removed.

For us, despite our appreciation of The Doors, we found such worship of the wormy carcass of this OD'd decadent as that performed by the greasy-haired Euro-hippies and cigarette-smoking American teenagers whom we found massed before Morrison's grave a somewhat pitiful spectacle. But, then again, yours cruelly has a jar of moldering earth dug from the grave of Poe in our Charnel House, so who am I to judge!

We spent the mourning walking down Père-Lachaise's winding, tomb-crowded paths and looking out upon the tree-shrouded expanses of this mammoth cemetery. It was a truly unforgettable experience to wander amidst the cemetery's seemingly endless acreage of extraordinary tombs and vaults whose stone façades had been cast an eerie greenish hue by moss over the years.

Making our tour even more otherworldly was that it reminded yours cruelly in no small part of the grand graveyard from Michele Soavi's zombie masterpiece, *Dellamorte Dellamore*, although I had my doubts whether its soil had the same re-animating properties as Rupert Everett's! Père-Lachaise was a truly sumptuous feast for any aficionado of old cemeteries and enthusiasts of tomb art.

LES CATACOMBES
1 Place Denfert-Rochereau
Montparnasse
+33 (1) 43 22 47 63

After a few hours within Père-Lachaise's sooty walls, we got on the Metro and headed back across Paris to Montparnasse, the neighborhood whose cafés had once been the stomping grounds of the 1920s American expatriate set. But we had not come to this former heart of Paris's intellectual vigor to debate literature and painting as T. S. Eliot and Pablo Picasso had done decades before. No, the delightfully rotten morsel that had brought us to Montparnasse lay across from the Metro stop on Place Denfert-Rochereau: Les Catacombes!

The entrance was remarkably unassuming, its green-painted front adorned with only a simple bronze plaque inscribed with the place's hours of operation. It would have been *very* easy to miss were it not for the line of the morbidly curious stretching down the block and worming its way around the corner, a telltale sign to the unknowing that something . . . *extraordinary* . . . lay beyond those staid green doors. And we knew what that "something" was indeed, as this was perhaps the most anticipated curiosity of our whole blood-spattered excursion throughout Paris's rank, grue-engorged bowels.

After waiting in that very same line for about half an hour and paying the pittance of an entrance fee, it was our turn to descend the stone spiral staircase down into the cryptic belly of Les Catacombes. The electric light from the foyer above died a little more with each downward step we took, a foreboding dampish chill creeping into the air all about us. When we reached the bottom, some 80 or so feet below the bustling streets of Paris, we stood before a dark stretch of low-ceilinged tunnel and, with no tour guide or signs to direct our course, we headed into that black maw carved out of the limestone bedrock.

Our procession to Les Catacombes took us down a few such corridors, each lit only by a small electric bulb every 20 yards or so. Our journey was made all the more creep-ridden by the fact that we had somehow become separated from those who had gone down before us, and those behind had not yet caught up.

After perhaps a 10-minute walk that felt much longer because of these gloomy subterranean environs, we joined the party who had descended ahead of us before a pair of wooden obelisks and, beyond these, a simple, short door. Above this passageway was a sign emblazoned with but a few French words, their translation: "Halt! Here is the Empire of the Dead." And as we stepped through that door beneath those very words, we saw the utter undeniable truth of them.

No matter how many photos we had seen before leaving for Paris, no matter how many vivid descriptions we had read, *nothing* could have prepared us for Les Catacombes. It was as nothing we had experienced before. The very walls were fashioned of thigh bones that had been stacked upon each other like cordwood. Jawless skulls lay in a row atop these femur-made walls. In some places, the skulls had been fit into the walls themselves, fashioning patterns such as crucifixes. Strewn haphazardly behind these walls was an endless mass of human rubble, the remains of approximately *six million* Parisians, a number too staggering for us to even *conceive*.

This mortal debris and the bone-walls that held it had once resided within the Cemetery of the Innocents, Paris's medieval graveyard of yore

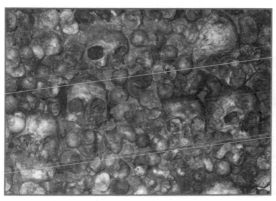

which had stood at the very heart of the city, shopkeepers and prostitutes alike peddling their wares alongside it. The dead from nearly 20 parishes were brought to Innocents and, as Paris grew, so too did it. But after some time, the eldritch boneyard grew unable to properly house the unending stream of cadavers delivered unto it. Because of mass burials and poor sanitation, the cemetery became choked by a mephitic odour of putrefaction, a literal fog of death that is said to have been *so* utterly repellent that it curdled fresh milk and made vinegar of wine!

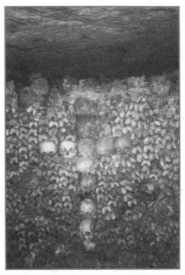

The Cemetery of the Innocents was finally closed in 1785 following an infamous incident in which a common grave laden with rotting corpses burst forth, emptying its foetid contents into the basements of neighboring homes! Out of an overwhelming fear of pestilence, an alternative to Innocents had to be devised and a series of ancient Roman quarries dating as far back as 60 B.C. were chosen as the makings of a mammoth ossuary. A massive exhumation of the cemetery began in 1786. Once night fell, priests led pall-shrouded carts filled with bones to these quarries by the light of torches. Such processions would continue for nearly two years until Innocents had been completely emptied and, thus, Les Catacombes was born!

As we walked through the dank, bone-lined halls of Les Catacombes, we passed locked gates beyond which laid pitch black tunnels, legs of the immense place into which the general public is forbidden access. For while the tour spans little more than a kilometer, the entire ossuary is made up of more than *11,000* square meters. Intrepid explorers known as "cataphiles" break into these unauthorized tunnelways some-

what regularly despite the plethora of hazards that face them in these unkempt regions.

It was a truly surreal experience to be surrounded by *so. . . much. . . death*. No words can describe the emotions that coursed through yours cruelly as we stood within those stretches of the nameless dead. As we journeyed deeper and deeper into Les Catacombes, the ceilings overhead began to weep, dripping a mineralized water which had further darkened the green, moss-covered bones, giving them an almost fossil-like appearance. Because of this, it seemed as if these osseous ramparts had reigned since the dawn of time itself, deepening the atmosphere of unreality that surrounded us down in that dour, tenebrous underworld.

As odd as it may sound coming from my horrors-dripping pen, it was with a sense of *relief* that my abominable bride and I came to the spiraling staircase that would lead us back out into the Parisian sun. Perhaps because of feelings of claustrophobia amidst those grim tunnels of endless death, my thirst for the macabre had been glutted and I wanted no more of this place! More so than even Père-Lachaise, Les Catacombes was a true and utter herald of the triumph of Death, an inexorable charnel house built from the very bones of the dead. Even now, I get the heebie-jeebies just thinking about it. Don't *you*, Creepy Reader?

MONTPARNASSE CEMETERY
3 Boulevard du Edgar-Quinet
Montparnasse
(01) 44 10 86 50

Once we climbed out of Les Catacombes, we sat along a wall and warmed our flesh from the cold grip of Death. After stopping back at the entrance to procure a few postcards and a little book on the history of the place for our Krypt's collection of creepy curios (for some reason, Paris's museum commission, which operates Les Catacombes, had deemed it wise to situate its small gift shoppe not at the *end* of the tour as logic would seemingly dictate but at its beginning!), we reckoned we would end our visit to Montparnasse with a visit to, unnaturally, *another cemetery!*

Found within the confines of a somewhat residential district on Boulevard du Edgar-Quinet, the Montparnasse Cemetery was but blocks from Les Catacombes. Less expansive and tree-shadowed than Père-Lachaise, the stately graveyard was reminiscent of those we had espied in New Orleans. Although the relatively tourist-free Montparnasse Cemetery had a wealth of its own funerary decor, it paled in comparison to the sombre splendor and bemossed magnificence of Père-Lachaise. But it was a single grave that had drawn us to this lesser known of Paris's cemeteries: the final resting place of Charles Baudelaire!

We found Baudelaire's unassuming plot at the far side of the tombyard; it actually would not have been hard for us to walk past it had we not asked a security guard to point it out on one of the free maps that were available at the front gate. Baudelaire's remains had been interred within a family

vault, his name and the dates of his life etched upon the face of a common marker. Aficionados of the writer's infernal works had left offerings of letters and notes upon the face of this familial sepulcher. A red rose lay amongst them, perhaps in honor of his very own "fleurs du mal."

As devoted acolytes of that Master of the Macabre, Edgar Allan Poe, we paid homage to Baudelaire, who himself prayed to Poe each night for morbid inspiration, for the invaluable part he played in keeping alive Poe's legacy through his French translations of the writer's works. But Baudelaire was not merely an adorer but an adept himself in the black literary arts. He introduced the world to absinthe-tainted vistas of malignancy the likes of which it had never seen before. His work today is placed on the same pedestal as Poe by lovers of all things morbid such as us, something that would fill olde Charles's black heart with pride I am sure.

My only regret about our visit to Baudelaire's grave was that, as it was an above-ground stone vault, I could not retrieve a bit of putrid charnel dirt from it as we had done after our communion at the final resting places of Poe and his other protégé in all things horridly weird, H. P. Lovecraft. Alas, we had only photos by which to remember our time with Baudelaire.

For the first offering of our ensanguinedly hideous expedition's cadaverous artistic curiosities, we lurched back onto the Metro and headed towards Montmarte. Exiting at Place Pigalle (or "Pig Alley" because of its red light offerings), we were just below Montmarte itself. But don't believe that this made the remainder of our journey any easier! For you see, Creepy Reader, Montmarte was settled some strange eons ago high above the rest of Paris on one of the city's two extant hills as a site of pagan worship and we would have to trudge up that very (and very steep!) hill to get there.

Undaunted explorers into the darkest depths of the morbid that we are, we wormed our wicked way up to Montmarte, only to later learn that, for the mere cost of a Metro ticket, we could have ridden there on a "funicular," a sort of glass-covered ski lift, something most—if not *all*—of the tourists we found strolling about the ward's quaint shoppes and eateries had done. Where it had taken us almost half an hour to walk up from Place Pigalle, we could have caught that tram-like thing at the foot of Rue Tardieu and been carried to the streets of Montmarte in but a fraction of that. Alas, had we only known about it!

Still cursing ourselves, we walked amongst the picturesque, aged buildings that filled Montmarte and took in the charming atmosphere of this former late-nineteenth-century home of Paris's Bohemian set. We wondered how it all would look if seen through eyes blurred by absinthe, as those painters and writers had eras before us, their work influenced by the green glassfuls of wormwood they drank while sitting at some of the same cafés that cater to tourists today.

ESPACE MONTMARTE — THE SALVADOR DALÍ MUSEUM
11 Rue Poulbot
Montmarte
(01) 42 64 40 10

But what shuddersomely tomb-escent secrets awaited us in Montmarte that had made that awfully arduous ascent so worthwhile? Well, the Salvador Dalí Museum of corpse! Also known as the Espace Montmarte, the Dalí Museum was settled on Rue Poulbot, just around the corner from the quarter's main avenue, Place du Tertre, which was teeming with tourists lunching at small cafés and sitting before portrait artists. The museum was one grand exhibit called "The Phantasmagorical World of Dalí" and was comprised of over 300 original pieces: pen-and-ink illustrations, etchings, watercolor paintings, lithographs, and even sculptures, apparently the largest assemblage anywhere of the artist's three-dimensional renderings.

Of all the works on display at the two-floor museum, those that caught our bloodshot eyes were, naturally, those that showed the master of madness reveling in the grotesque. First there were the drippingly lurid watercolors of John the Baptist (our second audience with the decapitated disciple, his head here being held aloft by Salome) and a similarly ruined seraph with a crimson font where its own head should have been. More surrealist horrors came in the form of a series of large lithographs featuring a repugnant cast of the freakishly malformed who looked as if they had stepped off a Hieronymus Bosch painting and then been slathered with Dalí's own brand of nightmarish eroticism. Although small, the Espace Montmarte was a fine encomium to the mustachioed Spanish madman.

For Dalí devotees with a taste for the morbid who find themselves in the South of France, there is the Perpignan Railway Station. To Dalí, the red brick station in Perpignan was the veritable center of the universe, an "esoteric monument" that sent him into orgasmic rapture. This adoration was captured in his 1965 painting, *The Railway Station at Perpignan.* In an extraordinarily bizarre instance of "life imitating art," almost as if torn from the nastiest of Giallo shockers, the station has

seemingly had the same effect on a Jack the Ripper-esque butcher known as the "Mutilator of Perpignan."

Since 1997, the "Mutilator" has slaughtered three young women, the murders curiously mirroring sexually explicit images from Dalí's own paintings, most notably 1934's *The Spectre of Sex Appeal.* Because the victims, found with their breasts, hands, heads, and genitals removed with almost surgical adeptness, were reminiscent of Dalí's own dismembered female nudes, French authorities believe that these atrocities are blood-swathed tributes to Dalí, left at the very site that the artist himself had so worshipped during his life.

MUSÉE DU LOUVRE
Pyramide (Cour Napoléon)
(01) 40 20 57 60

Ah, the Louvre! After killing some hours with Dalí amidst Montmarte's Bohemian haunts, it was here that we sought our next course maggot-infested curiosities. Creepy Reader, you may be asking yourself, what does the Louvre, the largest museum, art or otherwise, in all the world have to offer ghastly ones such as we in terms of a frightfully gruesome fare? Well, coffinfuls! Among the 30,000 works that fill this former twelfth-century fortress was a septic sundry of necrosed artwork that would sate our less wholesome hungers because, aside from nude loungers, artists seem to love nothing more than to portray tableaux of death, carnage, and chaos in all their belovedly lurid glory.

As we exited the Metro into the bottom floor of the Louvre, we knew that our thirst for the macabre and the morbid would be drawing us to cobwebbed corners of the palatial museum's three wings that are rarely traveled by the herds of tourists who congregate without end before the *Mona Lisa* and *Venus de Milo*, the museum's most famous attractions. After a rather lengthy wait in one of many lines that snaked across the reception foyer, we finally bought our tickets and began our very own tour of the Louvre's astoundingly atrocious artworks.

The Louvre was a truly immense institution, dwarfing even the likes of New York's Metropolitan Museum of Art. While it would literally take days, if not weeks, to take in all of the museum's offerings, we had but a day to spend within its walls and so had to concentrate our darker attentions on those verily vermiceous works of art we had read about before embarking on this expedition of ours through Grim Paris.

Passing through an astounding collection of Greek marble antiquities which filled the ground floor of the Louvre's Richelieu wing, we came to our fiendishly favorite sculptures, those French pieces from the early Renaissance with their gloriously macabre aesthetic! After the Black Death gutted much

of Europe during the fourteenth century, many of the medieval artists who witnessed millions laid to waste by the virulent and rat-born *Yersinia pestis* made their art a mirror to this insatiable pestilence.

These appalling sculptures from fifteenth- and sixteenth-century France were the very epitomes of this exquisitely grim trend. The first of these carved foetid beauties was the white stone effigy of Jeanne de Bourbon. Following the death of Jeanne de Bourbon, Countess of Auvergne, in 1511, this funerary high relief was made to adorn the recesses of her

tomb. It was a rather skin-crawlingly bizarre tribute, though, as it depicted the half-decomposed flesh of her belly ridden with worms as well as giving egress to an impertinent loop of intestines!

Further evidence of the period's death-obsession was the blackened alabaster statue that stood beside wormy Jeanne: *Dead Saint Innocent*. This somewhat modest grotesquerie had reigned above Paris's eldritch Cemetery of the Innocents atop a shuttered tower, his cadaverous countenance exposed only once a year on All Saint's Day. The Carrion-Lord reigned over that grand medieval cemetery until 1786 when the cemetery was emptied of its posthumous contents (thus making way for Les Catacombes). The skeletal Dead Saint Innocent was draped in human skin and his arm was raised over his head, a now-lost dagger once held in his skeletal fist. On a shield resting against his bony leg were carved some lines in French, their rather ominous translation: "There is not a single being alive,/however cunning and strong in resistance/whom I will not slay with my dagger/and give to the worms as their pittance." Indeed, Saint—*Bon appétit*!

We had to go to the second floor of the Richelieu wing and the hall of Northern European paintings to find more delectably horrid artistry. There we found works by the ungodly triumvirate: Hieronymus Bosch, Albrecht Dürer, and Pieter Breughel! While their works hanging in the Louvre (*Ship of Fools, Self-Portrait*, and *The Beggars*, respectively) were in no way comparable to their more grotesque and grisly masterpieces (most notably Breughel's *The Triumph of Death*) which are imbued with

that same medieval brand of artistic necrophilia, it was a true pleasure to stand before actual paintings by these masters, three of yours cruelly's most revered painters.

For a more blood-slathered fare, though, we did not have to look very far, as the Louvre's walls were rife with them. Most of these were religious in nature, such as *The Martyrdom of Saint George*, *Salome with the Head of John the Baptist* (our *third* encounter with the headless preacher!), and countless depictions of the crucifixion of Christ. However, some of the museum's more gruesome works were by those painters whom we did not normally associate with such an unnatural penchant for the repellent. Such is the case with Rembrandt, whose lovely *Flayed Ox* was bought by the Louvre at a bargain price because its rather unpalatable subject matter was seen as offensive to bourgeois tastes. I ask you, Creepy Reader: how could you *not* buy a painting of a gutted and exsanguinated ox carcass? I would think no ghoul's abattoir would be complete without one!

LE THÉÂTRE DU GRAND GUIGNOL
(Now "Theatre 347")
7 Cité Chaptal (Off Rue Chaptal)
Montmarte

The last course of our creep-ridden carrion campaign would treat us to a foul taste of Parisian theatre. And so we gruesome twosome journeyed to Pigalle and, passing all the sex shoppes and porno theatres therein, we lurked down to Rue Chaptal where the Grand Guignol had once chilled and thrilled

GRIM PARIS + 123

scores of theatre-goers. Born in 1897 from the mind of playwright and tabloid journalist Oscar Méténier and later swathed in gore by Max Maurey, the 285-seat theatre—a former church, of all things, deep down within the shadows at the end of an alleyway off Rue Chaptal—took its name from a traditional "Punch and Judy"-like puppet show; however, while the "puppets" here were in fact live actors and not marionettes (thus the "grand"), the madness and violence that delighted children in a typical puppet (or "guignol") performance were here amplified to dizzyingly disgusting degrees for the morbid pleasure of those very same children's parents with the Grand Guignol.

The disturbing, blood-drenched dramas performed on its stage were a cathartic means of slaking its patrons' bloodlust. Unspeakable acts of sadism and butchery were enacted before their very eyes, the cast's crude yet convincing, sleight-of-hand stage effects a closely guarded secret, the dark, sticky blood recipe rumored to be the most prized of them all.

Aside from original scripts penned by the theatre's own stable of ghouls, the Grand Guignol adapted the works of authors who themselves dabbled in bloody excess. The most infamous of these would no doubt be that of Octave Mirbeau's long-censored novel, *The Torture Garden*, in whose stage adaptation strips of fake flesh were peeled from an actress's back to the horrified squeals of the audience; as yours cruelly truly worships Mirbeau's masterpiece of eroticized slaughter, what I would not give to have seen this sanguinolent spectacle with my own eyes, Creepy Reader!

To further the infamy of the theatre, one of its managers adopted the tactic of having a "physician" examine would-be attendees lest those literally faint of heart die from the Grand Guignol's gorily gruesome goings-on, a trick borrowed some years later by horror sinema's consummate showman, William Castle! But, alas, because of the rising popularity of films and post-World War II audiences having become jaded to the theatre's antics, the Grand Guignol—now only a pale likeness of its former gloriously grisly self—closed its doors in 1963.

In a curious twist of fate, this was the very same year that Herschell Gordon Lewis released his low-budget gore epic, *Blood Feast*, the now-classick celluloid atrocity that earned him the title of "The Godfather of Gore"! *Blood Feast*'s then-appalling acts of revoltingly riotous repulsion were Lewis's homage to the Grand Guignolian tradition of theatrics, something he would do again more overtly some years later with the drive-in shocker that some horrorphiles deem his *true* masterpiece, *The Wizard of Gore.*

Despite the influence that the Grand Guignol has had on the horror genre beyond H. G. Lewis, from the bewitchingly abominable stageworks and films of Clive Barker to even horror-fied "shock rockers" like Alice Cooper, the theatre was much maligned and vilified during its egregiously emetic heyday. Because of this and the still-pervasive aversion to all that is blood-splattered that we were experiencing on our terror-tour of Grim Paris, when we finally arrived to Rue Chaptal, we were truly shocked to find a commemorative historical marker placed there by Paris officials in honor of that former human slaughter-playhouse! Like that marker, we two gorehounding purveyors of the gruesome paid tribute to the sneeringly transgressive fiend that was the Grand Guignol and dreamed of savoring its "venerable filth," as Anaïs Nin once called it, in the proverbial flesh.

**OPÉRA NATIONAL DE PARIS—
OPÉRA GARNIER
Place de l'Opéra
+33 (1) 44 73 13 00**

Leaving the Théâtre du Grand Guignol and Pigalle's porno splendor behind, we took the Metro to the final stop of our journey through Paris's repugnantly rotted horror-realms: the Opéra Garnier! Emerging from the subway station to Place de l'Opéra, the grandiose opera house with its gilded marble façade loomed before us in all its wondrously overstatedly stately glory. But the outside would prove to be but a mere *taste* of its ornateness, as its design and decor only grew more so once we made our way inside. The guided tour costing a pretty penny, we decided to only pay the meager entrance fee and lurk about the place on our own.

As we walked past the ticket booth, we were stopped by what we saw before us, as the Opéra Garnier was *the* definition of ostentation! The main hall was distinguished by a cascade of gray marble that was the grand staircase. With its ornately carved banisters, arched columns, marvelous stone statuary of cherubs and other mythic beings, all illuminated by a multitude of massive chandeliers and candelabras, the flamboyantly imperial double staircase was like something out of ancient Rome. Since it was built for the pleasure of Napoleon III, nephew of Napoleon Bonaparte, who, like his more infamous uncle, had declared himself Emperor of France, this reminiscence was perhaps fitting. And if there ever was an opera house fit for an emperor, this was it!

Designed by Charles Garnier in 1861, the lavish Opéra Garnier took 14 years to complete, finally opening its doors in 1875 and soon becoming Paris's premier stage for opera and dance. But the opera house *truly* came to fame thanks to the depraved doings of the one and only Phantom! While the Phantom was himself made a household name because of the award-winning "Lite FM" romance of the Andrew Lloyd Webber musical (and, now—egads!—the Joel Schumacher film), the Phantom's true origins were rooted in the pages of Gaston Leroux's classick 1911 novel, *The Phantom of the Opera*.

Some years before writing the sensation-heavy novel, Leroux, an avid theatre-goer himself, had heard some rather unsettling tales from the opera's cast and crew of a mysterious revenant whose malicious presence had been linked to a handful of inexplicable accidents and deaths! Intrigued by such creepy accounts, Leroux decided to flesh them out on the page and thus the Phantom—"Erik": Persia-born ventriloquist, inventor, trickster, assassin, and "living corpse"—was born!

However, Leroux's original work is veritably unknown to all but the most learned of horror devotees such as we, his creation turned into a fiendish icon within the fright-choked halls of horror history instead by its sinematic adaptations. The most celebrated—and inarguably best—of these was the 1925 silent film made classick by the ineffable talents of that "Man of 1,000 Faces," Lon Chaney. Many other celluloid Phantoms would come and go over the years, but the role will forever be Chaney's in the bloody annals of Horror. Walking about the Opéra Garnier, there were indeed quite a few little corners where a bemasked phantasm could lunge out from the shadows and this "threat" made our self-guided tour all the more spooky—and fun!

The ostentatious décor became, if possible, more so once we entered the concert hall itself, with its endless giltwork, red velvet upholstery, and Marc Chagall-painted ceiling. The grand chandelier hanging from the very center of the hall's high ceiling looked as if it easily weighed a few tons and could indeed splatter many an opera-goer if it fell from such a height, as it did in both Leroux's tale and its adaptations by the wrathful hand of the Phantom. While we are far from avid opera aficionados, I would definitely be there if promised such a sight, especially if it were the finale of some symphony of sickness by the likes of a slaughter-cult like Funebrarum. Now *that* would be a night at the opera worth seeing, would it not, Creepy Reader?

Ah, *Grim Paris!* Our horror fiend's creepy crawl throughout the dank diabolic depths of Paris's rotted offerings had come to an end. And so, bidding farewell to the gargoyles of *Nôtre-Dame* and the piles of bones in Les Catacombes, we returned across the cold, churning Atlantic to our Charnel House, our exhumation of Paris's putrescent viscera for traces of the horrific leaving our bellies filled with repellent French delicacies and our thirst for the necrosed sated. . . *at least for now!* It was a fiend's nightmare come true to be able to feast upon such legendary locales as Nôtre-Dame, the Grand Guignol, Les Catacombes, and other such horrid Parisian haunts!

Creepy Reader, you may be asking yourself, aside from this putrid slew of atrocious locales, what did we *really* think of Paris? Well, I must tell you that my appalled bride and I had heard *many* things about Paris before departing from our Krypt (and not all of them pleasant!), but we, explorers in the nether regions of the macabre, decided to venture deep down into the blackly foetid bowels of Grim Paris with proverbially open minds. However, upon our return from this expedition amidst the city's dreadful underbelly, we realized that Paris has such a reputation for a reason! Mind you, we *did* encounter *some* rather helpful and friendly Parisians, but they were, sadly, few and far between.

While it *would* have helped immensely if we had spoken at least *passable* French, it was not the language barrier that hindered our exhumation of Paris' store of pestilence and putrefaction but, rather, a *cultural* one. For you see, Creepy Reader, the culture of Paris is one of conservatism, tradition, and pretension. As we experienced firsthand, theirs is definitely *not* one that revels in the macabre history of its past! Contrary to the impression you may have been left with by these pages, finding these horrific sites about Paris was not an easy undertaking!

Unlike London, Paris would rather *not* hang its proverbial grue-besmeared laundry out for the eyes of tourists. And so there were *no* haunted tours, *no* chambers of horrors, *no* museums of death, *no* guillotine souvenirs, nothing but that which we dug up ourselves! We were not looking for tacky commercialism and tourist traps but something *real*, something with a little olde fashioned guts and gore to make the heart skip a beat and the skin crawl, for was this not the stomping grounds of Quasimodo and the Phantom of the Opera? 'Tis a pity, Creepy Reader. Well, as the French say, *c'est la vie* . . . !

But despite all this, my unspeakable wife and I *did* have an unforgettable excursion—and would indeed like to return someday. But should you decide to undertake such an excursion to Grim Paris, don't forget to bring a shovel because you're going to have to do a lot of digging to feast as ravenously as we two gorehounds did! And before I bid you a gruesome *adieu*, Creepy Reader, you must know that, as much as I would have been truly *thrilled* to stroll down it, despite what Poe and his tale of the razor-wielding orangutan would have you believe, there is *no* "Rue Morgue" in Paris!

PART TWO

Creepy Crawls of Horror in Literature:
In Search of the
Leprous Lords
of Laudably
Loathsome
Letters

Chapter Three

SLEEPY HOLLOW:
AMIDST THE HEADLESS HAUNTS
OF THE HUDSON VALLEY

C reepy Reader, yours cruelly must begin this chapter with a most black heart-rending confession: my unspeakable wife is fiendishly addicted to all that is Tim Burton. While I have been loath to admit it, all the telltale signs have been there lo these many years: descending into a drooling delirium at any mention of *The Nightmare Before Christmas*; the start of a distempered sweat upon news of a strange new shudderific picture show; a compulsion to consume any and all cadaverously creeptacular Burton-esque curios.

My black bride's reaction to the creepmeister's 1999 morbidly fanciful monster-piece, *Sleepy Hollow*, was no different. Burton's films have always displayed a beautifully grim aesthetic and atmosphere, but, for yours cruelly, *Sleepy Hollow* was one of the loveliest of them all. Even so, the film used only the bare bones of Washington Irving's classick tale of tenebrous terror, "The Legend of Sleepy Hollow," as its basis—the literary gateway unto a world of a profoundly more pathological horror that definitely would have paled Irving's Yankee skin. As the posters had promised, Burton had indeed sent many heads a-rolling!

Despite this, the film, from a screenplay by Kevin Yagher and Andrew Kevin Walker—the former having done the special effects for some of Horror's most infamous franchises, from *A Nightmare on Elm Street* to *Friday the 13th*, as well as, of corpse, *Sleepy Hollow* and the latter having written the utterly hideous and horrific non-"Horror" likes of *Se7en* and *8MM*—verily captured the dark fantasy within which Irving's tale dwelled.

The gloomily gray skies, the foreboding forests of untold fear, and, of corpse, the Headless Hessian hurtling through the night: all of it embraced the "drowsy, dreamy" and haunted spirit of Irving's tale. And Burton's decision not to shoot the film on location amidst the suburban serenity of the very real Sleepy Hollow, New York, but, in its stead, at both Leavesden and Shepperton Studios in England was, in the end, a wise one, as the man-made exteriors steeped *Sleepy Hollow* with an eerily otherworldly essence reminiscent of those early Hammer Gothic horrors as well as Mario Bava's *Black Sunday*, which is, by his very own acknowledgment, one of Burton's very favorite spookshows.

It was truly ironic, though, that not only my Burton-carnivorous crepuscular bride but yours cruelly as well had been so thrilled by this celluloid adaptation of Irving's tale when neither of us, in all our years upon this graveyard Earth, had ever, up until that time, journeyed to its actual Hudson Valley haunts. And what, exactly, is the irony of this, you may ask, Creepy Reader? Well, Sleepy Hollow, just north of New York City along the eastern shore of the Hudson River, is, in truth, but miles from where we had been reared into the gruesome twosome you love so very loathsomely.

Although I can say that I was never drawn to the real-life town of Sleepy Hollow, the tale that Irving had set in this secluded Dutch village he'd visited in his youth—known to me at first by the fearful fun of Disney's 1949 animated classic, *Ichabod & Mr. Toad*—had always lingered in the dark recesses of my gray matter. Amidst the dreadful bottom of that dark and dank well in which yours cruelly deposited notions of what defined "Horror" was, verily, Irving's tale of the Headless Horseman. I can even recall a Halloween night from when I was but a wee fiend when another trick-or-treater dressed as Irving's cranially-challenged Hessian mercenary had scared the candy corn out of me.

This shadow of Irving's "The Legend of Sleepy Hollow" upon my consummately creepified childhood is not so very surprising, as it is, possibly, America's only faerie tale. Along with the macabre masterworks of Poe and Lovecraft, Irving's fright-fanciful literary fabrication, first published sometime around 1819 as a part of *The Sketch Book of Geoffrey Crayon, Gent.*, afforded some of the only Horror archetypes that are truly "American," verily born and bled on this side of the Atlantic.

And so what of that *real* Sleepy Hollow, the Hudson Valley home of this bona fide, and bona fidely bone-chilling, Yankee-born spookiness of Washington Irving's? Well, not so very long ago, my noctiflorous bride and yours cruelly decided, the weekend before our repellently riotous Halloween revelry, to journey north unto the once-bucolicly backwoods burgh at the black heart of all this wraithen Burton-y weirdness my bride craved so accursedly, that very same locale that had inspired Washington Irving's seminal tale: Sleepy Hollow. So join us then, won't you, Creepy Reader, for yours cruelly's deliciously dreadful date with that hellaciously hellish Hessian, the one and only Headless Horseman!

That autumnal season of the dead having fallen upon our severed neck of the East Coast like a funeral pall, we gruesome twosome took our camera, a map, and our creepy thirst for all that is crawly and so began our day's exhumation of those eeriest Hudson Valley horrors. A moribund vista of mountains bathed in the melancholic reds and oranges of October was a veritable feast for our bloodshot eyes as our butchermobile motored north along Route 9 into New York State. As we traversed the churning Hudson River by means of the Tappan Zee Bridge, yours cruelly wondered why this expedition into the ancestral heart of all-American haunts had been so long in coming.

The traffic being on our side that nippy November mourning, we found our loathsome selves in Tarrytown in less than half an hour. Crawling down Tarrytown's single-lane main street, which was home to a succession of small but somewhat swank eateries and shoppes, it was but two miles further along Route 9 before we were greeted by a signpost welcoming us to historic—and hopefully, for our sake, horrendously horrid!—Sleepy Hollow.

Before our noisome travel narrative continues, Creepy Reader, I would share with you a curious fact: Sleepy Hollow was not, in fact, "Sleepy Hollow" until 1996. In 1874, the village was incorporated, along with the nearby hamlet of Beekmantown, into "North Tarrytown." What exactly had brought about this change of names all those years ago is unbeknownst to yours cruelly. But, verily, it was not until only recently that residents of that centuries-old village decided to officially adopt that profoundly more prominent and, in the end, pleasing name of "Sleepy Hollow," no doubt not only to boost tourism but, simply, to bestow upon the place and its living inhabitants an identity all its own.

Whatever the reason, it would seem to have simply made the village easier to find, something I could truly appreciate as, having at first studied some useless pre-1996 maps, I was unable to find it myself and, thus, had I not known that it had once been but a small stretch of Tarrytown, we would have wandered about "higgledy-piggledy," as Irving would have said, in search of it!

As we two foully fiendish fright-fan-addicts ventured deeper into those eldritch Horseman-haunted environs of Sleepy Hollow, we passed Sleepy Hollow High School—its blood-red Headless Horseman mascot carved upon the school's very own lawn-marker—and Street Mark's Episcopal Church, that stone temple built in 1868 as "The Memorial Church of Washington Irving," and it fast became obvious why Burton and his creep-mongering crew had opted *not* to shoot their film here on the soil that Irving had once trod himself.

Since the time he captured the rustic charm of the place in his 1819 tale, the population of both Sleepy Hollow and neighboring Tarrytown have swollen, something owing to the constructions of the Tappan Zee Bridge and the New York State Thruway earlier this century. The thick expanse of forest that had once filled Irving with a disquietingly nameless dread as he journeyed through them on full-mooned nights are, now, inhabited by blocks of suburban houses and small businesses. The only locale that has remained veritably untouched by the passage of time—and the production of man—and that could indeed cause you to feel the cold, cadaverous fingers of Irving's Horseman upon your back amidst the nightmareish gloom of an October night was the Old Dutch Church and Burying Ground.

THE OLD DUTCH CHURCH & BURYING GROUND
Route 9 North (within Sleepy Hollow Cemetery's South Gate)
Sleepy Hollow
(914) 631-1123
(Friends of the Old Dutch Burying Ground)

We gruesome twosome pulled off Route 9 and crawled through the iron gates of the Sleepy Hollow Cemetery, within whose limits the Old Dutch Church and Burying Ground fester still, and onto Sleepy Hollow Avenue, which overlooked the picturesque Pocantico River below. Further down this very same road, we would later espy an aged wooden bridge that traversed the Pocantico's waters.

While this was not, verily, the eldritch bridge "famous in goblin story" over which "horror-struck" Ichabod Crane made his final (and failed) attempt to escape the clutches of that hideously daemonic Horseman in the last few pages of Irving's tale—this actual specimen, long ago lost to roadway redevelopments, had most likely been located but south of the Old Dutch Church, a blue-and-yellow historical sign marking its approximate location—that extant replica with its rough-hewn planks afforded some skin-crawlingly splendid musings upon that ancestral structure.

Back at the cemetery's gated south entrance, the small, one-story church fashioned out of stone and brick sat atop a modest green knoll, which we gruesome twosome had to surmount so that we could explore that Old Dutch Church. An affeared night-traveler seeking sanctuary from the Horseman within its walls today would have to suffer the cruel kiss of a Hessian axe's cold steel, as we found its front doors locked and barred and learned that the church was not regularly opened to visitors.

This was not a surprise, as the Old Dutch Church was declared a National Historic Landmark in 1963.

Construction of the church began almost 300 years earlier, in 1685 to be exact, under the authority of local Dutch trader and landowner, Frederick Philipse.

It was built with timber culled from the local forests, stones quarried from nearby farmlands, and yellow bricks imported from the home country of Holland. Ownership of the church and its lands were given over to the town proper after Philipse's ancestors, loyalists to the Crown during the Revolutionary War, were tried and convicted, in absentia, of treason against those newly founded United States of America.

Over the years, it has undergone various renovations and remodelings, such as an enlargement of its windows and the movement of its front doors so that they would face Route 9. As the community it served swelled over the years and three additional churches were built to meet the spiritual needs of that burgeoning populace, the Old Dutch Church was used less and less frequently, services held there now only on holidays.

After examining the Old Dutch Church, our morbidest of curiosities beckoned us to inspect its gravestone-covered grounds. The Old Dutch Burying Ground, one of the oldest in America, stands not only as a record of the bygone settlers of Sleepy Hollow and its surrounding communities, but also, verily, as a funerary museum, displaying some of the earliest examples of American folk art still in existence.

Although the oldest gravestone dates back to 1750, it is unclear exactly when the place was first used as a burying ground, as the gravestones from those earliest interments disappeared so very long ago due to their construction out of wood and other decayable materials. It is speculated that burials could have begun as early as 1645 or as late as 1700. The earliest of the extant gravestones in the burying ground reside closest to the church and can be distinguished by their reddish-brown sandstone, which was the preferred headstone-making material during the eighteenth century.

A great many of these goregeously ruddy gravestones, more than a dozen in all, were inscribed in Dutch, a testimony to the prevalence of the community's ancestral heritage and traditions. The adornments—or, better yet, the lack thereof—on these gravestones of yore followed the founding settlers' Protestant beliefs, which frowned upon religious iconography as false idolatry.

These most aged gravestones were carved with simple "soul effigies"—human faces with wings symbolizing the soul's passage to heaven upon shedding that mortal coil—below unfurled banners bearing traditional funereal mottoes in Latin, such as "Memento Mori." Unfortunately, although these sandstone memorials have endured much longer than their wooden predecessors, they too have suffered from the hands of both time and nature, as most that yours cruelly's bloodshot eyes espied were split and cracked, rendering portions of their carved façades wholly unreadable.

The most contemporary of the Old Dutch Burying Grounds head-stones, those from the late eighteenth and early nineteenth centuries, were fashioned from much sturdier stuff, such as granite and marble. However, these too have fared only somewhat better, as acid rain has dissolved their stony gray faces over the years. Further damage to the tombstones, regardless of the material of their manufacture, can be blamed upon the nineteenth-century practice of clearing graveyards of weeds and thickets by setting the grounds on fire.

What an extremely eerie spectacle that must have been, Creepy Reader! These nineteenth-century gravestones mirrored the different aesthetic sensibilities of Sleepy Hollow's inhabitants of that more modern age. Common funerary imagery, such as weeping willow trees and cinerary urns, was born out of a popular veneration throughout that still-young republic for all things Roman and Greek.

In 1947, William Perry, a Boston architect, recognizing the importance of the burying ground, undertook a preservationist's project that lasted six years and resulted in the restoration of almost 116 gravestones. Further efforts to preserve this historic site have been made by The Friends of the Old Dutch Burying Ground, a local voluntary organization supported by member contributions. Any fervent graveyard-feeding ghouls who come to lurk about the Old Dutch Burying Ground can help to support its Friends with the purchase of their immensely informative "Tales of the Old Dutch Church" handbook, a walking-tour guide which we gruesome twosome bought at a little shoppe in Tarrytown for but a few dollars.

"Tarrying," as Irving would have called it, about the Old Dutch Burying Ground, my black bride and yours cruelly came upon a handful of graves that would fire the fright-fiending fancies of "Legend of Sleepy Hollow" enthusiasts. But south of the church stood a cinerary-urn-topped marble monument of truly impressive measurement. It had been erected by the Brush family in memory of their deceased, one of whom was Eleanor Brush, who died in 1861 at the age of 97. Eleanor Brush was born Eleanor Van Tassel, the most likely real-life model for Irving's Dutch coquette, Katrina Van Tassel.

Although Irving refused to reveal the source of his, seemingly beloved, inspiration for the "blossoming lass of fresh eighteen, plump as a partridge" so as not to lose the favor of other local ladies, Eleanor was a very good possibility since she not only shared Katrina's surname but was herself a beautiful Dutch maiden. According to legend, her beauty was so striking that those "Red Coats" raiding her father's farm during the Revolutionary War could not resist trying to carry her off along with their other plunder until some related womenfolk beat them off with brooms and rolling pins.

This tale would later find itself woven into Irving's "Wolfert's Roost." Irving's purchase of the Tarrytown acreage upon which that abode at the whimsical heart of his tale was founded—and which he would replace in 1835, with the "little nookery somewhat in the Dutch style, quaint, but unpretending" that he would call "Sunnyside," which stands still upon Sunnyside Lane—would only further the connection between the writer and the Van Tassels, their Eleanor most of all.

Only some yards north of the Old Dutch Church lay the gravestone of Catriena Ecker Van Tessel. While it read "Van Tessel," yours cruelly espied at least three different variations of that very same family name: Van Tessel,

Van Tassell, and the most commonly known Van Tassel, all Anglicized from the Dutch "Van Texel," "Texel" being, actually, an island amidst the North Sea.

Regardless of the different spellings of their surnames, Creepy Reader, Catriena was in fact Eleanor's aunt. However, unlike her niece, Catriena can be ruled out as the flesh-and-blood model for Irving's Katrina, despite the similarities of their first names, because of the simple fact that she would have been dead by the time Irving first visited the Hollow sometime in the early nineteenth century, as she died in 1793 at the age of 56. Her sanguine sandstoned tombstone, sadly decayed so very severely since her sepulture, was carved with a simple soul effigy, something, again, common to the time of her burial. Above this was inscribed the Latin phrase "Mors Vincit Omnia." Translated, it read, "Death Conquers All." Indeed!

Another inhabitant of the Old Dutch Burying Ground would disagree with that depressingly dour and dismal and death-definitive declaration— at least according to his would-be biographer, Washington Irving—because he, housed in a shuddersomely mystery-shrouded grave only east of Catriena Van Tessel's, could very well be the fearfully horrid fiend known as . . . *the Headless Horseman*! We gruesome twosome found this unnamed "Hessian Soldier" in a grassy tombstone-less plot, a copper nameplate bearing the years of his factual life, 1752 to 1778, the only thing marking the final rotting place of his war-ruined earthly remains. In "The Legend of

Sleepy Hollow," Irving never described the burying place of that "Hessian trooper whose head had been carried away by a cannonball in some nameless battle during the Revolutionary War."

Yours cruelly examined his grave for telltale signs of

the supernatural, such as earth scorched by Hell's fire or the smell of brimstone tainting the air, but, sadly, found none. But it is, in the end, from the imagination that ghosts and goblins— and Headless Horsemen!— derive their *true* power. So if

you, Creepy Reader, should find yourself before this very same burial plot in the blackness of night, perhaps you could witness with your very own disbelieving eyes the depravedly dreadful and doom-bearing midnight rising of the Headless Horseman as he drags his vilely vermiceous corpse from the Old Dutch Burying Ground's charnel earth to ride forth in search of his long lost lopped-off head!

Beside that of this nameless Hessian Soldier was another curious grave, that of "Hulda the Witch." Yet again, like her Hessian neighbor, her grass-overgrown grave was distinguished from the cemetery's lawn only by a copper placard embedded into the earth. Hulda's story was unfortunate but truly interesting. According to the story handed down from colonial times, Hulda was Sleepy Hollow's resident witch, not unlike those inhabiting every superstitious village along the East Coast at the time. An immigrant from Bohemia who lived a very solitary existence within her woodland cabin, Hulda was a collector of local herbs and a trader with the Indians. Because of such, then, odd habits, she was branded a witch and her home was heaped with fear and ill-repute.

However, unlike her sisters, likewise accused of practicing the blackest of magicks, Hulda was, eventually, granted burial in a Christian graveyard. This "honor" was bestowed upon her posthumously after she was killed by a British rifleman during the Revolutionary War, in which, verily, she fought in defense of that very same community that had villainized her so viciously. Upon her death, a compromise of sorts was reached by Sleepy Hollow's townfathers: in honor of her combat-proven patriotism, Hulda's body was allowed to be interred here at the Old Dutch Burying Ground—but without a tombstone. Well, she was a damnable heathen after all, wasn't she?

SLEEPY HOLLOW CEMETERY
540 North Broadway
Sleepy Hollow
(914) 631-0081

As my unspeakable wife and I lurked further and further from the Old Dutch Church, its olde burial ground gradually worked its way up a small hill. And it was at the top of this rise that the Old Dutch Burying Ground became the exceedingly more expansive and elaborate Sleepy Hollow Cemetery. It was a necropolis of respectable size, dwarfing the three-acre burying ground of the village's ancestors below. As the "cemetery" was a Victorian concept, the Sleepy Hollow Cemetery was a fine reflection of those nineteenth-century sensibilities about death and the dead. With elaborate mausoleums and monuments of neoclassical design adorning the cemetery's winding paths and well-manicured hills.

The cemetery was founded in 1849 by a local committee that was headed by Washington Irving himself. It was at Irving's suggestion that its proposed name of "Tarrytown Cemetery" was changed, unsurprisingly, to "Sleepy Hollow Cemetery." His reason, simply, was "to secure the patronage of all desirous of sleeping quietly in their graves." Furthering the cemetery's non-utilitarian scheme, it was laid out like a park, making it a sedate and serene place for the living to appreciate nature's beauty amidst a true city of the dead. And we gruesome twosome were verily doing but that, enjoying autumn's crisp air rustling through the trees overhead as we lurked amongst

the vaults and headstones, when we came upon the burial plot of Washington Irving himself.

It had taken us a bit of time to find Irving's final resting place. The map we had been using as a guide was unclear when it came

to the exact location of his grave, leading us to believe that it was much deeper into the cemetery than it actually was. Finally, having returned to the Old Dutch Burying Ground so that we could start our search anew, we walked up an old brick path made somewhat treacherous by a pall of wet, fallen leaves and, at the top of it, espied the Irving family graveplot before us. It resided on Beekman Walk, atop that small hill that witnessed the gradual blending of the olde and the new: the aged Old Dutch Burying Ground with the comparatively more modern Sleepy Hollow Cemetery.

A short, blackened iron fence surrounded the plot, its locked gate bearing the Irving name. On the inside of this fence was a metal plaque donated by Irving's extant relatives upon the site's designation as a National Historic Landmark in 1972. The humble gravestone of that most famous Irving, inscribed with but his name and the dates of his birth and death, sat amongst those of his ancestors. A moss of some kind had

turned its white marble an earthy—and yet utterly unearthly—shade of green, bestowing upon it an eerieness truly befitting the legendarily literature-loathsome earth in which its dearly departed tenant had been buried.

From Irving's burial plot, we gruesome twosome could look down upon the Old Dutch Church and its Burying Ground, upon the graves of Van Tassels, Cranes, and Van Brunts, even that of an unnamed mercenary from the German kingdom of Hesse who fought, died, and was buried here in New York—very well without a head atop his unhallowed shoulders! Irving had made each of them as well as the little valley known as Sleepy Hollow, whose dreamy contagion they had all once breathed, immortal through his tale of fantastic terror. In turn, they helped to assure an august place amidst American letters for that author who had written so very worshipfully of their frolickingly fright-filled fictional exploits.

As yours cruelly surveyed the graved-lands about my black bride and I, with the Old Dutch Church of the Hessian and his Sleepy Hollow prey behind us and the latter-day Sleepy Hollow Cemetery before us—which Irving had not only helped to plan but, later, to populate—I truly experienced the bewitching influence of that particular Horror-hallowed portion of the Hudson Valley which Irving had himself felt oh so long ago, one that "breathed forth an atmosphere of dreams and fancies." Beyond Irving's grave, further into the Sleepy Hollow Cemetery, as the dates of death upon its tombstones approached the present day, this spell seemed broken, yours cruelly's communication with that haunted past utterly severed as if by the Horseman's very own axe. Perhaps it was the groundskeeper's lawnmower. . . .

Creepy Reader, should you find yourself lurking towards these parts of the Hudson Valley that Washington Irving had made his own, in life and in literature, do take the time to visit that tiny village of Sleepy Hollow as we gruesome twosome did and drink in the dreamy atmosphere of the Old Dutch Church and Burying Ground like some thick, autumnal cider shared before an open fire over haunted tales of scrawny schoolmasters, brawny Bones, and, of corpse, Headless Horsemen.

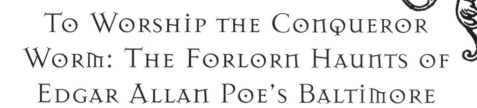

Chapter Four

To Worship the Conqueror Worm: The Forlorn Haunts of Edgar Allan Poe's Baltimore

"[A]nd yet it is but a thought, although a fearful one, and one which chills the very marrow of our bones with the fierceness of the delight of its horror. It is merely the idea of what would be our sensations during the sweeping precipitancy of a fall from such a height. And this fall—this rushing annihilation—for the very reason that it involves that one most ghastly and loathsome of all the most ghastly and loathsome images of death and suffering which have ever presented themselves to our imagination—for this very cause do we now the most vividly desire it. . . ."

—Edgar Allan Poe
"The Imp of the Perverse" (1845)

Yours cruelly was but a wee ghoul when I was introduced to the dank and forbidding world of horror. It was Halloween and, to commence the day's ghoulish festivities, my eighth grade English teacher decided to read us a tale culled from a "quaint and curious volume of forgotten lore." And so she began, the aged, musty words filling our ears, and what I heard as she read page after page was horrific. *Truly horrific.* The words she spoke were as the whispered utterances of the damned, the restless dead. I had never before heard such things. The word "dismember" was unknown to me and I can vividly remember pondering its meaning, its torturous letters burned into my adolescent brain.

This tale that my teacher was reading to us that All Hallow's Eve was coursing with a terror that was thick, utterly palpable and eerily so, like cold, carrion flesh. Those words that seemed to live and breathe on the page reeked of the grave and that foetid odour burrowed itself deep into my subconscious like tombyard worms. That tale of terror that ushered me into the hideous kingdom of the macabre was "The Tell-Tale Heart." And its author . . . *Edgar Allan Poe*. I was 13 years old and Poe, dead for more than 100 years, lured me with his sweetly decayed prose into the tenebrous realms of all that is horror. And I have dwelled there, a fiendish devotee of the shroud-draped writer, ever since.

The influence of Edgar Allan Poe upon the sanguinolent genre that is horror knows no bounds. Although Poe's pestilential touch extends well beyond the funereal halls of the horrific, having influenced all of literature, it is within that grotesque domain that his impious presence is the most distinctly felt. His works have been hailed as monstrous masterpieces of morbidity by those who are themselves icons in the vermiceous annals of horror: H. P. Lovecraft, Lucio Fulci, Vincent Price, Clive Barker, Dario Argento, Stephen King, George Romero, and so on. The list has no end; these immortal names are but a few atrocious adepts who praise his rotted name.

Poe's gloomy and grim Gothic terrors are nothing but seminal to the pantheon of horror. His fevered pen loosed upon the page a host of grotesqueries that had as yet been unheard, his words overflowing with an unwholesome fear-fascination with death. They plumbed the very depths of madness and sin, embracing the night-darkness of the human soul. Poe welcomed the abyss with open arms and drank deeply of the bitter wormwood of sheer and utter ghastliness. To read Poe is to feast upon the grave-blackened heart of Horror itself.

Poe's tales were about as sordid as his own life. Since his untimely death in 1849, his name has been sullied by endless (and endlessly lurid) accusations. Rumors of alcoholism, drug addiction, and madness have been his legacy. But no aspect of Poe's life is more speculation-ridden than its end. And it was in Baltimore that he met his death.

Although the author had claimed New York, Philadelphia, and Richmond as his home during his 40 years, it is Baltimore, that city that saw Poe through only six of his years, that has become so inseparable from Poe's name above all these others. And "Charm City" truly celebrates his life and work. It boasts an array of Poe-named haunts: restaurants, bars, pool halls, and other such attractions. The city even went so far as to change the name of the local football franchise to "The Ravens," an homage to the ebon-winged creature that lurked amidst Poe's renowned lyrical work.

As life-long connoisseurs of all that is dead and decomposing, my black bride and I, woefully devout worshippers at the moldering altar of Poe, yearned to exhume and consume the shadow-weltered Baltimore haunts about which Poe himself had once lurked. And so we gruesome twosome traveled down to Baltimore to these very same forlorn locales that Poe had known in life. . . *and death!* So join us then, won't you, Creepy Reader, as I take you with us on our creepy-crawly sojourn amongst the dreadful realms of the one and only *Edgar Allan Poe.*

When my unspeakable wife and yours cruelly lurched into Baltimore, the casket-plundering strains of Ghoul announcing our arrival, the city on the Chesapeake Bay was still thawing from winter's frost and beginning to prepare for the throngs of tourists that would soon populate the place in a few month's time, while also taking advantage of the somewhat mild early spring clime.

Most of our visitations were secluded to Baltimore's Inner Harbor, a scenic waterfront district along the city's southern extent. Where used to lie row upon row of abandoned warehouses and factories are now some of Baltimore's most desired attractions. Tourists flock to the Inner Harbor, drawn by the glamour of little boutiques, swank bars and restaurants, and posh hotels and the mammoth thrills of the National Aquarium, the Maryland Science Center, and famed baseball stadium Camden Yards.

But our interest in Baltimore lay with none such sites. We had not come down to Baltimore for its rancid crab cakes and pricey wares over which all these other less diabolic visitors fawned. No, we had come for a much more putrefied fare and so, casting our morbid appetites elsewhere, we embarked on our own dreadful tour of Baltimore's cryptic depths in search of the vermilion traces of Edgar Allan Poe.

THE MARYLAND HISTORICAL SOCIETY
201 West Monument Street
(410) 685-3750

We began our expedition of Poe's Baltimore with an examination of some of its awe-ful holdings of the worm-eaten author's artifacts and so made our way to the Maryland Historical Society. The three-floored museum on West Monument Street is dedicated to the preservation of Maryland's historical and cultural past. The museum's various galleries and exhibits display its collection of art, furniture, clothing, and sundry other antiquities that offer visitors a glimpse into the state's bygone years. But as interesting as all of these items may no doubt be, the main interest of this place to fine goremets of the foul such as we was the Society's venerable library.

This repository tucked away on the museum's second floor housed a truly envious collection of Poe first editions and manuscripts, extremely rare, sepia-toned photographs and daguerreotypes bearing the author's famously staid countenance, and a slew of newspapers and journals for which Poe had written during his days in Baltimore. The Maryland Historical Society's entire collection of Edgar Allan Poe rarities was the pride of its holdings; this wormy hoard made us, the fiends that we were of the author's written word, drool with absolute envy! Creepy Reader, we were standing at the putrid brink of the utterly *macabre*!

Once we had decided upon which artifacts we desired examination and had filled out all the necessary forms to attest that we were indeed very much "qualified" to handle them, we were allowed an audience with a few of these frightful treasures. The most magnificent of the lot was a marvelously decayed 1840 first edition of Poe's *Tales of the Grotesque and Arabesque*, which featured such tales of terror as "Morella," "Ligea," and "The Fall of the House of Usher"!

But our enthusiasm at basking in the black radiance of such a thing was all but garroted by the overzealous monitoring of the Gestapo-esque special collections librarian! As we feasted upon these rarities that we had summoned up from the bowels of the place, she eyeballed us rather intently. Did she think *us*, grue-spattered epicures of all manner of the macabre, mere thuggish dilettantes? But as collectors of curiously cadaverous curios ourselves, we understood the necessity of such scrutiny and it was worth bearing the brunt of it just to hold in our own blood-besmeared hands works that Poe himself had seen published! It was an unforgettable experience to feel beneath my fingers the time-worn parchment and to inhale the eldritch stench of their very ink! As Charles Baudelaire, who used to pray to Poe each night for ungodly inspiration, once wrote, "Decadent literature"!

The Maryland Historical Society was a very interesting stop on our tour of Poe's Baltimore, but I would only recommend it to his most rabid followers, as the confines of the museum's library, a secluded haven for those deeply entrenched in academic research, were not truly conducive to invoking the crepuscular spirit of the dead author. Having enough of such stiff scholarship, we took our leave of the museum and descended to Amity Street and the residence that Poe had once called home.

EDGAR ALLAN POE HOUSE & MUSEUM
203 North Amity Street
(410) 396-7932

One of the most curious, and at times unsettling, aspects of Baltimore is the way its wards change drastically within only the space of a few blocks, something we would soon learn as we made our way to our ghastly tour's second destination. While Poe's former home at 203 Amity Street was only five minutes from the polished tourist digs of the Inner Harbor, the neighborhood that housed Poe's aged domicile was not wholly dissimilar from that of a war zone! The realms that surrounded the residence were a truly startling vista of burnt-out tenements, abandoned lots strewn with rubble and debris, and dubious denizens lurking about the middle of the streets. And amidst all this urban decay, the small two-and-a-half-story red-brick house that was the Edgar Allan Poe House and Museum.

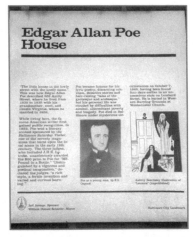

Perhaps needless to say, we two grue-somest ghastliness-glutting ghouls were the sole visitors at the locale that fair afternoon. We rapped upon its white wooden door and, as it creaked open ever so slowly, were met by the welcoming yet apprehensive smile of the home's hostess, who was dressed in a raven-black gown true to the mid-nineteenth-century age during which Poe himself had known this small abode. The charming usher beckoned our entry and, with a sense of dark flair that accented her melancholy garb, told us that although "Mr. Poe" was unfor-tunately not able to greet us in the flesh, he had invited us to partake of the comforts of his home all the same.

In 1832, Edgar Allan Poe came to Baltimore, to this very house, to live with his widowed aunt, Maria Poe Clemm, and her young daughter, Virginia, both of whom would become the writer's mother-in-law and his ill-fated wife, respectively. A little more than a century later, many of the residences in the neighborhood were torn down to make way for the tracts of housing that exist there today.

The house was to follow a similar fate until it was spared in 1941 by the city at the pleadings of the Edgar Allan Poe Society of Baltimore. It was

not until 1949 that the home was opened to the public as The Edgar Allan Poe House and, after further exhaustive renovations, continues to this day as a tribute to Poe's applaudedly loathsome achievements in American letters.

After viewing a rather interesting video presentation on Poe, we made our way about the small house. Although the brick structure itself was the primary display here, it housed within its modest walls a wealth of memorabilia related to both Poe's life and death. An artistic rendering on the first floor that caught our bloodshot eyes was the eerily vivid portrait of Poe's child bride, the only one of her

known to exist, painted mere hours after her death in 1847, having fallen to consumption. Some of the other more interesting Poe-etic curios hung upon the walls of the second floor's parlor: a set of beautifully detailed illustrations by noted French artist Gustave Doré that accompanied an 1884 edition of Poe's most well-known poem, "The Raven."

Also grasping our curiosity were several bottles of cognac left at Poe's grave over the years on the nineteenth of January (the writer's birthday) by the enigmatic "Poe Toaster." Since 1949, the centennial of Poe's death, the "Toaster" has left a bottle of the spirit along with three red roses upon the author's final resting place under the cover of night. Although this celebrant has never been confronted or identified, *LIFE* magazine did manage to photograph this annual ritual of his in 1990, a copy of which accompanies the partially-filled bottles in a display case on the museum's second floor.

It is believed that Poe's quarters within this home's meager walls was the solitary bedroom on the third floor. This cramped space, a veritable "narrow house" that comprised the entirety of the house's uppermost extent, had barely room enough for a simple desk and bed. But it was there, in that same claustrophobia-inducing chamber at the top of a narrow set of

stairs, that Poe's creative urges took him away from the poetry with which they had until then been occupied to the short story.

Although Poe may have mastered the short-story form with such tales as "The Masque of the Red Death" and "The Black Cat" some years later while living in Philadelphia, it was in Baltimore, in that very room we crept about that afternoon, where Poe would embark down the redoubtably repellent road unto utter godhood within the blood-drenched annals of literary horrors. One of the tales born out of the hours Poe spent cloistered in that tomb-esque room was "Berenice." It was with this simple tale that Poe would begin his unnatural affair with the unwholesome, his thoughts consumed with the grave — and all that awaits beyond it. With "Berenice," Poe's writing would become flavoured by an appallingly Gothic aesthetic and atmosphere, his words rank with the macabre and absolute madness.

But it would seem that Poe's audience had not the constitution for the likes of "Berenice," as the editors of the Southern Literary Messenger who published the tale received scores of complaints objecting to its gruesome demeanor. Fearing for the future of his career, Poe made amends by deleting several offending passages and swore that he would "not sin so egregiously again." Fortunately for all goremands of charnel delicacies such as we, Poe was not a man of his word! Had he been, there would have been no Ushers, no pits and no pendulums, no Rue Morgues, and no black cats. *Nothing*. And what a dull world *that* would be.

The Edgar Allan Poe House and Museum on Amity Street was a splendidly ghoulish attraction for any Poe disciple and well-worth weathering the hazards of the unwelcoming environs surrounding the place simply to dine upon a Poesque locale such as this that witnessed the master's work begin its descent into a tarn of the morbid. Two occasions make for ideal, and ideally fiendish fun, visitations: Halloween (the weekends before and after) and Poe's birthday.

It is the latter that is the grander of the two, as The Edgar Allan Poe Society of Baltimore hosts a celebration of the most reverent and reveling sort throughout the weekend closest to the nineteenth of January. To commemorate the author's birth, the Poe Society devises a menu of truly macabre merriment, including lectures by notable Poe scholars, musical recitals inspired by Poe's life and work, actors and actresses portraying the most infamous denizens of Poe's tales of terror, such as Madeline Usher and The Red Death. Recently, John Astin of *The Addams Family* renown was on hand with his celebrated performance as Poe himself! Gomez Addams reading "The Tell-Tale Heart" beats the hell out of cake and candles, does it not, Creepy Reader?

RYAN'S "FOURTH WARD POLLS" TAVERN
44 East Lombard Street, between High & Exeter Streets
(Former Location)

Our cadaverous tour of Poe's Baltimore now took us eastward across town to the locale where the mystery-enshrouded events of Poe's ever-controversial death had begun over 150 years ago, and so we headed across town for the third chapter of our grim expedition through Poe's haunts, the former location of the Fourth Ward Polls Tavern. When we came to Lombard Street, reminiscent of the neighborhood we had just left, we were faced by rows of low-income housing projects.

Many decades before city planners decided to turn the landscape of the ward into a red-brick ghetto, the tavern of Cornelius Ryan had stood on this same road between High and Exeter Streets in what was then known as Gunner's Hall; Ryan's pub, known by the moniker "The Fourth Ward Polls" because of its proximity to a voting site, had stood at 44 East Lombard Street, a few doors down from the corner of High Street.

Gunner's Hall and its neighboring establishments long since torn down, the urban setting we surveyed that afternoon was much different from its incarnation of 1849 when Poe was found before the seedy pub on October 3. When he was found by an acquaintance of his, Dr. Joseph Evans Snodgrass, the author was delirious and raving madly. His body was battered and bruised; his clothing filthy and torn. Because of his already infamous (and arguably unwarranted) reputation as a drunkard, his sorry state was thought the result of some hell-raising debauchery of his.

What had happened to Poe? What horrors had befallen him before he was found at Ryan's tavern, teetering on the brink of the grave? It is known that Poe, two years widowed after the lamentable passing of his Virginia, had become engaged that same year to his childhood sweetheart, Elmira Shelton, and that they had planned to wed on the 13th of October. Poe had left Elmira and Richmond for New York on September 26 so that he could fetch Mrs. Clemm, his aunt and mother-in-law, who was to live with the newly wed couple in Virginia. But what occurred between his departure for New York on the 26th of September and his discovery in Baltimore on October 3 has become the topic of much fervent debate and lurid conjecture.

Some speculate that Poe, because he was found before a voting site mere days after a city-wide election, had been the victim of "cooping," an all too commonplace gang-like means of accruing votes for some office seeker by using violent ruffians to coerce drugged street urchins into casting ballots for the unscrupulous candidate. Others believe that Elmira's vehemently disapproving brothers, not wanting their family's name sullied by their sister's nuptials to such an ill-esteemed man as Poe, had savagely beaten the writer, their vicious molestation proving ultimately fatal. Still others look to medical causes for Poe's death, seeing him as suffering from either a diabetic coma or, perhaps most absurd of all, rabies!

Despite all of these theories, well-founded or not, the most commonly held scenario, then and still to this day, was that Poe had danced macabre for the last time with that "fiend Intemperance" as he dubbed it in "The Black Cat," welcoming oblivion at the mouth of a bottle.

What happened to Poe during his journey from Richmond to New York? With what terrors did he rendezvous on that fateful trip north? No one will ever truly know, Creepy Reader. Seven of Poe's last days were lost and will remain so no matter how long the debate rages. The answers to the mystery of Poe's demise are now so much worm-food, long buried with the writer himself beneath cemetery dirt. Resigning ourselves to the never-ending mystery that surrounds this stretch of Lombard Street that once housed Ryan's Fourth Ward Polls, we traveled now to the very Baltimore hospice where Poe was carried on that afternoon of October 3: Washington College Hospital. No one will ever truly know, Creepy Reader.

WASHINGTON COLLEGE HOSPITAL
(Now "Church Home Hospital")
Broadway & Fairmont Avenues
(410) 522-8000

We had only to drive a handful of blocks from the urban vista of Lombard

Street to come upon the grand and looming Washington College Hospital, now known as Church Home Hospital. It was here, to this venerable institution with its Gothic towers and gables on the corner of Broadway and Fairmont, that Poe was taken by carriage on that third of October. It was perhaps macabrely appra-Poe that the writer was brought to this particular hospital as it had in those days of gore a blood-drenched reputation that rivaled the ghastly horrors of Poe's very own works.

Opened in 1836, the then Washington College Hospital had by Poe's admission earned for itself a rather ghoulish reputation for body-snatching! It was rumored that bodies of the deceased buried in a close-by cemetery were not in the ground for a whole day before they were on a slab in the hospital under the scrutiny of anatomy students.

Far more sinister murmurings surrounded the place though. Whispered accusations arose among Baltimoreans of the place's doctor-butchers abducting unfortunate souls who perchance found themselves about its premises at night, their still-breathing bodies making far fresher specimens for the cutting examinations of would-be physicians.

The blood-chilling atrocities that were said to have taken place within the walls of Washington College Hospital were *so* horrific that, when the place went bankrupt and was abandoned in 1855, local residents, still affeared of the majestically fiendish sick house, tried to bring its unhallowed halls down in flames on several unsuccessful occasions. It was *here*, to this same hospital with its repulsive history, that Poe was brought on October 3, 1849. For a lover of the funerary such as Poe, the surroundings could not have been more fitting.

When Poe was brought here, he was put under the care of Dr. John J. Moran. Although Moran has been deemed by much of Poe scholarship as unreliable despite the fact that he made a fine living towards the latter half of the nineteenth century lecturing on the author's final days, he remains the only source of information on Poe's state upon admission. His testimony, albeit fanciful and at times downright absurd, is all that exists of a portrait of Poe's final days. According to Moran's accounts, Poe was taken to a room in one of the hospital's towers, where those ill from drink were confined so their behavior would not disturb the convalescence of the other patients.

Over the course of the following four days, Poe is said to have sunk in and out of unconsciousness, rising from this darkness only to wake into a frenzied derangement. Dr. Moran could not determine exactly what had so enfeebled the author. Nor could he seem to effect his recovery because, in the dawn hours of October 7, after murmuring weakly, "Lord, help my poor soul . . .", Edgar Allan Poe, one of America's finest writers and the undeniable father of the horror genre, shed his proverbial mortal coil and ventured forth into the vast, black beyond that had so molded his work.

Poe's death went uninvestigated, "congestion of the brain" the only cause of death officially attributed to his case. It would seem that hospital officials and Baltimore police were satisfied that his unfortunate demise was born out of his self-consuming debauchery with the bottle. To most, his death seemed so sadly inevitable, an act of suicide begun many long years before. And so it came to be that perhaps one of Poe's most grim tales was that of his own death, here at what once was Washington College Hospital all those long years ago.

Church Hospital was opened within the remains of Washington College Hospital in 1943. The institution recognizes the part its ancestor played in the life and death of Edgar Allan Poe with two plaques that hang on the hospital's walls to commemorate the stay of its most famous patient. The first of these tributes adorns the lobby and the other, on the second floor in one of the hospital's two towers, marks the purported site of Poe's deathbed, the small room where the writer drew his last breath in that forlorn life of his. If this locale *truly* is where Poe took his leave of this world, what an experience it would be, would it not, Creepy Reader, to spend a night within those same four walls?

After taking in old Washington College Hospital, we departed for the final destination of our tour of Poe's Baltimore and the last place he, or better yet, his corpse, ever saw: Westminster Cemetery, the final resting place of our adored scribe, the cemeterially wondrous Edgar Allan Poe.

WESTMINSTER CEMETERY
Fayette & Greene Streets
(410) 706-2072

We parked our touring hearse along Fayette Street and disembarked for the final chapter of our grimly fiendish expedition to Baltimore. The grandiose and towering Westminster Cathedral lurked behind a tall stone wall topped by a wrought iron fence, its concrete pillars carved with weather-worn winged hourglasses whose sands have run out, time-honored memento mori befitting the church's venerable cemetery.

While modest in size, the churchyard was adorned with a fabulous array of monuments, from mammoth, rounded sepulchers to distorted table-like headstones whose inscriptions have long since been rendered illegible. Among the inhabitants interred within its ground are patriots of both the Revolutionary War and the War of 1812 as well as some of Baltimore's most respected forefathers.

The final resting place of the burial ground's most well-known denizen lay at the corner of Fayette and Greene Streets: the tall, white marble memorial of Edgar Allan Poe. Three of its four faces were inscribed with the names of the dead: two were those of Poe's own family, Maria Clemm and his dearly beloved, mournfully departed bride, Virginia; between the two, as in life, was Poe, his name chiseled into a marble tablet on the monument's rear aspect. The letters were sadly worn away, their edges smoothed from endless rubbings done upon the author's name and the dates of his life by droves of tourists over the years. The sun-bleached face of the cenotaph was decorated by Poe's own: a circular, copper bas-relief of the author's stoic façade hung upon the front of the monument. The material for the sculpted portrait was provided by the pennies collected by Baltimore school children some years ago.

As beautiful to our bloodshot eyes as this towering tribute was, Edgar Allan Poe's remains and those of his loved ones did not find themselves beneath it until 1875, even though Poe cast off his corporeal shell nearly 30 years earlier. On November 17, 1875, Poe's remains were exhumed from the soil in which they had been interred rather unceremoniously about three decades before and, with those of Maria Clemm, who had also died in Baltimore some years after Poe, were reburied beneath this marble monument.

Poe's reburial, a commemoration of the author's contribution to Baltimore and all of American literature, was heralded by much fanfare. This new location in the corner of the cemetery was dedicated through a succession of elaborate ceremonies attended by admirers of the writer, his extant relatives, and American poet Walt Whitman, sadly the only man of letters to attend.

The reinterment garnered attention the world over, helping not only to give rise to a renewed interest in Poe's works but also, perhaps more importantly, to help redeem his much-slurred name. For Poe, dead now almost 30 years, such honor heaped upon his name was long overdue. Ten years later, Poe would be reunited with his lost Virginia when her remains were brought to Baltimore from Fordham, New York, to be mingled with those of her forlorn groom and doting mother beneath the solitude of this same obelisk. But from where had Poe's remains been removed, you may be asking yourself, Creepy Reader. Well, we two graveyard lurkers would only have to turn the corner of the old church to find the very place.

We wove our necrophilous way amidst the graveyard's aged décor and about the side of the steeple-topped temple to the remainder of its properties. It was there, hidden behind the church and its encroaching stone walls, that we found it: *the primeval grave of Edgar Allan Poe!* The grassy, square plot was surrounded by a metal fence only inches tall. At the head of the burial lot was a rounded gravestone, its gray, water-stained face engraved with a few simple words distinguishing it as Poe's original burying place along with the years his body had lain there. Atop it was a solitary raven, perched in stone not upon a bust of Pallas but Poe's very name, the

name that had become so synonymous with that black-winged beast. A
single, withered rose had been left at
the base of the headstone.

Another offering left by some
worshipper such as we lay curled at the
corner of the plot: a birthday note
messily scrawled upon a small slip of
paper, its utter devotion sealed by the
smeared lipstick of kisses, no doubt
truly meant not for the parchment upon
which they were left but rather Poe's
own phantasmal, postmortem lips.

It was in this very earth before which we stood that Poe was buried
in the bleakness and gloom on the afternoon of October 8, 1849. Only a
small congregation of mourners, less than half a dozen, were assembled
at the family burial plot, Lot 27, in the dreary rain that day. As news of
Poe's death only the day before had not yet reached his friends and family
in Richmond or New York, only a handful of Poe's relatives and acquain-
tances from Baltimore and surrounding parts attended the scant ceremony,
which is reported to have lasted only minutes.

And with this feeble, rain-spattered memorial, the remains of the man
who was Edgar Allan Poe were lowered into the cold earth, his mortal
pangs swallowed up by the gaping maw of the grave and the curiosity of
vermin. It would be many long years before this writer, this man, would
rise up from out of this grave, from deep within these six feet of tombyard

earth, and, conquering the worm, dwell
atop literature's throne as the master of
the macabre, purveyor of sundry grim
nightmares, the inexorable lord of the
charnel house. This man was, and will
forevermore be, Edgar Allan Poe. And
it was he whom we worshipped that
day in Baltimore.

After some moments communing
with Poe at the site of his primordial

grave amidst the serenity of the Westminster Cemetery, we took a few photos of the funerary grounds, paying particular attention to both of his burial sites. But photos were not enough to satiate my thirst for the grave! No, I had to have more. And so my monstress and I bent down upon that burial plot of Poe's and collected a bit of the wet, graveolent earth.

Although Poe's human remains were deposited beneath it no more, yours cruelly *knew* that some semblance of his essence, the most minute trace of his rudimentary carbon, having been shed from his flesh some 150 years ago, still lingered in that same graveyard dirt. And my purpose for this ghoulish endeavor? Did I intend through some sort of vile necromancy to bring the author back from beyond the grave to weave further tales of the macabre? No, we yearned not to cloister the revivified Poe beneath our very own Charnel House. I had seen the dire results of such black witchery with Peter Cushing and Jack Palance in "The Man Who Collected Poe," the extraordinary final chapter of Amicus Films' *The Torture Garden*. Rather, this charnel dirt would be bottled like a fine vintage, its bouquet so putrescently sweet, and laid to rest before our cherished editions of the writer's works, the festering centerpiece of our altar to that forever ensanguined father of horrors: Edgar Allan Poe.

If you have ever been thrilled, chilled, and dread-filled by Edgar Allan Poe's ruminations amidst madness and the macabre, then a purulent jaunt such as ours into the depths of Baltimore's more antique wards will surely not disappoint. But as I said earlier, as are most urban settings, Baltimore is a city of extremes. So be prepared for a fine dose of the city's grittier, less touristy offerings. To assure that the only horrors you savor while there are those of the imagination is to realize exactly where you are traipsing about and let your behavior follow suit. And it would most assuredly be best to go about such a sojourn in numbers, not merely by your forlorn lonesomeness.

But it is fitting to have such grim settings as these as the backdrop for a tour of Poe's tenebrous Baltimore haunts, such as those on which we ravenously gorged ourselves that day. A safer and crime-free time would no doubt be spent among the bland fare to be had at the Inner Harbor, such as the pretentious yuppie stomping grounds of the Edgar's Place restaurant-bar, but where is the funereal festivity in that, Creepy Reader? So if you are a *truly* abominable Poe aficionado such as my noctiflorous bride and yours cruelly, do give old Eddy A. a visit the next time you find yourself in Baltimore. *He'll be waiting for you . . .*

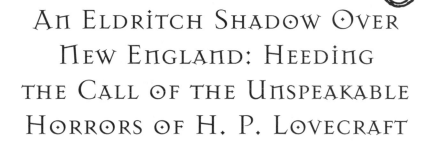

Chapter Five

An Eldritch Shadow Over New England: Heeding the Call of the Unspeakable Horrors of H. P. Lovecraft

"Children will always be afraid of the dark, and men with minds sensitive to hereditary impulses will always tremble at the thought of the hidden and fathomless worlds of strange life which may pulsate in the gulfs beyond the stars or press hideously upon our own globe in unholy dimensions which only the dead and the moonstruck may glimpse. . . ."

—H. P. Lovecraft
Supernatural Horror In Literature (1927)

Providence, Rhode Island's weirdest son, Howard Phillips Lovecraft, who, almost seventy years ago, died the most despicably painful of deaths—from long ignored intestinal cancer—was and still is one of most important writers the hideously unhallowed halls of Horror have ever known. His cadaverously Cosmic Chaos-worshipful contributions to loathsomest American letters is second only to that of Edgar Allan Poe, which Lovecraft, the nineteenth-century author's devoted disciple in deepest dread, esteemed "a master's vision of the terror that stalks about and within us, and the worm the writhes and slavers in the hideously close abyss."

Verily, for some of Lovecraft's very own devotees, his influence upon Horror indeed surpasses Poe's. Regardless of his exact ranking, he was, truly, a horror writer's horror writer, having savored what he called the "weird tale" since his youth and who, throughout his life as both an appreciator and an adept, studied the aesthetics of that literary subspecies in order to survey what made a work "true" or not, ultimately concluding— in his essayistic genealogical examination, *Supernatural Horror in Literature*— that it was a matter of "a profound sense [. . .] of contact with unknown spheres and powers."

Thus having tutored his shudder-sensitive self, he swore, so very satisfiedly, that, "there is no field other than the weird in which I have any aptitude or inclination for fictional composition." Lovecraft would then go on to write some 109 of his very own wretchedly "weird" works within which he can be witnessed worshipping his forefather's of the form—the Reverend Charles Maturin, Arthur Machen, Lord Dunsany, Algernon Blackwood, and, of corpse, Poe—and from which, begot a horrendous singular hybrid of science-fiction, fantasy, and horror that is simply . . . Lovecraftian!

Although Lovecraft died, at the age of 47, essentially unknown to all but a coven of Cthulhu Mythos-crazed protégés—his work then having mostly appeared in throw-away "shudder pulps"—that self-proclaimed "Old Man of Providence" slumbered not unlike his very own Great Old Ones—"dead but dreaming"—until, as he wrote in 1926's "The Call of Cthulhu," Creepy Reader, "the stars had come round again to the right positions in the cycle of eternity" for his influence upon "modern horror" to be truly understood.

Within that lousy league of horror literature, the specter of Lovecraft seeps from the works of those writers who have been themselves relished and revered as masters: Lovecraft's contemporary correspondents in the creepiest of confederations, such as Robert E. Howard and Robert Bloch; those of that dreadedly doomed "Third Generation" of Lovecraft's disciples, such as Brian Lumley, Graham Masterton, Ramsey Campbell, and even Stephen King, who, after spawning youthful simulations of his strangest style and symbology, would themselves become the ghastliest of horror gods; wondrously well-known comic book writers, such as Alan Moore, Neil Gaiman, and Mike Mignola.

Celluloid would also become a medium through which Lovecraft-mad horror movie mavens could offer monstrously macabre tributes to their

Master: John Carpenter; Stuart Gordon; Dan O'Bannon; Lucio Fulci; Sam Raimi; and Guillermo del Toro. Lovecraft's weirdness has also been transduced into the most morbidly unmelodious strains of musick by such cults as Black Sabbath, Metallica, Gwar, Electric Wizard, Engorged, and The Black Dahlia Murder.

Verily, Creepy Reader, if there is a reference in a book, film, or song to odiously otherworldly gods, the eeriest of eldritch grimoires, namelessly noisome places, unspeakably unnatural abominations, and the hideous horrors of all things tentacled, it is because of Lovecraft. As Neil Gaiman has said of Lovecraft, "He's all over the cultural landscape." Indeed!

And so, Creepy Reader, perchance you are curious about when yours cruelly, like Cliff Burton or John Carpenter or Alan Moore before me, was ushered into the woe-begettingly weird world of H. P. Lovecraft? I was not introduced to his work until I was in high school, but, in truth, I could not *truly* behold what was before me, in the form of Del Rey's *The Best of H.P. Lovecraft: Bloodcurdling Tales of Horror and the Macabre*, which I had bought, so very simply, because of its cursedly lurid Michael Whelan cover.

Being that I was still but an unfostered young horror fiend, perhaps my gray matter was not yet prepared for what Lovecraft's profoundly putrescent purple pulpy prose—with the exquisitely florid excesses of its dauntingly dense, delectably dreadfullest descriptions—required from me. All was "nameless, unexplainable," "alien and aberrant," "blasphemous," "abominably repellent," "unnatural," and, more than anything else, "unknown." The odd words of that Lovecraftian lexicon—"eldritch," "gibbous," "ichthyic," "batrachian," and so on—were unknown to me. And so I put Lovecraft on a shelf and there he would fester, forgotten yet unfading, until those "stars had come round again" for me to read him once again.

It was then that I became indoctrinated: ill-fatedly infected by his words as if I had inhaled through them the fiendishly foulest of fatally foreign fungi. In short, Creepy Reader, yours cruelly was obsessed. And it was some years later, indeed not so very long ago, that I began to hear the call.

Now and again I would hear it, some scarcely audible yet atrociously shuddersome sound, like whispering wraithen words upon a radio frequency that refuses to tune. Despite my most desperate efforts to shut that chillingly ghastly call from my mind, I could not. My sleep was restless, my dreams ridden with tenebrously terror-torturous tableaux: moldering graves shadowed by grotesquely moribund trees; olde abandoned and atrocity-abased Victorian abodes whose paint was peeling off like the skin from a shriveled corpse; nauseously notorious and nameless New England towns whose roots are rotted with the most repellent ill-renown.

Whilst awake, I would hear that call as well—croaking, gibbering, baying—in the rustling of dead October leaves and the howl of bitter December gusts. And so, finally, unable to free my unfortunately meanly mortal mind from that maddening call—Lovecraft's call!—my black bride and yours cruelly followed it north unto those "nameless cities"—the all-too-real inspirations for his "Arkham," "Innsmouth," and "Dunwich," as well as his very own home, Providence—where he worshipped his Old Ones, his Deep Ones, and all things scuttling and shambling decades and decades ago. Won't you join us then, Creepy Reader, on our journey into the monstrous mouth of madness that is H. P. Lovecraft's weird New England!

Our butchermobile had motored northeast from our Charnel House, through Connecticut and then into the Bay State, Massachusetts, for almost four hours before we finally found our repugnantly Horror-ravening selves in ill-rumored Salem. As we crawled further and further into the cursedly cryptic heart of the town, we espied innumerable olde Colonial houses with their fancifully gabled façades, all of them making for a picturesque backdrop for that so-called "Witch City."

The profoundly venerable presence of those houses all throughout Salem was evidence of exactly how olde it was. The settlement was founded in about 1626 by a crew of Plymouth colonists, headed by Roger Conant—who was in search of more freedom than his family's former Puritannical home had furnished—and, later, came under the governance of the Massachusetts Bay Company.

While the town played a vital part in early America's trade in the East Indies and China because of its many ports, it would be those terribly torturous witch trials of 1692, in which 20 unfortunate townsfolk died so very detestably because of the bizarre and "Bewitched!"-branded behavior of two pre-adolescent girls, that would assure Salem's widespread notoriety.

Although many of those wrongfully accused "witches" were residents of Danvers, known then as Salem Village, rather than Salem, then called Salem Town, it was upon the latter that the most impious of iniquity-imbued infamies have been heaped since the late seventeenth century. And, verily, it was because of Salem's profoundly ill-rumored past—its nature defined by black magick and even blacker murder—that H. P. Lovecraft made it the all-too-real model for his very own Arkham!

Despite the fact that Lovecraft did indeed often reference Salem alongside his Arkham—which he had founded so very foully not so very distant from its inspiration within Massachusetts's Essex County—this does not belie the latter's real-world roots in the former. It was in 1920's "The Picture in the House" that Lovecraft first wrote of Arkham, whose founders, "strange people, whose like the world has never seen," had escaped from beneath the austerity of their prohibitive Puritan peers into the spooksome sylvan shadows of the Miskatonic Valley—yet another fabrication—where, "in their isolation, morbid self-repression, and struggle for life with relentless Nature, there came to them dark furtive traits from the prehistoric depths of their cold Northern heritage."

While he would return, again and again, to that "changeless, legend-haunted city of Arkham, with its clustering gambrel roofs that sway and sag over attics where witches hid from the King's men in the dark, olden days of the Province" in "The Dreams in the Witch-House" (1932) and "The Thing on the Doorstep" (1933), it was not indeed the most unspeakable of his hideously Horror-fied yet bogus New England burghs—a dread-ridden distinction that would definitely go to neighboring "Innsmouth."

Regardless, Creepy Reader, Arkham is indeed at the eerie and eldritch black heart of his Cthulhu Mythos: the home of his Miskatonic University, that ill-famed institution of the most appalling of academics, and his Arkham Sanitarium, that most Mythos-macabred madhouse that would, in the decades following Lovecraft's death, take on a loathsomely lunatic life of its own as the Arkham Asylum of *Batman* comic book lore. And it was for that very reason, Creepy Reader, that we gruesome twosome made Salem, that "Arkham" of Lovecraft's terrorizingly weird tales, our crypt-away-from-krypt whilst exploring that severed neck of Lovecraft's noisome country!

"ARKHAM"

After we had stowed our bags at the Suzannah Flint House, a three-story Essex Street home built in 1808 and then restored, only some years ago, into a quaint bed and breakfast, my black bride and yours cruelly went out in search of Salem's creepily cryptic occult curiosities. Although Salem was indeed Lovecraft's precursor for Arkham, there was, verily, nary a one true Lovecraftian location throughout the town, the inspirations for Arkham's fiendishly distinguishing features, such as Miskatonic U. or Arkham Asylum, not found in Salem itself, albeit not so very distant from it.

But Creepy Reader, this by no means meant that our terror-tour's blood-feasting chopping block was to remain so sorrowfully unensanguined whilst in Salem. No. For as we gruesome twosome walked amidst "Arkham," we found our abhorrently atrocity appalled selves beset by witches! There were witches on the awnings of shoppes, witches upon sundry Salem souvenirs, and even upon the doors of patrol cruisers, in the form of the Salem Police Department's official logo.

It was truly evident that Salem has profited well from its infamous past by turning the macabre and the morbid into the most convivial of tourist commodities. According to pamphlets, there was a slew of witch-themed attractions, from walking tours to museums, that do a bountiful Horror business in Salem from May through Halloween, October naturally being the town's most popular time of year. Yours cruelly had no doubts that such a debasing bacchanal of deepest All Hallow's Eve devilry was not the sort of legacy that its founding Puritan fathers wanted for their sleepy little village of Salem!

SALEM WITCH MUSEUM
Washington Square
Salem
(978) 744-1692

Across from the picturesque Salem Common, but a block from the Suzannah Flint House, we gruesome twosome espied the Salem Witch Museum and it seemed like a properly bedevilled place to begin our black-hearted Salem witch-hunt. With its so very fanciful stone façade and turreted roof, the hulking Salem Witch Museum, which looked like some sort of grim olde Gothic church, was perhaps the most eye-catching edifice in the whole town, at least to yours cruelly's bloodshot eyes.

After paying the pittance of an entry fee and waiting for a few minutes within the dimly lit foyer—wherein the churchly aesthetic was furthered by its pew-like benches and wrought iron wall sconces—my unspeakable wife and I, along with that hour's other visitors, were ushered into the shadow-bathed, cavernous belly of the museum's auditorium. And in but a few minutes time, the Salem Witch Museum's presentation began.

The horrendously ill history of 1692's Salem Witch Trials was unfolded through, so very aptly, 13 staged sets—which looked verily like life-size dioramas—installed high atop our heads within the auditorium's walls. That almost three-century-old troubling tale of twistedly "pious" transgression and terribly pitiless tribulation—began with, Elizabeth Parris, the nine-year-old daughter of Salem Village minister, Reverend Samuel Parris.

The series of sets started with Elizabeth Parris, and her 11-year-old cousin, Abigail Williams, being regaled with the most superstitious of fireside folk stories by the Parris' West Indian maidservant, Tituba, all the while building up to the hanging of 19 of the harshly-hunted accused witches—each set was spotlighted one after another as a verily educational and engaging prerecorded dual narration-and-dramatization was played in the background. The petrified three-dimensional "players" in the Salem Witch Museum's drama of deadly seventeenth-century "Devil!"-dread had been fashioned out of some sort of wax-like material which gave them a weirdly "wrinkled" appearance.

Amongst the museum's displays, yours cruelly's favorite, Creepy Reader, would have to have been the extremely more macabre chamber of horrors-esque exhibition of the "pressing" of Giles Corey, who had vigorously refused to answer his accusers' unfounded charges. Thus, he could not be tried as a witch, and was instead "press'd to death for standing mute," heavier and heavier stones heaped upon his slowly crushed body until he pled for mercy and admitted his guilt, which, in the end, Corey defiantly refused to do, his only request, at least as the story goes, being for "More weight." Also calling to our nastily nefarious natures, of corpse, was the staged set of Satan himself, in all his garishly red-lighted infernal glory!

Between those eerily odd effigies and the relishingly atmospheric background recording that let them "speak," my black bride and I were thoroughly entertained by the Salem Witch Museum, which, whilst verily a popular attraction, avoided the hokiness of Salem's other supposedly Horror-fied tourist traps, at least for yours cruelly. The only thing lacking for us, though, was the whining and whimpering of some affeared youngsters, which we had no doubt was not such an uncommon hurly-burly to hear there in the pitch blackness of the museum's auditorium!

When the Witch Museum's remarkably bewitching retelling of the Witch Trials had indeed been told, we gruesome twosome were let out into—so very coincidentally, Creepy Reader!—the gift shoppe. After browsing for a short while through the shoppe's selection of Salem sundries, we crawled out onto Washington Square for the repulsively accursed remainder of our exploration of the wickedly witch-horrid whereabouts of Lovecraft's Arkham.

OLD BURYING POINT & SALEM WITCH TRIALS MEMORIAL
Charter Street (between Central & New Liberty)
Salem

Lurking down Hawthorne Boulevard towards the less than sinister sight-seeing spot that is Salem Harbor, my unspeakable wife and yours cruelly came upon Charter Street and it was there, in but two blocks, that we found ourselves before the so very grimly funereal grave-plotted grounds of Salem's Old Burying Point. Eleven years after Roger Conant brought his faction of former Plymouth fishermen to that unsettled country along the craggy Massachusetts coast called *Naumkeag* to local Indians—thereafter known as Salem and, later to Lovecraft, as Arkham—this somewhat small piece of land along Charter Street was allotted for the burial of that young colony's dead and dubbed the Burying Point.

The Burying Point is not only the oldest boneyard in all of Salem but, at least according to some histories, the second oldest in all of America, that latter assertion not so difficult to believe as we gruesome twosome wormed our nauseatingly necrophilous way amongst Old Burying Point's simple gray, slated gravestones with their ascetically Puritan aesthetic. Although a good many of those headstones' inscriptions had been almost utterly worn away by well more than three centuries worth of severest weathering, yours cruelly could still espy, upon their folksily foreboding faces, many deeply delectable memento mori.

In "Pickman's Model," Lovecraft wrote that his 1926 tale's ghastly artist of the most grievous grotesqueries, Richard Upton Pickman, was "of old Salem stock, and had a witch ancestor hanged in 1692." While there are indeed nine Pickmans recorded amongst Burying Point's 347 burials, nary of them are, so very sadly, Creepy Reader, the "four-times-great-grandmother"—who was "hanged [. . .] on Gallows Hill"—of he who produced such perverse paintings as *Ghoul Feeding*.

While the signpost but within the tombyard's black wrought iron fence would seem to declare Mayflower passenger Captain Richard Moore as its most famous posthumous holding, its most *infamous* was not a witch—particularly not of Pickman blood!—but, verily, a witch-hunter: "The Witch Hanging Judge," John Hathorne. Along with his fellow magistrate Jonathan Corwin, it was Hathorne who not only interrogated those original three woefully-accused women—Sarah Good, Sarah Osborne, and that Caribbean-born slave, Tituba—imputed of unspeakable impieties by the

Satan-possessed Elizabeth Parris and Abigail Williams as well as all the others similarly baselessly branded, but, throughout the spring of 1692, who also presided upon those infamous Witch Trials.

And as my black bride and yours cruelly crawled past Old Burying Point, we beheld a truly poignant testimonial to the utter tragedy of those Trials of 1692 in the form of Salem's Witch Trials Memorial. Although none of the 20 "witches" whose deaths had been decreed so very deludedly by Hathorne and Corwin were indeed interred here at Burying Point—or within Salem at all but, in its stead, in Danvers, where they were hanged, all save for Giles Corey, upon "Gallows Hill"—Salem's town-fathers decided to finally acknowledge the unjustice meted out during the Witch Trials by memorializing its victims. The tribute—dedicated by Nobel Peace Prize winner Elie Wiesel upon the tercentenary of their deaths— was founded here, alongside Burying Point.

The memorial was fashioned, out of simple gray stones, in the form of a somewhat horseshoe-shaped wall abutting that aged graveyard, along which had been affixed slab-seats carved with not only the names of the victims, but the dates—and means—of their deaths as well. Even the most horrendously foul of horror fiends such as we gruesome twosome, Creepy Reader, sat there, amidst the shadowed solitude upon one of the Witch Trials Memorial's stone benches, in reverent remembrance of those 20 poor Salem residents who lost their lives in that archetypal 1692 witch-hunt.

THE WITCH HOUSE
310 Essex Street
Salem
(978) 744-8815

After whiling away some time amidst the lonesome ceme-terial loveliness of the Old Burying Point and the Witch Trials Memorial, we two most tenebrous of terror-touring thanatologists lurked towards Salem's charmingly shoppe-tenanted Essex Mall and, from there, along Essex Street for perhaps a block or two until we espied the eldritch black-painted and fancifully gabled façade of Salem's so-called Witch House.

In 1932's "The Dreams in the Witch-House," Lovecraft wrote of accursedly horrid Arkham's "centuried house"—the titular Witch-House, its seeming black roots in Salem so very apparent—wherein dwelled that mad metaphysics-minded Miskatonic mathematics major, Walter Gilman, so very deliberately within "the moldy, unhallowed garret gable" of "queerly irregular shape" that had been, in 1692, the abomination-adumbrated abode of Keziah Mason.

It was indeed this wretched accused Arkham witch, Creepy Reader, who had confessed to Witch Trials' Judge John Hathorne "of the Black Man, of her oath, and of her new secret name of Nahab," and who had escaped from her seemingly inescapable jail cell by means of "curves and angles smeared on the gray stone walls with some red, sticky fluid," thereafter to haunt Lovecraft's belovedly bewitched burgh as the most perverse of midnight phantasms.

As my unspeakable wife and yours cruelly entered Salem's Witch House, it was to so very egregiously edify our eeriest selves with those otherworldly occult secrets of Keziah Mason that the all-too-curious Walter Gilman had himself sought within Arkham's very own Witch-House. But, alas, we would find such morbidly black magickal mysteries so very unfortunately absent here, as the seventeenth-century Essex Street home was not inhabited by a witch—as its name might very well lead tourists to believe—but, in Mason's macabre stead, a very real witch-finder, in particular Judge Jonathan Corwin. Corwin bought the house—which is, today, the only extant edifice in all of Salem with direct ties to those 1692 Witch Trials—in 1675 and lived there with his family for almost 40 years and it stayed in the Corwin Family until the mid-1800s.

Unfortunately, it would seem that, thereafter, the Witch House fell into a sad state of disregard and disrepair and, by 1944, was threatened with demolition. Wanting to preserve that oldest structural artifact from their town's Puritan antiquity, Salem's residents raised almost $45,000 to renovate Corwin's former abode, something that brought about a "new wave of restoration" throughout Salem. Thusly refurbished, Salem's Witch House was opened to visitors in 1948.

While our comely Puritan-costumed tour guide showed us throughout Corwin's Witch House, yours cruelly was looking forward to witnessing the troublingly terrifying torture tactics wielded by some of Horror's most horrendously notorious witch-hunters—such as repellently ugly Reggie Nalder's Albino from *Mark of the Devil* (1970) or that "Witchfinder General" himself, Matthew Hopkins, as played by a delightfully despicable Vincent Price in, of corpse, *The Witchfinder General* (1968).

However, such a disturbing desire for all that is dreadful was thwarted yet again, as the primary purpose of the home is as an exhibit of life in the Salem of the seventeenth century through "examination of the material culture of the period." What this meant was that our tour guide explained to us the furnishings and architectural features about the Witch House that help to portray the profoundly practical Puritan lifestyle during those dark, bedeviled days of the Salem Witch Trials. And because of this, Creepy Reader, we gruesome twosome were treated to your average 1692 household accoutrements rather than implements used for the punishment of the "impious."

And so, although we were now verily knowledgeable of the history of seventeenth-century Salem life, our hideously unwholesome hunger for Horror had, here, not been as well fed as our gray matter had. After we had been shown the whole of the Witch House, my black bride and yours cruelly, having found there neither Lovecraft's Keziah Mason nor the tools of the witch-torture trade of those woe-begettingly bloodthirsty witchfinders we were all too familiar with, we departed to appease so very atrociously our Horror-fiending appetites elsewhere amidst H. P. Lovecraft's eldritch New England.

The mourning after that first day's worth of weirdest Arkham witch-hunting, our loathy ghastliness-gorging Lovecraftian journey would bring we two most execrable explorers of all that is eerie from Salem to its neighbor but eight miles to the north: that purportedly witch-plagued Salem Village of 1692, known instead to its present day inhabitants as Danvers. And perhaps, Creepy Reader, you would ask exactly what my crepuscular bride and yours cruelly sought in Danvers. While, again, it was there, upon Gallows Hill, that those 19 "witches" had their scandalized necks so shockingly stretched, we were not in search of its whereabouts but, rather, someplace where we gruesome twosome could commit our curelessly creeps-crazed selves: that morbidity-shadowed sanctuary for the most shuddersomely Cthulhu Mythos-maddened known to decades of Lovecraft's disciples and D.C. Comics' *Batman* devotees as . . . Arkham Asylum!

As Lovecraft had based his very own strange primordial specimen—which he himself had called Arkham Sanitarium—upon the all-too-real mammoth Massachusetts madhouse known as Danvers State Insane Asylum, it was thither that we were shambling as our butchermobile motored out of Salem.

"ARKHAM SANITARIUM":
DANVERS STATE INSANE
ASYLUM
Hathorne Circle
(off the intersection of
Highway 1 & Route 62)
Danvers

At the very beginning of 1926's "The Call of Cthulhu," Lovecraft's narrator declares, affearedly, that, if man were to see beyond the "veil" that separates humanity's reassuring definitions of reality to its terrifyingly revolting truth, the only consequence, due to the finitude and fragility of the human mind, is madness. That is why, throughout Lovecraft's weird tales, those foully ill-fated few who indeed behold the loathsome, unspeakable things that lurk beyond that very same "veil"—the unknown Great Ones and all their otherworldly offspring—descend into utter disturbingly dreadfullest derangement.

To house those unfortunate lunatics of his, Lovecraft turned to Danvers State Insane Asylum, a massive neo-Gothic mental hospital built between 1874 and 1878 after the aesthetic designs of Nathaniel Bradlee and the psychiatric dogmas of Dr. Thomas Kirkbride. Called the Witch's Castle, so very aptly, by locals, the asylum must have seemed like New England's very own Bedlam—the very loathsome embodiment of extremest lunacy— to Lovecraft when he espied the enormous, eldritch edifice with his very own eyes sometime before writing "Pickman's Model" in 1926, the short pulp story that would usher the madhouse into the monstrous stygian maw of his Cthulhu Mythos.

In that work, Lovecraft's narrator, in his attempts to portray the abhorrent artistic aberrance of that titular Pickman, attests that, "Before long I was pretty nearly a devotee, and would listen for hours like a schoolboy to art theories and philosophic speculations wild enough to qualify him for the Danvers asylum."

Lovecraft would return to Danvers five years later in what is perhaps one of his most popular tales, "The Shadow Over Innsmouth," wherein its ill-fated narrator, hearing for the very first time of the repulsively

rumored reputation of "shadowed Innsmouth," is told by a railway ticket-seller "of more'n one business or government man that's disappeared there, and there's loose talk of one who went crazy and is out at Danvers now." But after such appearances, it would seem that Lovecraft wanted to relocate the awfully Horror-apalled asylum from the Danvers of Massachusetts fact to the Arkham of his Mythos's fiction because, with 1933's "The Thing on the Doorstep," he began to house his luridly terror-tormented lunatics at his very own Arkham Sanitarium.

But perchance, Creepy Reader, you are all too curious about how Lovecraft's Arkham Sanitarium became Arkham Asylum, that most macabre Gotham madhouse wherein the legendarily villainous likes of The Joker, Two-Face, and The Scarecrow were, again and again, locked away in Batman comic books and films? While it is sometimes said that Bob Kane, Batman's creator, founded that institution for the criminally insane after Lovecraft's death in 1937, as a tribute to the writer whose work Kane verily respected, such a story is as much of a fabrication as anything either of them ever fathered.

In truth, it was not until 1974, with *Batman* #258, that then-current writer Dennis O'Neil introduced an Arkham Hospital—or, variously, Arkham Sanitarium, recalling Lovecraft's very own name for the psychosis-plagued place—into the fabric of the D.C. Universe and, after some years, its name became the more deeply macabre Arkham Asylum. After it had been named thusly, Lovecraft's Mythos-madhouse was brought to Gotham in 1980 by Swamp Thing-creator Len Wein in *Batman* #326, who also, in 1985, elucidated the now abidingly D.C. asylum's repulsively mad roots with the creation of Amadeus Arkham—such an exquisite example of "retroactive continuity" fleshed out, so fiendishly finely, by Grant Morrison and Dave McKean in 1989's *Arkham Asylum*. And so, while it was indeed a sanitarium to Lovecraft—one, verily, in his very own Arkham!—it has become, perhaps, an even more greatly grotesque Gotham-haunting asylum, and so it shall remain, even, seemingly, for a many a less learned Lovecraft-lover.

And it was there, Creepy Reader, to this horrid and thusly historied Danvers State Insane Asylum—which also had been the spook-ridden setting for 2001's post-*Turn of the Screw* celluloid ghost creepshow, *Session 9*—that we gruesome twosome were motoring from Salem to explore. While Danvers was but eight miles northwest of that former Salem Village, the journey there was almost as tortuous as its ill-rumored Arkham Asylum incarnation's pedigree.

When our meatwagon had motored for a few miles along Route 114, yours cruelly wheeled us onto, one after the other, Highway 1 North, then Route 62 West, and then, finally, Highway 1 South. It was from there that we exited onto Maple Street, which seemed to be a service road of sorts on the eastbound side of Route 62. Almost at once thereafter, our touring hearse veered onto Hathorne Circle, along which, after motoring but a short way, we passed a rusted black-and-white sign for "Danvers State Hospital." We knew, then, that high upon the hill before us—the very same hill upon which it is said "Witch-Hanging Judge" John Hathorne had once lived—was indeed, hidden beyond a thick moribund veil of thickets and trees, Arkham Sanitarium.

As we crawled, so very slowly, closer and closer to the hill, from Hathorne to Kirkbride Road, we began to espy some of the asylum's towers and spires emerging before us. But it was there, upon Kirkbride Road, that my unspeakable wife and yours cruelly found our wretchedly Lovecraftian weirdness-worshipping selves before not simply a No Trespassing sign, but also a steel gate upon a stretch of road that would indeed usher us out upon the hill's very head and, there, to the asylum. But because that gate was opened wide and there was nary a security guard in sight—and because we were racked worse than ever before by our hideously ravenous hunger for all things Horror-fied—we let our butchermobile creep all too curiously unto Lovecraft's macabrely ill-renowned madhouse, Arkham Sanitarium!

And as we gruesome twosome wormed our woefully Horror-fiending way further up the hill, we passed, on the right-hand side of the road, a squat brick structure that I would later learn was once housing for the nurses of the lunatic hospital. But it was thereafter, as our meatwagon slowly lurked out into what had been the institution's parking lot—whose wide black face was split-open and sprouting weeds—that my black bride and yours cruelly saw it looming before our expansively awe-appalled eyes, Creepy Reader, so very stunning in its utter shuddersome sublimity: Danvers State Insane Asylum!

It is said that Danvers State was, in its day, the greatest mental hospital in America, if not, very possibly, the world. As we gruesome twosome stood there before what is known as the Kirkbride Complex—a shocking, sprawling congregation of 17 conjoined structures, each fashioned out of red Danvers brick—such an estimation was not so very difficult to believe. But what was so frankly affearingly fascinating about the monstrous madhouse was not simply its sheer size but, verily, its deeply dread-disposing design.

While acclaimed Boston architect Nathaniel Bradlee was responsible for the asylum's blueprints and building, its astoundingly peculiar aesthetics were born of the progressive psychiatric philosophies of Dr. Thomas Kirkbride. To Kirkbride, who was widely held as the "guiding spirit of model-hospital building" of the late nineteenth century, there were several architectural stipulations for a truly healthful lunatic hospital. Amongst them was that it should be a profoundly private place and, thus, should be located in isolation. Another was that, in order to assure that fresh air flowed through all of an asylum's various wards, they should not be laid out so linearly. Because of that, his Danvers State Insane Asylum was not only founded here upon this wooded hill, apart from the rest of Danvers, but was fashioned in such a wholly weird way that its wards spread out from a main structure.

Verily, Danvers State's wings—their foundation's walls featuring almost 240 angles—were unfurled—yes, Creepy Reader—like "wings." Perhaps those of a bat . . . ? And with its fancifully Gothicized façade—ornamented so very oddly by a grandly grotesque slew of gables and steeples—this singularly designed Danvers State would seem to have been an insane asylum liable to produce, simply by its very construction, profoundly more insane patients.

Despite the fact that nothing in Danvers State's history—from when it opened in 1878 until when it was, indeed, abandoned in 1992—would suggest that it was the scene of the same species of infamously sordid iniquities that turned London's very own Bethlehem Hospital into the deeply despicable Bedlam, the atrociously atmosphered asylum before us could not have been a more forbidding and frightful thing.

And as my unspeakable wife and yours cruelly stood there amidst the strange and surreal shadow of this very same Danvers State Insane Asylum—

that Castle of the townsfolk, that Arkham Sanitarium of Lovecraft, and that Arkham Asylum of O'Neil, Wein, and Morrison—we two most cryptic of Horror-fied curiosity-mongers were indeed, Creepy Reader, witnessing a monstrously macabre, maddening madhouse upon the very borderland of wholly alien worlds: the Danvers of fact and the Danvers of Lovecraft's fiction; the Arkham of 1933 and the Gotham of the 1970s and '80s.

We gruesome twosome were thusly ruminating before the rotting remains of "Arkham Sanitarium" but some minutes before, from that very same road our butchermobile had taken there as well as from the opposite side—as that hill-topping hospital was hemmed by a circular driveway—came down upon us, at the very least, four patrol cars and out from them, once they had pulled to a stop all about us, stepped security guards, some local Danvers constables, and even one or two Massachusetts State Troopers.

Needless to say, Creepy Reader, yours cruelly's horrendous black heart stopped—and not from any eerily abhorrent effect of eldritch "Arkham Sanitarium" upon me! We had very well known, before leaving on our expedition to Lovecraft's New England, that not only was Danvers State abandoned but that, elsewhere upon its enormous acreage, had been housed a drug rehabilitation clinic. Whether or not those No Tresspassing warnings were in place to keep unwanted visitors from investigating the former or to preserve the privacy of the latter's patients is unbeknownst to me.

Regardless of their raison d'etre, we had not heeded them and so had to answer for not doing so. But after realizing that we were, in the end, harmless and had no intentions of breaking into the boarded asylum, they sent us on our way, in fact actually ribbing the security guard who should have stopped us at the gate below. And so did yours cruelly wheel our meatwagon around and motor back down whence we came.

While our exploration of Danvers State Insane Asylum had been unfortunately interrupted, it was truly an indescribable experience to worship, if only for a short time, at the weird altar of Lovecraft's abomination-weltered Arkham Sanitarium. Neither of us had seen its like before and so very unfortunately, Creepy Reader, you may never even have that opportunity—tresspassing or not!—as yours cruelly learned that, some years, in fact, after our fiendishly unforgettable yet all-too-fleeting committal there, that the former mental hospital and its abundantly appreciated acreage had been bought by a Virginia-based developer known as Avalon Bay, who plan on building apartments and condominiums not simply on the property but—egads!—perhaps even within remodeled portions of that Kirkbridge Complex!

There had been various preservation-minded parties who had fought to have Danvers State refurbished for not only its historical and architectural value but because its grounds have been buried with the bodies of some 768 patients who died during their time at the asylum. However, their efforts were, so very obviously, all for naught. But if, within the horrid annals of Horror, abodes founded so very simply upon ghastly forsaken graveyards become haunted by the spirits of the disgracefully desecrated dead, can you conceive, Creepy Reader, what will become of these residences built atop the boneyard of this most morbid of madhouses?

"INNSMOUTH"

It was in late 1931 that H. P. Lovecraft introduced readers of his terribly tenebrous weird-terrored tales to what is— more than Dunwich and its natives whose "annals reek of over viciousness and of half-hidden murders, incest, and deeds of almost unnameable violence and perversity," and even more than "witch-cursed, legend-haunted Arkham"—his most horrendously eldritch New England home of Cthulhu Mythos horrors: "the ancient Massachusetts seaport of Innsmouth."

In "The Thing on the Doorstep," it is attested that "Arkham folk avoid going to Innsmouth whenever they can." Similarly, it is called "that ancient, half-deserted town which Arkham people were so curiously unwilling to visit" in "The Dreams of the Witch-House." Despite these two references, which indeed sink Innsmouth's ill-historied infamy into the deepest stygian depths, it is in but one of Lovecraft's works, 1931's "The Shadow Over Innsmouth," that the repellently ill-rumored renown of his town was rooted.

While the horrors of Arkham may be more curious and cryptic, those of Innsmouth have always seemed more deeply, disturbingly dreadful. And because of this and the simple fact that "The Shadow of Innsmouth" is yours cruelly's favorite of Lovecraft's weird tales—"The Hound" being its rival!—

it was on that third day of our expedition throughout the foetid bowels of his fiendishly fabricated New England burghs, after returning from our time at Arkham Asylum, that we gruesome twosome journeyed to Newburyport, Lovecraft's real-world inspiration for his very own Innsmouth!

NEWBURYPORT
Market Square
State Street at Merrimac
Street & Water Street

Found almost 25 miles north of Salem upon the southern shore of the Merrimack River where its mouth yawns unto the Atlantic, Newburyport was first inhabited by the Pawtucket Indians, who were followed, in the 1630s, by fishermen from England. Those earliest Colonial settlers made thorough use of the town's prodigious maritime potential and turned it into a ship-swarmed seaport, the very first wharf having been built in 1655 by Captain Paul White.

Fishing and sea-trade flourished there so very fortuitously into the eighteenth century that, in 1764, the port seceded from greater Newbury to become Newburyport. Such sea-going successes continued after the Revolutionary War until the town was all but crippled by a devastating conflagration in 1811 and the trade embargoes born of the War of 1812. Although, towards the latter half of the nineteenth century, Newburyport did rise somewhat from such ruin, by the 1900s, it suffered yet more depression.

It was to this thusly ill-fated Newburyport—its ports decayed, its streets dingy, and its once dignified townsfolk downtrodden and disenfranchised—that H. P. Lovecraft visited for the very first time before 1931 and his writing of that tale that would immortalize its monstrous Mythos morbidity upon the

maps of Horror history, "The Shadow Over Innsmouth." While in that story Lovecraft had written of factual Newburyport alongside his fictional Innsmouth, as he had with Salem and its iniquitous Arkham incarnation, the former's decline—"civic degeneration" and "communal decay" as Lovecraft referred to it—verily inspired Innsmouth, that "seaport of death and blasphemous abnormality," that "festering city of death and decay," in which the tale's nameless, naïve narrator was so very unfortunate to find himself.

After my unspeakable wife and yours cruelly had left "Arkham" that mourning and had motored northwards along Route 95 until, after perhaps 30 minutes, our touring hearse began creeping down Merrimac Street into downtown Newburyport. And what we espied as we came upon Newburyport's Market Square was truly horrifying: a Starbucks! Yes, Creepy Reader, Newburyport had definitely risen from its former ruin and was nothing like what Lovecraft had made of it with his Innsmouth after first visiting there: "a community slipping far down the cultural scale," "a region of utter desperation which somehow made [that narrator] shudder."

Because of a 1970s urban renewal project, Newburyport, particularly the downtown quarter in the heart of which Market Square hunkers, was utterly revivified and, as we parked our meatwagon along State Street to walk about that Innsmouth-shadowed Newburyport, we witnessed the exhaustive extent of that renewal. With its scenic cobble-stoned streets and redbrick structures, downtown Newburyport was a profoundly picturesque place inhabited by a sumptuous slew of antique shoppes, gourmet grocers, foreign crafts boutiques, and little eateries.

Because of this, it looked as if, at least to yours cruelly's bloodshot eyes, the contemporary residents of this titillatingly traditional New England seaside town were actually somewhat affluent, and *not* because of disgustingly dreadful Deep Ones-deifying doings—the "sacrficin' [of] heaps o' their young men an' maidens to some kind o' god-things that lived under the sea" and, worse, "matin' with them toad-lookin' fishes," all to get "all kinds o' favour in return," particularly the "gold-like things"—which Captain Obed Marsh, that "old limb o' Satan," learned from the Kanakys of the "Saoth Sea islands" and which he brought back to Innsmouth.

Alas, Creepy Reader, Newburyport was nothing like how old Zadok Allen, "the half-crazed, liquorish nonagenarian," had so petrifyingly portrayed it to the tale's narrator as they sat amidst Innsmouth's deteriorated ports: "everything a-rottin' an' dyin', an' boarded-up monsters crawlin' and bleatin' an' barkin' an' hoppin' araoun' black cellars an' attics every way ye turn." And so, search as we did, yours cruelly found nary any "fish-like frogs or froglike fishes" in all of Newburyport, Lovecraft's Innsmouth.

After ruminating upon what Lovecraft would have thought of this reborn—and less than repugnantly rotted!—Newburyport and whether he would have sat within that Market Square Starbucks, sipping a frothy $5 frappucino, and been inspired to beget the same hideously blood-curdling Horror as he did with "The Shadow Over Innsmouth," we gruesome twosome returned to our butchermobile to journey southwards to Gloucester.

While Newburyport was indeed Lovecraft's inspiration for his Innsmouth, that latter terrifyingly shadowed town's most Horror-legendarily loathsome landmarks, such as the Gilman House and the temple of the unspeakable Esoteric Order of Dagon, were, in fact, Creepy Reader, not in Newburyport at all but in Gloucester, almost 25 miles to the southeast. And it was there we were bound when our meatwagon motored out of Newburyport's shuddersome Innsmouthed self.

THE LEGION MEMORIAL BUILDING
(The American Legion Post No. 3)
8 Washington Street
Gloucester

Like Newburyport, Gloucester, almost 18 miles northeast of Salem, was settled as a fishing port upon the Atlantic-scourged rocky shores of Cape Anne in 1623 because of its potentially profitable proximity to worthily fish-choked waters off the coasts of Nova Scotia and Newfoundland to the north. Its maritime trade was in fact so substantial and successful that it became, throughout the commercially-cast consciousness of popular culture, the home of that symbol of simplest seafood, Gorton's of

Gloucester, and its frozen prefabricated fish-food, which was founded there in 1849 as John Pew & Sons.

Gloucester's rife maritime renown was furthered more recently by *The Perfect Storm*, the book and the film both, that "true story" of a Gloucester fishing boat, the *Andrea Gail*, that was swallowed whole by the so-called Halloween Nor'Easter—the titular storm of the century—whilst on their way back to New England in 1991. And so Gloucester's thusly prominent seafaring past has continued into the present day.

But we two most monstrously morbid of Cthulhu Mythos-mongers had not come to Gloucester to scarf down enough slimy bucketsful of monkfish, crabs, lobsters, cuttlefish, squid, and other such deep sea denizens to have utterly disgusted poor fish-phobic Lovecraft. No, Creepy Reader. My unspeakable wife and yours cruelly had lurked into Gloucester and then to Washington Street because it was there, just off Middle Street, that we would find the Legion Memorial Building and, with it, the mammoth model for the horrid Innsmouth home of Lovecraft's very own Esoteric Order of Dagon!

With its wide, white façade and its two-story-tall pillars, it was not very difficult for yours cruelly to espy the Legion Memorial Building as our butchermobile motored down Washington Street. The stout, classically-designed structure reigned over most of its share of Washington Street, which was perhaps only natural because it had been built in the early 1840s as Gloucester's very first town hall, which it remained until 1867 when it was replaced by a second, more stately, version. In 1919, the building became the property of the American Legion and was made Gloucester's Post No. 3.

But, at least to Lovecraft in "The Shadow Over Innsmouth," such history was forgotten for something more Horror-fied. In his tale, 8

 Washington Street was, in its American Legion's stead, "the former Masonic Hall now given over to a degraded cult" and was indeed the very first thing in Innsmouth to fill the story's ill-fated narrator so very foully with a "very strong impression of poignantly disagreeable

quality." While Lovecraft's placement of the Order's terror-threatening temple was very—and very startlingly!—accurate, his ill-portending portrait of it did not resemble what we gruesome twosome saw before us. Whenever it was that he had himself first beheld that former Gloucester town hall, it must have been looked after with considerably less consideration than its current custodians obviously do.

Regardless, Creepy Reader, it was here in "The Shadow Over Innsmouth" that the terror-tale's narrator witnessed, with "bizarre horror," the "pastor" of that cursedly abominable Cthulhu Mythos cult, "clad in some peculiar vestments doubtless introduced since the Order of Dagon had modified the rituals of the local churches."

Worse, he would later learn, from drunk and daft old Zadok Allen, that it was from this foully horrid former Masonic Hall that "old man Mash," Captain Obed, spread his woe-begetting Deep Ones-worship to the once—*once!*—human inhabitants of Innsmouth. And so after lingering amidst Glouster's wicked Washington Street whereabouts of that degraded cult of dark dreadfullest Dagon, my black bride and yours cruelly shambled in search of that loathsome location that would make the nastiest of nameless nightmares of that narrator's night in nauseating Innsmouth: the Gilman Hotel!

THE SARGENT HOUSE MUSEUM
(The Sargent-Murray-Gilman-Hough House)
49 Middle Street
Gloucester
(978) 281-2432

Before leaving Newburyport for ignominiously unspeakable Innsmouth—borne there by the rickety and rusted old bus of loathly Innsmouth looking Joe Sargent—the narrator is told, with the least approving of appraisals, of "a hotel in Innsmouth—called the Gilman House [. . .] There was a factory inspector who stopped at the Gilman a couple of years ago and he had a lot of unpleasant hints about the place. Seems they get a queer crowd there [. . .]." But having abandoned his bus in Innsmouth, so very atrociously, because of a faulty engine—thus necessitating a stay at the Gilman—he would come to know that its other guests were grossly more gruesome and grotesque than simply "a queer crowd."

For it was indeed, Creepy Reader, his stay at the Gilman House that would be one of most horridly harrowing happenings in "The Shadows Over Innsmouth," if not all of Lovecraft's traumatically terrorizing weird tales, as, lying upon his room's ragged and mold-reeking mattress, Lovecraft's narrator's shrinking attempts at sleep would be worse than "rudely" interrupted by someone trying to unlock the door of his room.

And it was thereupon, after narrowly escaping from his shockingly sinister would-be sacrificers, that the narrator would steal through the dreadfully night-drenched town, only to witness the "things" that were Innsmouth's torturously twisted Deep Ones-transmuted townsfolk—"in a limitless stream—flopping, hopping, croaking, bleating—surging inhumanly through the spectral moonlight in a grotesque, malignant saraband of fantastic nightmare"—that would compel him to ask the question, "Where does madness leave off and reality begin?"

And so, Creepy Reader, after my unspeakable wife and yours cruelly adjourned our most abhorrently Horror-fied Esoteric Order of Dagon meeting before Gloucester's Legion Memorial Building, we lurked eastwards along Middle Street for but two blocks before we espied Lovecraft's Gilman House upon our right. The Sargent-Murray-Gilman-Hough House (which houses the the Sargent House Museum) was a truly magnificent Georgian mansion with a yellow-painted and paneled façade and white-stoned pilasters whose late-eighteenth-century grandeur hardly recalled to yours cruelly that "tall, cupola-crowned building with remnants of yellow paint with a half-effaced sign proclaiming it to be the Gilman House." The house was not, in fact, at any time a hotel but was the august Gloucester abode of Judith Sargent Murray, built by her first husband, Captain John Stevens, in 1782.

In her lifetime, Murray became one of America's very first woman authors, her feminist philosophies unfolded most famously in her 1790 essay, "On the Equality of the Sexes." However, while the museum—which was opened in 1919 or thereabouts after being restored—does indeed stand as a memorial to her literary legacy, its raison d'etre would seem to be, more so, as a domestic educational document of not simply early Gloucester history but, through it, pre- and post-colonial American life.

But, Creepy Reader, we gruesome twosome sneered at such unHorror-fied stuff because my crepuscular bride and yours cruelly were there—of corpse!—in search of the most atrociously unsettling of accommodations at Lovecraft's most infamously Innsmouthed Gilman House!

This former home of Judith Sargent Murray has become itself so sickeningly Mythos-shadowed to sundry scrutinizing Lovecraft scholars—despite the fact that it has two floors, a garret, and, possibly, a basement whilst the Gilman House had five floors with, at the very least, 28 rooms per floor, according to the narrator's statement that he was given "Room 428 on [the] next to top floor"—because of the simple similarity of the two edifices' names but, perhaps more so, also because of the sheer adjacency of the Sargent-Murray House to the Legion Memorial Building upon Washington Street. Its shorter stature, however, would have definitely made the narrator's escape through the window of his room here a less than formidably hair-raising feat, as he would have dropped but 15 feet to the yard below!

After investigating the "Shadow"-ed Sargent House scene of the start of that most unfortunate narrator's nightmarishly unnatural night in Innsmouth and finding, so very sadly, no room at Lovecraft's "Gilman House" for us two fearfully fanatical of Horror-fiends, we returned to the less loathsome likes of "Arkham" so that we could rest our repulsively weird-ravenous selves for the last day of our expedition amidst Lovecraft's eldritch Mythos-exalted New England and, with it, our journey throughout his very own beloved Rhode Island burgh of Providence.

"MY PROVIDENCE!"

Very early the next mourning, Creepy Reader, my noctiflorous wife and yours cruelly packed our most aberrant creepy-crawling accoutrements and parted from those horrendously witch-historied haunts of Salem for what was, for but two of his 47 years, the beloved lifelong home of H. P. Lovecraft: Providence. Our meatwagon had been motoring, out of Massachusetts and then into Rhode Island, almost an hour and a half before we eventually found our Horror-fiending selves amidst what is the Providence neighborhood of College Hill.

Settled by Roger Williams in 1636 atop a steep hill upon the eastern shore of the Providence River, College Hill was Rhode Island's very first permanent British province. In the years thereafter, this predominantly residential portion of Providence became the home to that "Beehive of Industry's" most remarkably prominent and prosperous residents, and it was their sundry massive houses and mansions that have made College Hill renowned for its admirable assortment of handsomely aestheticized and architecturally historical abodes.

But the neighborhood received its noticeably collegiate name because of the inhabitance of Brown University and the Rhode Island School of Design, the former founded in 1764 and the latter in 1877, the both founded but across Prospect Street from each other. But the steep and thusly settled streets of College Hill are lurked by scholars and students of a shuddersomely more strangeness-enshrouded species, Creepy Reader, because this was not simply where H. P. Lovecraft had set some of his most wretchedly Mythos-weird tales but, more importantly for devoted Lovecraft disciples such as us, where he himself had lived until his death in 1937. And as we gruesome twosome pulled our butchermobile to a dead stop before Brown University, it was these very same heinously Horror-fied haunts that we had come to explore.

BROWN UNIVERSITY
(Brown University Quadrangle)
Prospect Street between Waterman &
George Streets
Providence

Having stowed our meatwagon upon Prospect Street amidst the stately academic shadows of Brown University, yours cruelly thought it only fitting then, Creepy Reader, to begin our tortuously shambling terror-tour of Lovecraft's College Hill than with that illustriously ill-rumored institute of namelessly unnatural nefarious knowledge: Miskatonic University! Whilst Lovecraft's Horror-infamied college of black arts and weirdest sciences was said, throughout Lovecraft's Cthulhu Mythos cycle, to have been found amidst Arkham, its acknowledged ivy-adorned academic inspiration was, verily, Brown University, almost 80 miles south of Salem.

While Brown University—the third oldest university in New England and the seventh oldest in all of America—was founded in 1764 as, in fact, the College of Rhode Island in Warren, Rhode Island, it was not until 1770 that it was relocated to its present location amidst Providence's College Hill, and thereafter, in 1804, following a greatly generous gift from Nicholas Brown, renamed Brown University in recognition of his substantial remittance.

In addition to its distinguished undergraduate degrees, Brown began to grant master's and doctorate's as well as M. D. degrees in the late 1880s and, somewhat surprisingly, the mid-1970s, respectively. With such a highly regarded and recognized history as Brown's, it is not so very surprising that Lovecraft used it as his model for the much more macabre and morbid Miskatonic University—particularly since it was in his very own Providence backyard!

Yes, Creepy Reader, it was indeed this very same College Hill university that Lovecraft had metamorphosed, through miscellaneous tales, into mammothly notorious Miskatonic University. And the unspeakable horrors with which Arkham's very own dreadful den of dubious disciplines was veiled were things that would make even the most unpleasantly apathetic undergraduate vomit in utter revulsion.

In 1922's "Herbert West: Re-Animator," it was at Miskatonic's Medical School that the titular disgustingly all-too-curious doctor "made himself notorious through his wild theories on the nature of death and the possibility of overcoming it artificially" and, through his "abominable pursuits" of them.

And in 1933's "The Thing On the Doorstep," it was attested—perhaps upon West's nature-wronging wretchedness alone!—that, "there was even talk of black magic and of happenings utterly beyond credibility." But even more than such shocking stuff, Miskatonic University was utterly infamous—within and without Lovecraft's monstrous Cthulhu Mythos—because of its colossally ill-collectioned library.

From 1923's "The Festival" to 1928's "The Dunwich Horror," the library's hideously huge holding of "subterranean magical lore" is what brought a curious, unwholesome crew of Lovecraftian characters to Arkham's Miskatonic The collection included, as described in "The Dreams in the Witch-House," "the dubious old books on forbidden secrets that were kept under lock and key in a vault at the university library," such as "the dreaded *Necronomicon* of Abdul Alhazred, the fragmentary *Book of Eibon*, and the suppressed *Unaussprechlichen Kulten* of von Junzt," grand grimoires of grossest Great Old Ones obscene grotesqueries, one and all!

As my black bride and yours cruelly looked upon Miskatonic's true, and truly fine, Brown University face, it was—with its resplendently olde redbrick buildings overlooking its considerably picturesque campus— very much the Ivy League institution. But, alas, Creepy Reader, perhaps the sun was shining too brightly upon the quad, perhaps its halls of high- est education were less caliginously moss-crawled, perhaps the general atmosphere about its ample College Hill allotments was not so very gloomy enough—ghastly enough—for us to truly espy any vilely, very vermicious traces of its atrocious Miskatonic alter ego.

This prestigious and pre-eminent college was, in the end, simply that: only a college. But before we left Lovecraft's "Miskatonic University" for the rest of our Cthulhu Mythos-creeped tour of College Hill, yours cru- elly wondered, given the fact that, in its earliest days, Brown was the only university to welcome students of all religious persuasions, whether or not that included the worship of odiously tentacled otherworldly Old Ones as well . . . ?

THE FLEUR-DE-LYS STUDIO
7 Thomas Street
Providence
(401) 331-1114 (Providence Art Club)

After passing the repository of H. P. Lovecraft's profoundly profuse papers that is the John

Hay Library, my crepuscular bride and yours cruelly turned down College Street and put Prospect behind us. When we came to the corner of College and Benefit Street, upon which we found sitting the somewhat stately, classical Providence Athenaeum Library—America's fourth oldest library but, more importantly, a most favorite haunt amidst College Hill of both Lovecraft and his pseudo-autobiographical Providence-resident protagonist, Charles Dexter Ward, in 1927's "The Case of Charles Dexter Ward"—we began lurking down Benefit Street,

which is known as Providence's "Mile of History" because of the picturesque profusion of Colonial homes that can be found hemming the street's periphery.

It was but two blocks further upon Benefit that we gruesome twosome found ourselves before Thomas Street and, there, within the sanctified shadow of what Lovecraft had decreed "the finest Georgian steeple in America"—that of Main Street's First Baptist Meeting House, the oldest of the denomination in all of America, the Fleur-De-Lys Studio. At 7 Thomas Street, the Fleur-De-Lys Studio—constructed in 1885 from out of the artistic collaborations of painter Sydney R. Burleigh and architect Edmund R. Wilson, who were prominent members of the Providence Art Club—was very well the most strangely queer structure yours cruelly had ever espied.

With its olde world Europe architecture, its odd yellow-plastered ornamental panels, and its flat black-painted fringing, this extraordinarily singular Thomas Street edifice was utterly different than the abundantly staid and simply-styled Colonial abodes we had passed upon Benefit Street. And 7 Thomas Street, that peculiar art project of the Providence Art Club, must have also affected Lovecraft's foulest weirdness-fiending fancies because, in 1926's "The Call of Cthulhu," he would make it the horridly Mythos-enshrouded Providence home of dreadfully Cthulhu-dreaming artist, Henry Anthony Wilcox.

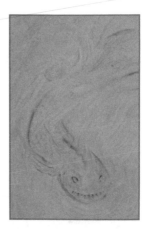

In that most abhorrently morbid Cthulhu Mythos archetype, the antiquarian and all-too-curious academic, Professor George Gammell Angell, is called upon by that very same Henry Wilcox, a student of sculpture at the Rhode Island School of Design. The young artist had brought with him a "queer clay bas-relief" which he had sculpted at his dwelling at the Fleur-De-Lys Building—a "hideous Victorian imitation of Seventeenth Century Breton architecture which flaunts its stuccoed front amidst the lovely Colonial houses on the ancient hill"—after "an unprecedented dream of great Cyclopean cities of Titan blocks and sky-flung monoliths, all dripping with green ooze and sinister with latent horror."

The resultant revolting bas-relief had depicted what "seemed to be a monster, or symbol representing a monster, of a form which only a diseased fancy could conceive." And the mysterious identity of that very same "monster" which the torturous remainder of Lovecraft's terror-tale worked to reveal—great Cthulhu, "that nameless sky-spawn"—would conjure from Lovecraft's chaos-creeping creativity the cryptically macabre core of his Cthulhu Mythos, within which he and that hideously unwholesome host of Lovecraftian horror-worshippers would dwell in demiurgic disgust. And, verily, Creepy Reader, if they had not, the heinously sanguinolent halls of Horror would be less horrific because of it!

Had it not had such ties to one of Lovecraft's most infamous weird tales, Thomas Street's Fleur-De-Lys Studio would have still been a deeply different dwelling. But then again, had that been the case, the sculpted abstractions amidst the abode's yellow-stuccoed adornments would have looked but like fish rather than a monster. But as this was indeed the very same Fleur-De-Lys Building of that appallingly Cthulhu-channelling artist, Henry Wilcox, yours cruelly took profoundly ghastliest pleasure from investigating the house's very own bas-reliefs for signs of any loathsomeness of a shuddersomely Lovecraftian nature.

But, alas, finding nothing either abominable or abhorrent therein that would have us Arkham Asylum-bound, we gruesome twosome each uttered our "Ia! Ia! Cthulhu fthagn!" before Providence's most eldritch Mythos edifice and returned to Benefit Street for the inhuman remains of our terror-tour of Lovecraft's College Hill.

**THE STEPHEN HARRIS HOUSE:
"THE SHUNNED HOUSE"
135 Benefit Street
Providence**

It was but a few blocks further along Benefit before my black bride and yours cruelly found, at No. 135, the alluringly Colonial yellow clapboard abode that had been fashioned not simply atop the small hill rising from the street but into it. No. 135 Benefit Street is known as the Stephen Harris House, named after its mid-eighteenth-century founder and first owner, and it was indeed this very same home that Lovecraft would make the dreadfully detestable titular dwelling of his 1924 weird tale, "The Shunned House," wherein the story's narrator attested that it "stands starkly leering as a symbol of all that is unutterably hideous."

However, it would seem as if the house did not need Lovecraft's perniciously unhealthy portraiture to pall with ill-renown for inhabitants of College Hill, at least those of Lovecraft's day, as its all-too-real history was indeed, as he himself wrote, "of a kind to attract the attention of the curious." In Providence's earliest days, Benefit was known as Back Street and, because the settlement's religious liberality forestalled the founding of a common burying ground, most of the families living along it had some acreage of their properties allotted for the deposition of their dearly departed.

But sometime in the eighteenth century, Back Street was renovated in order to meet the demands of Providence's pullulating populace and, because of such a reformation, the decomposed—or decomposing!—

remains of the deceased interred therein were dug out of those primeval family plots and reinterred within the newly settled North Burial Ground, Providence's oldest surviving cemetery. But, at least according to local College Hill lore, not all of those Colonially-coffined cadavers buried along Back Street—known thereafter as "Benefit"—were found, in particular those of a French-emigrated couple who had once lived upon the steep stretch of Benefit Street where—but of corpse, Creepy Reader!—Stephen Harris built his home, No. 135, before which we gruesome twosome stood, in 1763!

Having been rooted in such eldritch charnel earth, it is not so very surprising then that No. 135 would become a truly ill-renowned residence blighting College Hill so very repulsively. For Harris, it would be a less than happy home, as it would witness the unfolding of one tragedy after another, both financial and familial. Harris was a well-moneyed Providence merchant, but such prosperity all but faded shortly after the fabrication of his new abode was finished, as it was then that some of his trade ships were lost at sea.

To such monetary losses were added those of a more distressingly mortal sort, as within their very own appallingly ill-fated abode, Harris and his wife would lose child after child, most of them at birth. Perhaps under the weight of such seemingly inexorable woe, it is said that Mrs. Harris slowly succumbed to insanity. No. 135 Benefit Street thus having become her asylum, she shouted and shrieked at passersby from her room's windows, such a thing made all the more shuddersome to College Hill's residents because it is said it had been in French, a tongue that was not her own!

Regardless of whether or not Mrs. Harris had indeed so loathsomely learned the language from the property's original inhabitants, such rumors continued to shroud the Benefit Street residence throughout the nineteenth century and well into the twentieth. It was then, in the latter century, Creepy Reader, that No. 135—the disquietingly dilapidated and decrepit dwelling still owned by Harris' kin—became known to Lovecraft as he shambled along Benefit Street how the narrator of "The Shunned House" said Poe himself had discovered it.

In "The Shunned House," Lovecraft's portrait of not simply Benefit Street, but No. 135 and its history in the Harriss' most horrid of eighteenth-century hardships, was amongst the most authentic of his odiously otherworldly oeuvre—except, of corpse, for the house's dreadfullest cellar-dwelling "unknown horror": that, much like a vampire, fed upon all those unfortunate enough to find themselves living there.

And of this "shunned house" of Lovecraft's it was, as his narrator confesses, "the dank, humid cellar which somehow exerted the strongest repulsion on us, even though it was wholly above ground on the street side, with only a thin door and window-pierced brick wall to separate it from the busy sidewalk. We scarcely knew whether to haunt it in spectral fascination, or to shun it for the sake of our souls and our sanity."

And it was in that cursedly abhorrent cellar of 135 Benefit Street, wherein earlier Lovecraft's narrator had espied a "sort of cloudy whitish pattern on the dirt floor—a vague, shifting deposit of mould or nitre," that he found the "filthy thing" festering so foetidly in its utter foreign foulness within the house's very foundation. His disposal of that "unthinkable abnormality" by means of "six carboys of sulphuric acid" would be an unspeakably shocking thing known only to himself.

While at the end of "The Shunned House" Lovecraft, through his nameless narrator, foresaw 135 Benefit Street—the Stephen Harris House—being "torn down to make way for a tawdry shop or vulgar apartment building," my unspeakable wife and yours cruelly were indeed very happy that naught had come of his prediction, as the abode, with its fancifully aged and lively yellowed façade, was thoroughly bewitching. In fact, Creepy Reader, it would seem to be a reflection of that somewhat un-Lovecraftian sense of hopefulness with which Lovecraft ended his 1924 tale: "The barren old trees in the yard have begun to bear small, sweet apples, and last year the birds nested in their gnarled boughs."

Whilst yours cruelly did not witness any such less than Horror-fied stuff about Lovecraft's shunned house, neither did I—no matter how deeply I inhaled, Creepy Reader!—smell the shuddersome stench of the shockingly sentient, supernatural scum of which he wrote. After simple savoring its former "Shunned" atmosphere, we gruesome twosome continued our lurkings amidst that thusly Lovecraft-loathsomed Benefit Street.

STREET JOHN'S EPISCOPAL CATHEDRAL & CHURCHYARD
275 North Main Street (Church Street between Benefit and North Main Streets)
Providence
(401) 274-4500 (The Episcopal Diocese of Rhode Island)

In the beginning of "The Shunned House," Lovecraft, in order to temper the terrifying atmosphere of the tale, ruminated upon the common nineteenth-century Benefit Street crawlings that Poe—whom Lovecraft worshipped, verily, as a god—had himself undertaken "in the late forties [. . .] during his unsuccessful wooing of the gifted poetess, Mrs. Whitman." And during what Lovecraft declared as his favourite walk, Poe would inevitably find himself before the very same alluringly lurid College Hill locale that would have a "peculiar fascination" not simply for Poe but for Lovecraft after him and for my crepuscular wife and yours cruelly after Lovecraft: the "hidden expanse of eighteenth-century gravestones" that is Street John's Churchyard.

Having espied the stately towering steeple of Street John's Episcopal Cathedral well before turning down Church Street, we came upon its aged Churchyard exactly where Lovecraft had said it would be: "the hidden grove of giant willows on the hill where tombs and headstones huddle quietly between the hoary bulk of the church and the houses and the bank walls of Benefit Street." Thusly, the church and its cathedral did indeed all but hide that bewitchingly bygone boneyard from yours cruelly's bloodshot eyes until we were upon it and we gruesome twosome wormed our wretchedly necrosis-wanting way to it through a parking lot beside the church.

Street John's Episcopal Cathedral was one of four Colonial-era churches that, in 1790, assembled what is known as the Episcopal Diocese of Rhode Island. It was founded in 1722 as King's Church from the Anglican-faithed efforts of Gabriel Bernon, a French Huguenot who fled France in the late seventeenth century in search of religious freedom, eventually finding a home in Providence in 1718. Along with some other fellow Anglicans, Bernon began to raise the funds necessary for a church of their very own and, when they had amassed enough money, the small and simple wooden sanctuary that would be King's Church was built upon a plot of North Main Street property owned by parishioner Nathaniel Brown.

After closing for almost a decade with the very start of the Revolutionary War—because of the scandalously Loyalist sermons of its conspicuously British clergymen—the church was renamed Street John's Church in 1794. In 1810, its former wooden façade was torn down in favour of a stone masonry and mortar façade, an extravagant new addition to the edifice that would become the Cathedral of Street John, in whose sacrosanct shadow we stood that day.

While Street John's Cathedral continued to flourish for many years after its nineteenth-century reincarnation, it was finally faultlessly refurbished sometime in the 1970s, having been, for some decades, the religious and regulatory heart of the Rhode Island diocese. Its churchyard, of which Lovecraft wrote so lovingly in "The Shunned House"—where the tale's narrator "reared a marble urn to his [dead uncle's] memory"—was not so similarly revivified. Street John's plain yet picturesque grave-plotted yard was finely kept but was no less fantastically, fancifully phantasmic because of it.

As my unspeakable wife and yours cruelly shambled amongst the timeworn slate-gray tombstones that stuck up from the uneven charnel earth of that most hallowed College Hill haunt of both Poe and Lovecraft, images of Lovecraft, here, courting Sonia Greene—Brooklyn-settled and seven years his senior, she would be his life's one "sweetheart" and his wife for five years—as Poe had himself done, almost a century before, with that "gifted poetess," Sarah Whitman, were conjured in our morbidly ghastliness-mongering gray matter. It brought a smile to yours cruelly's fiendishly ghastly face to think of Lovecraft sitting with Greene amidst these very same Street John's Churchyard tombstones as he read to her—very possibly, Creepy Reader!—some of Poe's most profoundly poignant necrotic poetry. Oh, Lovecraft, you necromantic!

THE HALSEY HOUSE
140 Prospect Street
Providence

After whiling away some time amidst the less than shuddersomely sublime sepulchral solitude of Street John's Churchyard, my noctiflorous wife and yours cruelly returned to Benefit Street only to face, at the very next corner, Creepy Reader, what had to be the severely steepest street in all of College Hill, if not Providence: Jenckes Street. We took our time crawling to the very top of it, where we walked out upon Prospect Street yet again and where, for some minutes, we stopped until the heavy heavings of our oxygen-hungry lungs had stopped.

After we gruesome twosome had indeed gotten our breath back, we found our next creeps-moldering Cthulhu Mythos College Hill curiosity upon our left-hand side at 140 Prospect Street, known as the Halsey House to more pedestrian inhabitants of Providence, but to atrociously Lovecraftian-astute abomination-adorers as the home of his most autobiographical Providence protagonist, Charles Dexter Ward, in his 1927 "The Case of Charles Dexter Ward."

The extraordinary redbrick edifice that was the Halsey House—or the Halsey Mansion as some strange Lovecraft scholars have come to refer to it—loomed from behind a lush veil of vegetation and, with its white wooden balustrades, columns, and other architectural beautifications, looked, verily, as Lovecraft had described it with the weirdness-trailing, world-traveling Ward's return to his very own "Old Providence!"

What we beheld there at 140 Prospect Street, that haughtily handsome Halsey House, was a very fitting home for that "exceedingly singular person" of Lovecraft's. What made the home as singular as its foully odd, fictional occupant, and what truly set it apart from the rest of College Hill's Colonial houses, was, at least to yours cruelly's bloodshot eyes, that "bayed façade," the two front corners of the Halsey House's brick-face, of which Lovecraft wrote that bowed out very much like towers, an arrangement which furthered its stateliness.

But after not finding Ward—or the cursedly unspeakable Joseph Curwen, who wore the skin of Ward, his "double and descendent"—at home there at No. 140, we decided to darken his door no longer and, thus, returned to the repulsively loathsome remains of Lovecraft's College Hill.

H. P. LOVECRAFT'S HOME: 1926 TO 1933
10 Barnes Street
Providence

H. P. LOVECRAFT'S HOME: 1933 TO 1937
65 Prospect Street
(formerly 66 College Street)
Providence

H. P. LOVECRAFT'S HOME: 1904 TO 1924
598 Angell Street
Providence

After visiting the "Case"-horrid Halsey House of that woefully disappeared Charles Dexter Ward, all that remained upon our terribly ichorous College Hill terror-tour's itinerary for us two most morbid of Mythos monstrosity-mongers were two of three extant Providence edifices that H. P. Lovecraft had himself called home.

My crepuscular bride and yours cruelly would find the first of these across Prospect from the Halsey House but a short way down Barnes Street. It was at the squarish and somewhat shabby sallow structure that was 10 Barnes Street that Lovecraft lived, with his two aunts, Lillian D. Clark and Annie E. Phillips Gamwell, from April of 1926—when he left both New York and Sonia Greene, who would remain his wife, at least legally, until they divorced in 1929—until May of 1933.

While living here at No. 10, he would beget those wildly weird works that would make him, when "the stars came right," a most hideously unhallowed god within the horrendously ghastly halls of Horror: amongst sundry others, "The Shadow Over Innsmouth," "The Call of Cthulhu," "The Dunwich Horror," and his most renowned 1931 novel, *At the Mountains of Madness*. Thusly, Creepy Reader, this ample Victorian Era abode would witness Lovecraft, that letter-mad master of luridest macabre letters, write his way into Horror's loathsome halls.

Returning to Prospect Street, we gruesome twosome lurked back towards Brown and, therein, our butchermobile. But it was along the way that we found ourselves before the simple black and white house at 65 Prospect Street. The abode had actually stood in the substantially learned shadow of the John Hay Library at 66 College Street, until, in 1959, it was transported some blocks to its present plot upon Prospect for the founding of the List Art Building. But whilst at its former address, the home had been that of Lovecraft, where he lived, with his aunt, Mrs. Gamwell, after the death of his other aunt, Mrs. Clark, in 1932.

In 1935, he would make it, also, the home of Robert Blake—that "writer and painter wholly devoted to the field of myth, dream, terror, and superstition" in "The Haunter in the Dark." The story was, in fact, Creepy Reader, a small inside joke of sorts, as Blake, the author of such terribly weird tales as "The Burrower Beneath" and "The Feaster from the Stars," was based upon Lovecraft's pen pal and teenaged protégé, Robert Bloch, who, in his "The Shambler from the Stars," had killed off his macabrely Mythos-ian mentor's semblance—for which Lovecraft had given Bloch the authorization "to portray, murder, annihilate, disintegrate, transfigure, metamorphose, or otherwise manhandle."

And so, returning that humorously horrific homage, Lovecraft housed Robert Blake at his very own home that stood now at 65 Prospect Street and, at the end of the tale, had him exterminated by some nameless thing— "hell-wind—titan blur—

black wings [. . .] the three-lobed burning eye"—because of his shudder-somely all-too-curious investigations into the Church of Starry Wisdom.

But altogether more than its appearance in "The Haunter in the Dark," 65 Prospect Street is known to Lovecraft's disquietingly dread-devoted disciples such as us because this was, verily, his very last home. Having been wracked with pain for sometime because of the grievous cancer growing so very grimly within his gut, it finally became too much for him to bear so he left his house, then at 66 College Street, for John Brown Memorial Hospital. And it was there that he died five days later on the fifteenth of March, 1937.

As we gruesome twosome ended our revoltingly repugnant yet remarkably reverent reverie before that last earthly home of Lovecraft, yours cruelly espied that it did not, as with 10 Barnes Street, display any sort of historical marker, which was truly a conspicuous thing in this part of Providence, College Hill, where almost every other olde edifice was earmarked thusly. These were the places where some of the world's most archetypal, adept, and simply arresting literature, weird or not, were written: why should passersby not be made aware of that fact?

You must ask yourself, Creepy Reader, whether Providence is ashamed of, possibly, its most famous son. Had H. P. Lovecraft not begotten timeless tales of terrifically blood-curdling terror, would he then have been remembered with more regard and respect by that city he himself held so dear and honored throughout his works in his very own woefully Horror-fied way? 'Tis very sad, is it not, Creepy Reader?

Our horridly creepy investigation of Lovecraft's College Hill having ended with 65 Prospect Street, we lurked back to our meatwagon some blocks away near Brown. And as we motored out of College Hill and to the very last abhorrent Lovecraftian attraction of our extraordinarily eldritch-exploring expedition throughout New England's eeriest expanses, we gruesome twosome stopped at 598 Angell Street. It was here, at this dull, dismal tan-and-brown dwelling—which looked, at least to yours cruelly's bloodshot eyes, somewhat architecturally similar to 10 Barnes Street—that Lovecraft had lived for the longest stretch of his life: from 1904 through 1924.

With the death of Lovecraft's maternal grandfather, Whipple Van Buren Phillips, in 1904, his family, specifically his mother and his two aunts, fell upon severe dire straits and, thusly, had to move from the haughty Victorian home in which Lovecraft was born—torn down in 1961, it had stood at 454 Angell Street, at the corner of Elmgrove Avenue—to the more meager accommodations we found ourselves before. It was here, after emerging, in 1913, from what S. T. Joshi has referred to as his "hermitry," that Lovecraft put all his dearly departed grandfather's tireless "weird" tutelage to work by authoring his very own amateur fictional atrocities, something he had actually begun with the likes of 1905's "The Beast in the Cave" but with less constancy.

Lovecraft would continue to live—and write—within the exiguously cramped edifice here at 598 Angell Street until 1924, when he moved to New York to live with his new bride, Sonia Greene, following their marriage on March 3rd of that very same year. He would return to Providence only two years later, again, to live at 10 Barnes Street. And so after stopping at Lovecraft's most ancient surviving abode, Creepy Reader, we gruesome twosome continued on our wickedly weird-wanting way to that very last terrifying location of our tenebrously Lovecraftian terror-tour: Providence's very own Swan Point Cemetery and, there, the gloriously ghastly, gloomy grave of the one and only Howard Phillips Lovecraft!

SWAN POINT CEMETERY
585 Blackstone Boulevard
Lovecraft's Plot: Lot 5, Group 281
(Pond Avenue)
Providence
(401) 272-1314

After leaving 598 Angell Street, our touring hearse motored northwards along Blackstone Boulevard, and it was amidst its blooming residential breadth that we found the Swan

Point Cemetery. After coming through its grand rock-fringed front gates, we stopped at the cemetery's main office, because, while we knew that Lovecraft's regrettably cancer-ridden remains had been buried alongside that of his father, Winfield Lovecraft, and his mother, Sarah Phillips, within the Phillips family plot, we gruesome twosome did not know exactly where it was amidst Swan Point's abundant cemeterial acreage.

Once inside, yours cruelly asked the woman behind the counter that we gruesome twosome were in search of the Phillips family plot. "H. P. Lovecraft?" she asked us without hesitation, having seemingly faced inquiries about the atrociously godlike author's grave from his abhorrently gruesomeness-athirst adherents such as us many, many times before.

After we assented, she took out a photocopied map and plotted out the directions for us, something that yours cruelly learned, some time after our return from that most execrable New England, could be had from a computer housed within an addition built upon that main office. With those less automated directions, we returned to our butchermobile and journeyed out into Swan Point Cemetery for our meeting with Lovecraft.

Swan Point Cemetery was one of the biggest and most beauteous boneyards we two most foully necrophilous of Horror-fiends had ever experienced. A true city of the dead, it was founded in 1846 upon the distinctly welcoming designs of Niles Bierregaard Schubarth, in which Swan Point was not meant to be a gigantic bare bones graveyard—simply a depressive and dreary depository for the decomposing deceased—but, in its severely unhealthy stead, a picturesque place for a gay afternoon's pastimes. And because of this very common Victorian view of death, its original 60 acres—which have grown to some 200 in the years since corpses were first interred here—were turned into a grave-plotted garden away from Providence's increasingly more industrialized pollution.

As my black bride and yours cruelly motored deeper and deeper into Swan Point, it was an utter delight—albeit a less than dreadful one, Creepy Reader!—to descry Swan Point's wealth of funereal wonders, in particular many truly extraordinary and elaborate monuments. And we gruesome twosome had some extra time for such gravesite-seeing because, despite our map and the directions to Lovecraft's plot therein, we found ourselves lost at least twice. But then, as our butchermobile crawled down Pond Avenue, yours cruelly espied it looming before us

along Avenue B beneath the bare twisted limbs of a dead winter tree: the compelling obelisk-crowned monument that was the Phillips family plot-marker!

Yours cruelly stopped our meat-wagon along the side of Avenue B and we disembarked for our cursedly morbid communion with Lovecraft. Upon the front of that tall monument's face were engraved the names of Lovecraft's beloved grandfather, "Whipple V. Phillips," and his wife, "Robie A. Place"—who died and was buried here at Swan Point when Lovecraft was but six years old—and the dates of their lives.

But as we came about the side of the monument to investigate its tree-shaded rear side, it was there that we found, beneath that of his parents, "Winfield S. Lovecraft" and "Sarah S. Phillips," Lovecraft's name carved into its cold gray stone countenance: "Howard P. Lovecraft." There upon the base of the monument's back, some fiendish, unknown Lovecraft fan-addict had scrawled, in black marker, that motto from "The Call of Cthulhu" which is very well the most perversely portentous profanation of the whole Mythos:

'That is not dead which can eternal lie
And with strange eons even death may die."

Although such an embellishment was unauthorized—and perhaps, by the estimations of some, disrespectful—it seemed, at least to yours cruelly, Creepy Reader, an extremely fitting epitaph for that author whose greatest fear, the fear with which his weird tales' words brimmed and which begot the hideously unspeakable horrors that crept and crawled throughout them, was of that blackly baleful "unknown" beyond this world.

It was in the shadow of that magnificent Phillips monument that we gruesome twosome came upon Lovecraft's very own headstone. The small gray, granite-sculpted gravestone was inscribed with his whole name, the dates of his birth and his death, and, below all of this, "I AM PROVIDENCE," the declaration taken from one of his many, many (many!) letters. Although, as that so very humbly adorned headstone attested, Lovecraft left this world in 1937, it was not until 50 years later that he was given his very own gravestone.

When his cadaver was buried here at Swan Point—alongside his parents and his grandparents, almost 70 years ago—his interment was memorialized with but the addition of his name upon that already postmortemly populated Phillips family plot marker. But in 1977, to commemorate the fiftieth anniversary of his death, a small congregation of Lovecraft's deeply enterprising devotees collected, between them, the proper proceeds to procure for him, at last, his very own headstone.

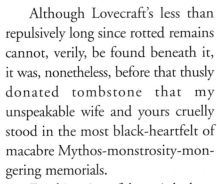

Although Lovecraft's less than repulsively long since rotted remains cannot, verily, be found beneath it, it was, nonetheless, before that thusly donated tombstone that my unspeakable wife and yours cruelly stood in the most black-heartfelt of macabre Mythos-monstrosity-mongering memorials.

For this writer of the weird whose worldwidely worshipped work was infused with an existential philosophy that professed man's utter cosmic meaninglessness, yours cruelly was very happy to belie, at the very least, Lovecraft's pitifully antemortem prophesied anonymity. Buried within some of Providence's most sepulchrally picturesque soil here at Swan Point with wintry New England winds whistling through the lifeless tree limbs overhead, we had little doubt, Creepy Reader, that Lovecraft would have been himself very pleased with this final resting place of his truly revered mortal remains.

And so, our communion with Howard Phillips Lovecraft having come to an end, so too did our expedition throughout the dark and dreadful depths of his most exquisitely noisome eldritch New England. Bidding our morbid Cthulhu Mythos-conjuring master a fittingly foul Horror-fiend's farewell, my black bride and yours cruelly returned to our butchermobile and wormed our wondrously weird-weighted way back to our Charnel House.

To explore Lovecraft's very own horrendously unhallowed haunts, whether the fictions of his Arkham, and Innsmouth or the facts of his very own Providence, was something we would never forget and, for the abhorrently ravenous Lovecraft aficionado, Creepy Reader, it is an utter dream—or nightmare?!?—to behold his "Arkham Sanitarium," that temple of his Esoteric Order of Dagon, his "Shunned House," and so on. But if you know of Lovecraft only through having watched *Re-Animator* or if you do not shudder in the very least upon hearing the foul chanting of "Cthulhu fhatagn!", then this would not be, verily, a creepily carrion campaign for you. But should you read an unwholesome slew of his shuddersomely weird tales, then perchance, you may very well hear that call to Lovecraft's curiously creepy Cthulhu Mythos country as well.

Before yours cruelly takes leave of you, Creepy Reader, I have a confession. It was after we gruesome twosome had worshipped in all our wickedly weird wretchedness before those once repulsively wormy remains of Howard Phillips Lovecraft that we, with but a taste of what he had called "the hideous extremity of human outrage"—egads!—dug up some of the eldritch charnel earth of his ghastliness-enshrouded Swan Point grave plot.

You must forgive me, Creepy Reader, but my hunger for the hideous, for the horrendous—for Horror!—was too severe. In the end, it was but a little and, upon our return to our Krypt, I stored it in a small cork-sealed vial, which stands before me as I write these words—as if abiding for my all-too-atrocious attentions. Perhaps some of Lovecraft's very own carbon—some of his very own extremely eldritch essence!—having been shed from his macabrely moldering mortal coil all those long years ago is within this very same specimen of most shuddersome soil.

I have the urge, though I know not why, to dislodge that disagreeable cork and inhale, deeply, of its foully inveterate foetidness. I slowly remove it. I—But . . . But I am affeared, Creepy Reader, that we have brought something back with us from New England. Something unnatural. Something unspeakable! Because why then does this detestable grave dirt of Lovecraft's pulsate as it does, as if roused from sleep? What of this darkness—this baffling stygian blackness—that puts out the sun outside my window? What of these sinisterly cryptic signs that have emerged, so eerily, upon my wall? What of this verily vague voor that, now, veils all about me? And what of of these hideously guttural howls that I hear, baying so blasphemously for blood? Oh . . . it's only the Abazagorath album coming on again. Never mind . . .

AND LEST WE FORGET, CREEPY READER, "DUNWICH"!

H. P. LOVECRAFT'S "DUNWICH"
Wilbraham, MA

"SENTINEL HILL"
"America's Stonehenge"
Route 111
Salem, NH
(603) 893-8300

In 1928's "The Dunwich Horror," Lovecraft offered very particular directions to his tale's titular Cthulhu Mythos-terrored town: "When a traveler in north central Massachusetts takes the wrong fork at the junction of the

Aylesbury pike just beyond Dean's Corners he comes upon a lonely and curious country." And amidst that "lonely and curious country" festers in all its infamous foulness . . . Dunwich! Many sagacious Lovecraft scholars assert that the author based it upon the small and sleepy Massachusetts burgh of Wilbraham, which can be found amidst, verily, the south central sylvan stretch of the state, not so very distant from Springfield, in fact.

Lovecraft visited the town just before writing "The Dunwich Horror," which seemed to have had an extremely shuddersome effect upon his weird-writer's sensibilities, particularly Wilbraham's very real "whippoor-wills," as he made the place the home of that "monstrous being known to the human world as Wilbur Whateley," who was "more and more hated and dreaded about Dunwich" and his twin brother, who "looked more like the father than he did."

But that hideous black heart of Lovecraft's Dunwich—Sentinel Hill, where Lavinia Whateley bore her two shockingly unspeakable sons and where, later, her Wilbur would conduct his repellently Old Ones-revering rituals—is not itself based upon anything in Wilbraham itself but, rather, what is known as America's Stonehenge, or Mystery Hill, in Salem, New Hampshire. A sublimely aged assemblage of astronomically-aligned stone architecture, they are the most primordial megaliths in all of North America—well over 4,000 years old—made all the more mysterious because their makers are unknown.

It was upon these that Lovecraft based Dunwich's very own "great rings of rough-hewn stone columns" [whose] "[d]eposits of skulls and bones [. . .] sustain the belief that such spots were once the burial-places of the Pocumtucks; even though many ethnologists, disregarding the absurd improbability of such a theory, persist in believing the remains Caucasion." So should you yearn to let fall your very own season of horror, Creepy Reader, by all means visit Wilbraham, but bring your sacrifices to Salem's Sentinel Hill!

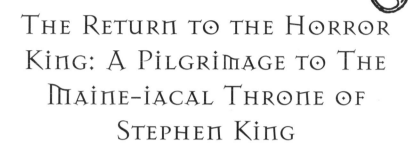

Chapter Six

THE RETURN TO THE HORROR KING: A PILGRIMAGE TO THE MAINE-IACAL THRONE OF STEPHEN KING

At the ripe olde age of 13, I had been ushered into the forlorn, funereal, and crypt-foetid world of Edgar Allan Poe. A year later, I began reading the burly, pop-culture horror yarns of that late-twentieth-century inheritor of Poe's moldering American horror throne: Stephen King. And while the sweetly putrescent odour of Poe's dreadful prose would come to be as opium to my unspeakably necrophilous senses and sensibilities, Creepy Reader, that earlier phantasmagorist's indubitable heir was my man—my Horror King, reigning as Lord and Master over an exquisite slew of sleepless nights.

When I was supposed to be reading dust-choked canonical tomes for my English classes, my days—and my nights—were spent reveling in the gleefully ghastly glory of King's sprawling novels. Instead of *The Great Gatsby*, it was *Pet Sematary*. Instead of *Great Expectations*, it was *The Stand*. While my would-be non-conformist peers were exercising their teenaged angst through Holden Caulfield's endless clamorings in *The Catcher in the Rye*, the anti-sociality of yours cruelly was blossoming through the likes of King's "Cain Rose Up," "Rage," and, dare I say it, "Apt Pupil." I devoured his writing like Pennywise the Clown, *IT*'s titular beastie, devoured children.

But as I got older, creeping my way through high school to university and then even *more* university, my unnatural predilections had drawn me away from King, that high school blackheart of mine, and towards the more obscure and obscene grotesqueries of Poppy Z. Brite, Edward Lee, Nancy Collins, Rex Miller, and so on. Maybe it was because of a hunger for more esoteric and extreme literary death-trips, but, alas, that same olde Stephen King magick had lost its daemonic spell on me.

But no matter how popular King may have become with a thoroughly "mainstream" crowd, no matter how purged his recent literary body may have become in recent years of that "horror" taint, he had not changed—he was still *Stephen King*. Those old classicks were still the primordial ooze from which much of modern horror was begotten, giving rise to notable adaptations from such celluloid dread-dealers as John Carpenter, David Cronenberg, and George Romero as well as suckling throngs of burgeoning would-be tellers of the written terror-tale.

It was only recently that I took those olde Stephen King creepshows off my Charnel House's shelves yet again. And rereading the books that made him a household name ever since *Carrie*, his first novel, was published in 1974 and which made that name utterly synonymous with all that is macabre and morbid, horrid and hideous, was like revisiting a childhood friend—a friend who keeps company with possessed '50s Plymouth Furys, hulking Saint Bernards seething with rabies, and rampaging, cabin-fevered hotel caretakers, but a friend nonetheless.

And so, with this unwholesome fiendship rekindled, I could conceive of no more fitting way to herald that turn than with a little pilgrimage to the throne of that King of my education in all things blackly ghoulish and bloodcurdling: Bangor, Maine. His home of 24 years, it is the seeming wellspring from which some of his most terrifying horrors have flowed, as King transposed the physical reality of Maine's third-largest city upon his writings' bloodied pages, most infamously in the form of "Derry," that town haunted by a veritable nameless Boogeyman for untold eons at the heart of King's epical monsterpiece *IT*. And it was the ghastly, grue-besplattered locations from what is arguably the writer's most nightmarish and horrifying book that my noctiflorous wife and I lurked deep into Maine to feast upon. Join me then, won't you, Creepy Reader, as we embark upon our sojourn amidst the land of the Horror King.

"The terror, which would not end for another twenty-eight years—if it ever did end—began, so far as I know or can tell, with a boat made from a sheet of newspaper floating down a gutter swollen with rain."

—*IT* (1986), page 3

When my crepuscular bride and yours cruelly arrived in Bangor, the nineteenth century's "Lumber Capital of the World," June was but dawning. But despite whatever month the calendar may have decreed it to be, the weather would have us believe otherwise, as we were welcomed by a somewhat dank northerly bleakness that spoke of nothing but autumnal moribundity: murky fog, interminable rain, chilling winds—and seemingly, the eerie cawing of crows all around us that adorned this grim and gloomy tableau that was Bangor.

But oh, Creepy Reader, what utterly sublime weather for our creepy crawl through Stephen King's Bangor haunts! And we could think of no more fitting a way to commence this tour of ours than with Betts Bookstore, a wormy wonderland for any true King aficionado, particularly those ridden with the frugality-debilitating collector's distemper.

BETTS BOOKSTORE
584 Hammond Street
(207) 947-7052

Built on Main Street in downtown Bangor in 1938, Betts is the oldest bookstore in town, having weathered, more or less, the corporate hurricane unleashed by the Barnes & Noble and Borders bookseller behemoths. It was bought in 1990 by Stuart and Penney Tinker with the intention of founding the very first Stephen King specialty shoppe, not only the first of its kind in Bangor but in all the world. The Tinkers' notion of capitalizing upon the frightful renown and the literary infamy of Bangor's most horrific resident by catering to the unquenchable thirst of King-aholics would seem to have been a successful one, as Betts has become known as *the* place for buying (and selling) anything and everything to do with the Lord of American Horrors.

Even though most of the dealings of this nasty niche are done through mail order and the internet, the Tinkers took it upon themselves to maintain a storefront so that Betts could exist as a den for all lovers of those darkest of delicacies. Six years ago, the Tinkers moved Betts's black roots from Bangor's downtown quarter to Hammond Street, which was where yours cruelly found it that dreary early-June mourning.

From outside 584 Hammond Street, Betts, with its wholly modest size and appearance, looks like any of the other small New England shoppes. But, Creepy Reader, as that old adage says, you cannot judge a book by its cover, especially if that "book" has "STEPHEN KING" pasted in foot-tall yellow letters upon its front window. For while Betts is indeed a true "hole in the wall," it is a hole dripping, with no exaggeration, from floor to

ceiling, from front to back, with Stephen King accoutrements and appurtenances. Shelves lining both sides of Betts's front room display what has to be King's whole literary corpse: all of his books, in hardcover or paperback, in English or otherwise, and in all their various editions.

With the exception of, oddly enough, a few books on aviation and automobiles as well as those from the fantasy imaginings of Terry Goodkind, there was little else there other than tomes by or about Stephen King. Besides these more commonplace editions of the Maine-born writer's wretched work, Betts also offered an assortment of rare special editions that would seem to be only for the true, and truly maniacal, collector.

The utterly gore-encrusted crown jewel in Betts's holdings of the Horror King's collectibles would, without question, have to be the Tinkers' singular edition of 1978's *The Stand*: it is bound in black leather, features gilt pages, comes interred in a small, black, coffin-like box that is lined with exquisite red velvet, and, last but not least, flaunts a $2,500 toe tag. Such a grand incarnation as this is absolutely fitting for what is touted by untold King-ophiliacs as their favorite novel of his, all well-over-1,000 pages of it.

No matter how extraordinary this coffin-kept copy of *The Stand* may have been, and no matter how extraordinary it would have looked displayed amidst the rest of the atrocious carrion curios deep down in the Krypt of yours cruelly, alas, in the end, our purchases at Betts had to be kept to less grandiose wares. Fortunately, Betts did indeed offer other less extravagant, yet no less horrid, sundries for the more thrifty King collector, from "Stephen King's Maine" t-shirts (which featured a bespectacled, smiling caricature of the writer alongside a sketch of his home state mapped out with the locations

of the towns King himself settled there, and then did in to gloriously unsettling effect) to charming little brass ornaments of King's own Bangor home in all its 1313 Mockingbird Lane-esque glory.

As we basked in this golden King idolatry, the truly phantastic thing about Betts Bookstore was not so much the wondrous possibilities it offered for mercantile gluttony but its existence as a veritable Stephen King museum, his legacy of literary dread spread throughout the shoppe beyond the consumable extent of such collectibles. The most curious of such macabre-born memorabilia were both on exhibit in Betts's backroom: a framed copy of the January 15, 1978 front page of *The Maine Campus*—the student newspaper of the University of Maine at Orono, where King taught as a writer-in-residence between 1978–79—which features the writer doing his very best Charles Manson impersonation, replete with the absolutely unhinged smile and double barrel shotgun, above the utterly pedagogically-sound headline, "Study Dammit!"; and a somewhat bizarre papier-mâché wall sculpture of King's face that would seem, with its leaf crown and feather adornments, to be some sort of ode to that eternal theme of "writer as shaman."

With a day of deeds of the foulest sort left yet to do, we could not tarry a moment longer amidst the King collector's candy store that is Betts. And so, after treating ourselves to a few small gleefully ghastly goodies, we bid farewell to the Tinkers' shoppe and lurched back out into the rain to explore the rest of Bangor's ensanguined bowels of fright-filled King-ly horror.

Creepy Reader, you may be asking yourself, "Pray tell, retch-worthy narrator, *what* did you and your monstrous bride purchase at Betts?" Appropriately, it was a wooden Maine-shaped ornament marked with the location of Derry, one of King's infamously terror-beset yet wholly fictional towns, neighbor to the likes of the ill-renowned Castle Rock and Jerusalem's Lot and the seemingly unassuming scene of *IT*'s unending hoard of villainous and vile supernatural wickedness.

Although King wrote that Derry was 30 miles from downtown Bangor, the rather explicit similarities between the geographical features of the two would prove otherwise, a fact that is not all that surprising when you consider that King wrote the book, his twenty-fourth in a little over a decade, here in Bangor between 1981 and 1985. But aside from these common landmarks, the similarities between them end there, as the rather sleepy reality of Bangor, despite the telltale signs that its fortunes are, unfortunately, ebbing in the shadow of a far more prosperous yesteryear, by no means jibes with the revoltingly eloquent description of Derry, very early in *IT*'s 1138 pages, as being "a sewer"—"a lot like a dead strumpet with maggots squirming out of her cooze." Yes, a nice place to visit . . . and visiting it we were!

Even though our expedition throughout Bangor would not throw us before the deranging gaze of Pennywise's "deadlights," we had little doubt that we could, at the very least, conjure a spookily savory semblance of *IT*'s unbound and ageless pseudo-Lovecraftian horrors of abysmal proportions from those real landmarks that circumscribed Derry's hideous underbelly and the King's kingdom of darkly fanciful dread therein. We began our disinterment of such doomful Derry depths with something cadaverous, and literally so: Bangor's Mount Hope Cemetery, America's second-oldest garden cemetery.

MOUNT HOPE CEMETERY
1048 State Street
(207) 945-6589

Past the mammoth remains of the (no doubt haunted) Bangor Water Works that rots along the Penobscot, the Mount Hope Cemetery is set apart from Bangor proper at 1048 State Street. In the fall of 1834, a consortium of well-to-do Bangor townsfolk bought 100 acres of land for $3,050 with the intention of founding a garden cemetery after the example of Massachusetts's own Mount Auburn Cemetery. These residents wanted to fashion a cemetery that was not only of a size considerable enough to contend with Bangor's blooming population, but also a place where their extant populace could taste a little bit of life amidst the dead.

And as we drove through Mount Hope's wrought iron gates and disembarked from our meatwagon to walk along its finely kept avenues, we truly appreciated the realization of their grand efforts, as a more lovely necropolis have we very rarely seen in all our years of grave-robbing. Sitting amidst the cemetery's lawns, decorated with a truly handsome host of shrubs, trees, and ponds, were rows upon rows of headstones and

other grave monuments hewn from marble and sandstone in that utterly comely classic nineteenth-century design.

What truly struck us, though, about Mount Hope's array of funerary slabs was the black scum that marked the previously pure white façades of what looked to be the cemetery's most eldritch gravestones. Some of the stones were utterly swathed in it, making the whole specimen look as if it had been charred rather than simply colonized by some unknown species of black moss that seemingly thrives in such a sodden New England clime. Whatever the true cause, the effect was an eerie marvel to behold, making Mount Hope a very fitting repository for some of the more unfortunate inhabitants of King's unusually unhealthy universe.

Based upon the "facts" of King's novels, it would seem that the grounds of the Mount Hope Cemetery have an unsavory taste for veal, as two note-worthy youngsters have found themselves interred here in Derry's own same-named cemetery. Six-year-old Georgie Denbrough came to inhabit a plot six feet below where we stood that mourning after chasing a paper boat made for him by his older brother, "Stutterin' Bill," into the wrong gutter during the fall of 1957 that dates the very opening pages of *IT*.

Because of whom—or, rather, *what*—little Georgie would meet down there in that dark drain—Mr. Bob Gray, also known as Pennywise the Dancing Clown—he would become the first of *IT*'s veritable morgue-full of victims, his arm ripped off by the book's titular Boogeyman as he saw Pennywise's once-smiling face turn into something "terrible enough to make his worst imaginings of the thing in the cellar look like sweet dreams" and heard him croak that now-infamous phrase, "Everything down here floats . . ."

Keeping Georgie company here some decades later would be Gage Creed from King's *Pet Sematary*. Little Gage, a mere toddler in the 1983 spookshow about why *no one* should play with dead things—particularly those interred in old, cursed Indian burial grounds—got away from his seemingly doomed parents and finally learned his lesson about why children should not play in the street thanks to a truck's careening tonnage. Poor Gage was buried—for the *first* time—here at Mount Hope, only to be exhumed and reburied by the hands of his woefully begrieved father, Dr. Louis Creed, with thoroughly horrid consequences, making for some of the most absolutely creepy moments in what is no doubt one of King's creepiest novels.

In 1989, Gage's burial was also actually filmed at Mount Hope for Paramount's adaptation of *Pet Sematary*. In the Mary Lambert-directed film, for which King himself not only wrote the screenplay but starred as the priest presiding over the mangled tike's funeral, Gage, played by 23-month-old Miko Hughes, proved yet again why dead little kids are *far* spookier than a cemetery full of axe-hacking lunatics.

KENDUSKEAG STREAM PARK
Valley Avenue (at the bottom of Nelson Street)

Having sated our unseemly saprophytic appetites upon such King-ly offerings, we left Mount Hope Cemetery behind us and made our wicked way west back into the vermicious heart of Bangor. Taking Nelson Street until it fed into Harlow Street to become Valley Avenue, we pulled our touring hearse into the Kenduskeag Stream Park, the hub of a two-and-a-half-mile walking trail that worms its way about the Penobscot tributary. Walking past a leg of the trail, we descended through the scrub that separated the trail from the Kenduskeag's bank to see what rotted wonders we might find floating there.

It was here, down along the banks of the Kenduskeag, where Bill Denbrough, little dead, one-armed Georgie's affeared yet vengeful older brother, and six other Derry misfits came together as "The Losers" during the summer of 1958. It was here, down along the banks of the Kenduskeag, that King had named "the Barrens," The Losers' hideaway from the switchblade-wielding teenage sociopath Eddie Bowers.

Down here amidst the Barrens, the Losers would commiserate about their, unfortunately common, appalling dealings with the atrocious embodiment of Derry's unspeakable terrors: It, the "Eater of Worlds," in all its manifold bloodcurdling manifestations—most infamous of all, Pennywise the Clown. Later that same summer of '58, the Barrens would be where the Losers would begin their retaliations against that shared Boogeyman of theirs, crawling their way through the Morlock Holes that emptied into the Kenduskeag to the labyrinthine sewers beneath Derry, the netherworldly monstrosity's abattoir, for what they would later think had been their last encounter with that child-eating fiend of all fiends.

Lurking along the Barrens, down that rather idyllic bank of the mur-muring Kenduskeag, not only did we not see any such Morlock Holes, within which to follow the sanguinolent traces of children ruptured like so many wineskins to the corrupted and corruptive belly of that Stephen King beast, but, wait as we did with fevered anticipation, we espied nary a dis-turbingly dread-filling circus clown to offer us a balloon. Perhaps, Creepy

Reader, if you should yourself visit these Barrens of King's in the dead of a moonless night, the sky as black as spilt blood, perchance you will have better luck than we. If so, tell Pennywise we sent our regards. . . .

THOMAS HILL STANDPIPE
Thomas Hill Road
(207) 947-4516 (Bangor Water District)

Leaving the banks of the Kenduskeag and the Barrens therein, we returned to our butchermobile for the next loathsome morsel on our utterly tenebrous King-ly terror-tour's itinerary: the Thomas Hill Standpipe. Driving to the very top of Thomas Hill Road, the Standpipe loomed before us like some sort of oddly stout New England lighthouse.

Along with the 31-foot, one-and-a-half-ton statue of Paul Bunyon, which commemorates Bangor's logging past, down on Main Street, the water tower, built in 1897, is Bangor's (and, by proxy, Derry's) most prominent landmark and was seemingly a tourist attraction of no little renown at one time. Standing well over 100 feet tall and holding some 1.75 million gallons of water, the Standpipe still serves Bangor and its surrounding townships.

Atop the Standpipe is a promenade, which is said to offer an astounding view to those who climb all the winding staircase's 100 steps. In the past, this promenade was open to visitors year 'round; however, because of the fatal plummet of a youngster in 1940, the Standpipe was closed by the Bangor Water District and is now open for tours on only four days out of the whole year. Alas, that dreary June day that saw us plaguing Bangor was not one of these and, thus, our visit would be an outside affair only. This was truly unfortunate, as an exploration of the Standpipe's beshadowed innards can be a somewhat spooky endeavor, or at least that's what some reports would have you believe.

If the fictional experiences of Stan Uris, one of the seven Losers, within the Standpipe's dark insides have any roots in the water tower's reality, a climb to that promenade could indeed be a truly harrowing and horrendous event. In *IT*, Stan, the most craven of all the Losers, was

undertaking such a visit to the Standpipe's summit when he came upon Pennywise in the form of a disgustingly putrid corpse.

While there were indeed innumerable cigarette butts about the parking lot that lay next to the Standpipe's granite base, we saw absolutely no fly-swarming traces of flesh blossoming with rot that day. Perhaps that is the real reason why the door is so rarely open: to keep all that lovely rot, all those lovely cadavers, from leaving the furtive morgue that is Bangor's Standpipe? But, then again, perhaps the Standpipe is not filled with dead and decaying clowns after all but only water—gallon upon gallon of drinking water. Sad but true, Creepy Reader. Sad but true.

BANGOR CANAL
York Street

After knocking one last time upon the Thomas Hill Standpipe's bolted black door just in case the corpse of King's Pennywise would let us in, we descended back down Thomas Hill Road to the repellent locale that witnessed the birth of *IT*'s "present-day" (circa 1985) horrors: the Bangor Canal. Cutting through the heart of Bangor and Derry both, the Canal funnels the waters of the Kenduskeag into the Penobscot. According to King, "it had been the Canal which had birthed Derry's boom years." Fittingly then, it was upon the York Street bridge, Derry's "Kissing Bridge," that spanned this very same Canal where the unspeakable horrors of King's other-worldly Boogeyman arose once more.

With the 1985 murder of the young homosexual Adrian Mellon, Pennywise revealed himself to have been foolishly left for dead by the Losers after their adolescent attack some 28 years before. Thrown from the York Street Kissing Bridge into the dark waters of the Canal by a handful of drunk, gay-bashing thugs, Adrian, dragged off to be flesh for that beast that dwells at Derry's black heart, is but the first of a new clutch of prey swallowed by the hungry maw of that arisen Pennywise, with "its shining silver eyes and its bared teeth—great big teeth."

Looking down into those very same dark waters of the Kenduskeag that flow through Bangor's Canal, it was not hard to imagine Pennywise down there, lurking among the shadows beneath York Street, waiting like a bridge troll of yore to suck the tender flesh from children's all-too-brittle bones— and the delicious fear from their frozen blood. But, alas, we had to leave such a meeting to our darkest fancies, Creepy Reader, as the only thing "floating" through the Canal that day were a few fallen leaves and the reflec-tions of our own hideously grinning mugs as we stared down into the Kenduskeag's murky waters in search of the sort of man-eating monstrosity that will hand you a balloon or two after tearing your arms from your torso.

BANGOR PUBLIC LIBRARY
145 Harlow Street
(207) 947-8336

From the York Street Bridge and the Bangor Canal beneath it, it was only a very short drive to Harlow Street before we arrived at the penultimate stop on our exhaustively ensanguined expedition through the extricated entrails of Stephen King's Derry.

In *IT*, the only Loser to remain in Derry after those dread-besmirched childhood years was Mike Hanlon. He would remain in Derry as a sort of burden-cursed chronicler of the town's unimaginably wretched past, dredging up and recording in his manuscript, "Derry: An Unauthorized Town History," It's eternally unwholesome and nightmarish stranglehold (for 14 to 20 months every 27 years) upon Derry's very soul since time immemorial. He would remain in Derry to witness, three decades after the Losers believed they had conquered Pennywise down in the sewers beneath that accursed childhood home of theirs, the reawakening of that ageless Boogeyman—It—with the slaughter of Adrian Mellon and nine of Derry's children. And Mike would do all of this remaining and recording, all this waiting and watching, here on Harlow Street, at 145 Harlow Street to be exact: the Bangor Public Library, King's inspiration for Derry's own library.

While the Derry Library, as described by King in *IT*, is a dark and dingy book repository befitting Hanlon's reclusive endeavors, Bangor's shares little with its fictive doppelganger other than their common address. In a woeful state of disrepair, both structurally and collectionally, it was not only renovated but also expanded and updated as well, this extensive project ending in 1997. During the planning stages of this renovation, King and his wife, Tabitha, pledged $2.5 million to the total cost of $8.5 million if the city of Bangor would put up the same amount, which they did. To commemorate their efforts, the library named its second-floor hall, Stephen and Tabitha King Hall, after the Kings and appointed Tabitha to the library's board of trustees. The Bangor Public Library's, and seemingly the whole town's, acknowledgment of their neighbor Stephen King, and his Bangor brood, is not so much because of his horrifying reincarnation of it—as well as veritably the whole state of Maine—throughout the blood-chilling pages of his many books, but the sheer philanthropy he has shown Bangor over the years.

It was from here, at this thusly reborn library before which we stood, that Mike Hanlon had called those former Derry outsiders who were his fellow Losers to warn them about It's return—telling them of the fresh atrocities that absolutely abhorrent abomination had wrought upon Derry's most innocent—and to get them to return to the town of their youth so that they could finish that shocking job of monster-hunting they thought they had finished back in 1958. And this those Losers did (all but two of them), descending into Derry's sewers to once more face It—the embodiment of their own deepest, darkest fears—seeing for the first time It's true nature: "a nightmare Spider from beyond time and space, a Spider from beyond the fevered imaginings of whatever inmates may live in the deepest depths of hell."

At the end of King's mammoth novel, with that nether-cosmic Boogeyman's arachnidian heart ripped out and crushed in the hands of Bill Denbrough for the death of his little brother all those long years ago, It—and Pennywise, one of the most utterly hellish, hideous, and horrifying figures in all of horror history, masterfully portrayed by Tim Curry in 1990 for the ABC mini-series adaptation—was no more. The thought always brings tears to my bloodshot eyes, Creepy Reader. 'Tis a pity . . . and all for eating some kids. . . .

STEPHEN KING'S HOUSE ("The William Arnold House") 47 West Broadway

Well, with the Bangor Public Library struck from our terror-filled tour of Stephen King's Bangor, there was but one locale left for my black bride and yours cruelly to exhume. However, this was not some mere ill-rumored landmark with which King had populated that most dread-ridden and accursed Maine burgh of his. This last locale can be found nowhere in the pages of *IT* because this was where *IT* was born. This was 47 West Broadway, the Bangor home—the dark and dreary domicile of dread-conjurings and horrid-doings—of that long lost fiend of mine, Stephen King.

In *IT*, King, perhaps in an attempt at self-portraiture, wrote that West Broadway was where Derry's mansions could be found. Bangor's West Broadway is no different. However, King's, an authentic mansion with its 23 rooms sprawled out over what has to be a whole block, was a little . . . *different*. As we slowly made our way down West Broadway that dreary June afternoon, divining which house was King's was no mystery. With its phantastically crafted black wrought iron fence inhabited by the dreadfully dubious likes of gargoyles, spiders upon their webs, and a three-headed griffin and its classically Gothic, almost Addams Family-esque architecture, this is *truly* a house fit for the King of modern American horror.

King and his wife bought the house, known as the William Arnold House to Bangor historians, in 1980 after his name, and his fortune, continued to be made upon the infamy of his work. After four years of renovations, their impressive tomb-sweet-tomb was done—or so they thought. For as King's notoriety grew, so did the draw of his wholly distinctive house to his devoted fans. While at first there had only been a sign to dissuade autograph-seekers and the all-too-curious from knocking upon their front door, that wrought iron fence, which took a year-and-a-half to finish, and which we gazed upon so droolingly, was put in place for those who seemingly could not (or simply chose not to) read. For a while at least, this was a sufficient means of assuring the privacy of King and his kin.

To the Bangor residents, the house at 47 West Broadway was known as "Spook Central" and, rather unshockingly, it was an absolute favorite trick-or-treating spot every Halloween for all the local Bangor ghouls and goblins, young and old alike. However, such haunting All Hallow's Eve revelry came to an end with the complete encircling of the Kings' house with not only a full fence but two rows of five-foot-tall hedges and the installation of various electronic security devices after the eventual encroachment of truly obsessed fans for whom not even a locked gate was enough to ward off their stalking. Unfortunately, it would seem as if King's very own literary monsters have made their monstrous maker a recluse in his Bangor crypt.

With this knowledge, and not wanting to pass from being Grand Guignolian gore-mands of all that is ghastly and ghoulish to all-out *weirdos*, my unspeakable wife and I did not stray far from our meatwagon, which we had parked across the street from King's enormous, and enormously grand, home—the Mansion that the Macabre Made.

As yours cruelly stood there in the dreary drizzling rain that June afternoon, I thought back to the first time I had read a Stephen King book, which, Creepy Reader, just so happened to be *IT*. While not my favorite of his bespooked oeuvre (that would be *The Dark Half* and its "high-toned son of a bitch"-ery for deeply personal reasons, as it was the book that made me want to be a writer myself), *IT* is, in my humble opinion, the most stomach-churningly, skin-crawlingly creepiest of them all and the novel that stands as the archetypal Stephen King novel, epitomizing, for me, why his name as the King of modern American horrors should not be tarnished by either monstrous mainstream success or artistic endeavors that take him, even if willfully, further and further from the horror business of his nightmare-bearing '70s and '80s heyday. With *IT*, the horrors that King invoked were so very *simple* and, thus, so *very* scary. As he himself wrote in the book, these horrors embody "the simplest thing of all: how it is to be children, secure in belief and thus afraid of the dark."

While King's horrors may not be the most "splatterpunk"-y extreme or the most finely written, he taught me, your sickness-spewing narrator, and a generation (or two or three) like me, what it *truly* means to be afraid of the dark—and those are lessons that I learned more than those of math or of science; lessons that no *Hearts In Atlantis,* no *Dreamcatcher,* can undo. Even if that once-terror-rousing pen of his will no longer call forth from the black ether of his immense imagination such mammothly macabre masterpieces as *Pet Sematary, The Shining,* or, of corpse, *IT,* he is still the one, the only . . . *Stephen King.*

And so, Creepy Reader, having paid our renewed respects to the Horror King, we returned to our monster coach and headed back towards I-95 for the 500-mile journey back to our atrocious Rot Island abode. Mind you, Creepy Reader, there are many, many other disguised Maine locales rooted in King's life and works: the town of Durham where King spent his formative years as a burgeoning Lord of Horror and where he was driven to high school in Lisbon Falls in a converted hearse with a weird girl named Carrie, who had an extremely Jesus-loving mother and who inspired, obviously, *Carrie*; the Shiloh Church in Durham that is said to be the inspiration for the vampire-lousy Marsten House from *Salem's Lot*; the home in Orrington that King and his wife rented while he taught at UMO and where he buried a family cat, which had been run over by a truck, at a little graveyard made by local children that became *Pet Sematary*'s namesake; and so on.

As a couple of days could easily be spent exploring all such King-ly Maine haunts, the expedition of yours cruelly was but a taste—but what a repulsive taste it was! So if you should find yourself in Maine and creeping past that spookhouse of Stephen King, please remember: look but don't touch or you just might get an arm or two torn off!

PART THREE

Creepy Crawls of Horror in Film:
In Search of the Cadaverous
Curiosities of Classick
Corpse-Mongering
Celluloid

Chapter Seven

Hollywood Deathtrip: Robbing the Graves of the Ghoulish Greats of the Ghastly Golden Age of Celluloid Horror

Why hell-o, Creepy Reader! The monstrously macabre meat-wagon that is *Creepy Crawls'* spooked-out motorkoach has arrived to take you on a torturously tenebrous terror-tour of . . . Hollywood! Yes . . . Hollyweird, Karloffornia, as Uncle Forry calls it: where not merely dreams are made but nightmares too—particularly those moldering classick creature-features that bathed the garish glitz and glamour of Tinseltown in a phantastic tarn of shocking frights and fearful spooks. From *The Old Dark House* and *House on Haunted Hill* to *London After Midnight* and *White Zombie*, this was where that gloriously ghoulish Golden Age of horror sinema was begotten all those many, many years ago.

But while you might suppose that shambling down the world-renowned Hollywood Walk of Fame would be a fine way of communing with the dread-mongering directors and actors who dwelled at the wormy, black hearts of those celluloid creepshows of yore, all you will espy along such stretches of Hollywood and Vine (with the exception of that altar to Fandemonium that is the Hollywood Book & Poster Company!) are sundry skid-row shoppes and tourist traps.

Standing before the Walk's bronze star plaques— even if they do bear the infamous names of such celebrated creep-meisters as Vincent Price,

Boris Karloff, and John Carradine—will be but the most meager of hors d'oeuvres to the necrophilous appetites of the true horrorist. Should you want to *truly* feed your fiendish fill upon a foul and foetid feast of Horrorwood's finest funereal fare, then you must make your wickedly wretched way to the *cemetery*, of corpse! And there are three boneyards both in and around Hollywood—Hollywood Forever, Forest Lawn, and Holy Cross—that have become the eternal festering place for some of horrordom's most deeply beloved bloodcurdlers. Won't you join me then, Creepy Reader, on yours cruelly's hideous and horrendous Hollywood Deathtrip!

HOLLYWOOD FOREVER CEMETERY
6000 Santa Monica Boulevard
Hollywood
(323) 469-1181

The Hollywood Forever Cemetery was not merely the first vermicious morsel on the morbid menu that was the Deathtrip's itinerary but, founded in 1899, it was the oldest of our three-course bloodfeast of horror-shrouded necropoleis. Mere blocks from the Walk of Fame at 6000 Santa Monica Boulevard, Hollywood Forever lay amidst what was seemingly one of the town's oldest quarters. Its southern extent actually abuts Paramount Studios's backlot, which was rather fitting because of the horde of Old Hollywood's most revered personages who can be found buried here.

The most famous of these "Immortals," as Hollywood Forever's proprietors call them, was no doubt the Italian-born "Sheik" himself, Rudolph Valentino.

When the boneyard was bought by Tyler Cassity in 1998 for only $350,000,

one of the oft-written of renovations and innovations that this English-literature-graduate-turned-funeral-director brought to the then sadly dilapidated tombyard that was "Hollywood Memorial Park" was the hosting of films amidst its gravestones and palm trees—upon the wall of one of its two grand  mausoleums no less—thus not only bringing a little life to this grand cemetery but also honoring those stars of yesteryear who now call the place "home."

While the most popular of these cemeterial celluloid screenings have been those from Valentino's rotted body of work, Cassity and his mortuary crew should offer something much more dread-weltered like *Mad Love* or, better still, the funeral home farce that is *The Comedy of Terrors* in tribute to one of Hororrwood's most ill-famed iconical boogeymen: Peter Lorre, whose remains were interred here after he died of a stroke in 1964.

Born László Löwenstein, the Hungarian actor's renown as an indubitable sinematic fiend was established in 1931, with his truly maniacal portrayal of the child-killing maniac in Fritz Lang's *M*. With the help of his bug-eyed physiognomy and singular European drawl, Lorre's on-screen

infamy was furthered by such black-and-white classics as *The Maltese Falcon* and *Casablanca* as well as a savory slew of sci-fi and horror features.

Walking into the shadow-drenched belly of Hollywood Forever's Hollywood Cathedral Mausoleum and down the right-hand corridor, Lorre's plot (which he shares with his wife, Anne Marie) was found along the lower-most tier of the Alcove of Reverence. Here, behind a square marble tile bearing two modest nameplates, lay perhaps the most mimicked and caricatured of horror sinema's spooks. After paying our darkest respects to "Dr. Gogol," Creepy Reader, we then left the deathly splendor of Hollywood Forever behind for the remainder of this damnably dreadful Hollywood Deathtrip!

FOREST LAWN MEMORIAL-PARK
1712 South Glendale Avenue
Glendale
(800) 204-3131

It was but a few miles before the butchermobile of yours cruelly crept into the Los Angeles suburb of Glendale and brought us to our Deathtrip's next awfully atrocious attraction: Forest Lawn Memorial-Park. Rotting away in that horrid California sun at 1712 South Glendale Avenue, Forest Lawn Memorial-Park, the very first of what is now a corporate quintet of burial grounds, was born in 1917 from Dr. Hubert Eaton's grandiose intentions of founding a cemetery that was "as unlike other cemeteries as sunshine is unlike darkness."

Eaton, who devoutly believed in a blissful afterlife, wanted to fashion a graveyard that shunned the classic boneyard aesthetic in favor of a park-like atmosphere, as its very name attests.

MESENKOP

Because of this, Forest Lawn had the appearance of some finely contrived, constructed, and maintained outdoor museum rather than a mammoth city of the dead that houses some quarter-million corpses. We did not experience the merest taste of either melancholy or  the moribund amidst the sprawling 300 acres that lie beyond Forest Lawn's grand wrought iron gates, which are purported to be the grandest in the world.

However, Forest Lawn's aversion to foul reminders of death—and the foetid whiff of decay therein—has not indeed rendered it truly "lively," as Easton's plan for it to be a place where the living could have a taste of life amongst the dead would seem to have been thwarted by the cemetery's extremely strict, and strictly enforced, rules and regulations, yoking visitors on matters ranging from plastic flowers and picnics to taking photographs within any of its buildings. Because of Forest Lawn's ordinances against all that is deemed unsightly, it is not so much lifeless as simply sterile, at least when compared to a tombyard such as Hollywood Forever, which seems to live and breathe with its postmortem inhabitants rather than exist as a mere repository, no matter how ornate or ostentatious, for their earthly remains.

While this proper pomp and pretension has attracted the celebrious burials of Clark Gable, Jimmy Stewart, Humphrey Bogart, and numerous other notables, for ghoulish graveyard-lurking gore-mands and ghastly ones such as yourselves and yours cruelly, a visit to Forest Lawn can be a less than macabrely merry time; however, it is an experience that any true fiend must suffer, as the stately cemetery is called tomb sweet tomb by a cadaverous collection of celebrity creeps.

We began our exhumation of Forest Lawn's putrefacted properties with the Great Mausoleum. Sitting at what seemed to be the very heart of the cemetery, the Great Mausoleum, whose architecture gave it the appearance of some medieval keep, is perhaps Forest Lawn's greatest tourist destination, as it is here where, in 1931, Eaton had enshrined his 15-foot-tall and 30-foot-wide Italian stained glass replica of Da Vinci's *The Last Supper*, but one of the cemetery's immense catalogue of museum-quality art.

While this enormous work, which is displayed with full, and fully hot-aired, narration every half-hour, is indeed impressive, its place amidst our Deathtrip was simply as an excuse, providing us with an easy answer in the face of questions from the security guard at the Great Mausoleum's entrance as to why we gruesome twosome were there.

After offering an impious wink to Judas, the *Last Supper* window was forsaken for the Great Mausoleum's *truly* abysmal frights. Feasting upon them, however, was by no means easily done, as it required dastardly dread-wreaking daring doings that were indeed less than permissible (and, thus, less than recommendable!), as these entombed treasures sat shadow-bathed in cloistered recesses of the Great Mausoleum that are off-limits to non-relatives. Such was the case with the lower leg of the Calumbarium of Memory, the mausoleum's right-most corridor, which was cordoned off with an olde chain. But so it went . . . and so under the chain we went!

Three plots in from the chained-off entranceway and five plots from the polished sheen of the marble floor was Forest Lawn's first offering of the Golden Age of Horror's ghastly greats: Theda Bara. Born Theodosia Goodman in Ohio, she came to fame after her turn as a vampire in 1915's *A Fool There Was*, for which the film's publicists bestowed her with the moniker "Theda Bara" (an anagram for "Arab Death") and an equally infamous, yet fictitious, biography. Because of the film's lurid publicity photos featuring her basking, relatively unclothed, amidst snakes and skeletons, she became the archetype of the silver screen "vamp."

Never working outside of the Silent Era, Bara's legacy was short but putrescently sweet, ending shortly after her marriage to director Charles Brabin in 1921. She died from abdominal cancer in 1955, and was buried here, within the Calumbarium of Memory

(niche #19565 to be exact). While Bara is known more for her portrayal of Cleopatra than of any frightful ghoul-mistress or goblin queen, her place as horror sinema's primeval monstress should not be forgotten.

Keeping Theda company within the dark belly of the Calumbarium, perhaps halfway down its length (niche #20076) was one of celluloid horror's most revered monster-makers, James Whale, the respected auteur who brought unspeakable life to some of Universal's most extraordinary fright-fests, most notably 1935's *The Bride of Frankenstein.*

After horror began to lose its favor with audiences at the dawn of World War II, Whale dropped out of filmmaking, returning to the director's chair now and again throughout the '40s but never again birthing anything truly bloodcurdling. He drowned in his own pool (an act of suicide, as poignantly dramatized in 1998's *Gods and Monsters*), and was interred here in 1957. Being that Whale was the man who handpicked Boris Karloff as his *Frankenstein's* "Monster," paying him tribute at this secluded burial plot was well worth the risk of such illicit lurkings, was it not, Creepy Reader?

Creeping back under that pesky chain, it was with nothing but the sheerest of dread-ridden delight that we descended upon the Great Mausoleum's last cadaverous curiosity, none other than the veritable Grandfather of Cinema Creeps, he who played the Phantom of the Opera, 'Dead Legs' Phroso, and the Beaver-Hatted Fiend amongst sundry others . . . Lon Chaney! But, alas, Creepy Reader, to meet the glorious "Man of a Thousand Faces" and master self-monster-maker would require,

sadly, much more than that last feat of below-chain creepy-crawling. For you see, when Chaney died from throat cancer in 1930, his body was interred amidst the Great Mausoleum's Sanctuary of Meditation, within a vault alongside that of his very own father.

Making his crypt a true macabre mystery for horror sinemaphiliacs, however, is that it is not only located amidst that extremely remote Sanctuary of Meditation, which is virtually inaccessible to those who are not ushered in personally, but was left unmarked (known only as C-6407), perhaps leaving it a fitting final resting place for the make-upped madman who pursued anonymity by refusing to sign autographs. Because of this, our Deathtrip's communion with the creep-lord himself was left to our phantastically fiendish fancies, as the likelihood of espying that unmarked crypt with our own bloodshot eyes was about as good as those lost *London After Midnight* reels ever being found. Thus, it was with no small regret that we left the Great Mausoleum for the remainder of our Deathtrip throughout Forest Lawn.

To partake of the rest of Forest Lawn's horrid posthumous holdings requires no such trespassing (such a horrible word for a worshipful act of *true* fiendom!) as they rot not within any of the mammoth cemetery's grand mausoleums but out amongst its sweeping green acreage. Leaving the Great Mausoleum, the meatwagon of yours cruelly wormed about the back of this crypt-keep and up through Forest's lawns to Cathedral Drive. We stopped across from the Garden of Ascension looming to our left and disembarked for our meeting with that consummate showman of celluloid horror's Silver Age: William Castle.

After a short but slow walk up Ascension's excessive steepness, we came before Castle's burial plot (L-8238 to be exact). The very simple plaque which marked it (inscribed with only his name, the years of his birth and death, and "Forever") was an oddly sedate memorial for the horror-maker, whose utterly sideshow barker-esque promotional mastery (as exemplified by the wraith-espying wonders of "Illusion-O," "Death-By-

Fear life-insurance policies, and, most infamously, in-seat vibrating contraptions) beshadowed his oh-so-screamingly fun spookshows such as *13 Ghosts, Macabre,* and *The Tingler.* Emulating the work and showmanship of Alfred Hitchcock and himself inspiring the likes of John Waters and Joe Dante, Castle died and was buried here, within Forest Lawn's Garden of Ascension, in 1977, leaving a legacy of horror biz hoopla that has very rarely been so fangtastically reproduced.

Leaving Castle's Ascension plot, there was but one more crypt at Forest Lawn to feast upon, and so we headed down Freedom Way towards the Dawn of Tomorrow wall-vaults. However, unlike the rest, this crypt lay somewhat *vacant,* not because its deceased inhabitant had been ill-fatedly pilfered by some resurrectionist, but because its owner has not yet taken up permanent residence there. For this was the future Forest Lawn plot of *Famous Monsters's* very own "Dr. Acula," Forrest J. Ackerman. While "Mrs. Science Fiction," Wendayne Ackerman, was buried here in 1990, Ackerman himself has yet to join her—not that there is any hurry to do so, Uncle Forry!

Even though his name has not yet been added to the front of their twin-crypt (C-3685), for true horror devotees such as we, it was a real macabre treat to visit the modest plot where this ultimate fiend's fiend, a true fan-addict if there ever was one, who helped to spread the horror-plague to at least three generations of would-be ghouls, will wile away his death—no doubt with a coffinful of his most cherished curios and collectibles.

HOLY CROSS CEMETERY & MAUSOLEUM
5835 West Slauson Avenue
Culver City
(310) 670-7697

With that (eventual) final resting place of Uncle Forry struck from our Hollywood Deathtrip's ill-rumored list of loathsome death-locales, and therein the whole of Forest Lawn Memorial-Park and its seemingly anti-sightseeing policy, there was but one

remaining boneyard for us to rob—metaphorically speaking, of corpse: Holy Cross Cemetery. And yours cruelly had saved this deliciously dreadful delicacy, this charmingly cadaverous curiosity, for last as it was the utter ensanguined icing upon our dead meat-cake of the graves of celluloid horror's ghoulish bygone greats.

It was less than a half-hour's lurch from Forest Lawn before our monstrous touring-koach arrived at 5835 West Slauson Avenue in the Los Angeles suburb of Culver City, the home of Holy Cross, our terrible terror-tour's last stop. While it was not as old as Hollywood Forever (founded in 1939, it is actually the youngest of the three on our Deathtrip's itinerary) nor as humongous as Forest Lawn (it is comprised of 200 acres, only half of which has become corpse-laden thus far), Holy Cross, a Roman Catholic cemetery, was extraordinarily lovely to the eyes of even the most worm-weary of cemetery-stalkers such as we. With its finely manicured grassy lawns, small ponds and waterfalls, sun-bleached ghost-white statuary, and serene grottoes hewn out of volcanic rock, it almost seemed to stand as the quintessential Southern California cemetery.

While the fetching boneyard did not have as many of the rich and famous to its name as Forest Lawn did, it was at Holy Cross's Our Lady of Lourdes Grotto where those who are indeed buried here can be found—and, thus, it was there to which our unappeasable ghoul's blood called us. Passing through Holy Cross's majestic gates, we took the left-hand path at the three-way fork in the road and headed towards that very same hilltop grotto. About it stood statues of the Virgin Mary and Saint Bernadette, whose ghostly meeting is the grotto's namesake. Near them, a very comely niche carved out of the volcanic rock housed a white altar adorned with flickering prayer candles.

But we had not come there to pray after all—at least not to any saints or virgins! Our Hollywood Deathtrip had brought us to the sloping lawn before the side of this rock grotto that faced Holy Cross's gates, to the fourth row of graves that lay between markers #126 and #127, and the plot there numbered L120, to the grave of the one and only Bela Lugosi! Perhaps not the most obscure offering on our Deathtrip's morbid menu, Lugosi's final resting place was perhaps the uttermost dreadfully delectable of them all, a true memorably macabre Mecca for any truly blood-splattered horror-hound who worships at the altar of that Golden Age of Celluloid Creeps, that eerie eldritch epoch when movie monster-men were carrion kings.

Along with Karloff and Price, Lugosi was, and still is, the most famous of horror sinema's ghastly Golden greats, the utter epitome of classic horror, this owed to his absolute embodiment of *Dracula*'s titular Phantom Lord of the Night-Creatures. As represented by Tim Burton's *Ed Wood*, Lugosi's popular reputation is largely (yet, sorely, narrowly) circumscribed about his later-life's morphine-addledness, his paupery, and, in the last sadly ironic turn in an already thusly-defined life, his burial in full Dracula regalia, cape and all. However, such a portrait, no matter how rooted in unfortunate reality, does little to honor the actor's *true* legacy within the World of Horror.

Born Béla Ferenc Dezso Blasko in 1882, Lugosi took his professional surname from the town of his birth: Lugos, Hungary. Beginning his acting career on the Hungarian stage and then in various European films, he emigrated to America in 1921 and worked as a character actor for many years. His name was finally established with Tod Browning's 1931 adaptation of Bram Stoker's novel, a fateful role for which he had prepared for three years by starring in a stage version of the classic book, in which he was cast after Browning's initial choice, Lon Chaney, died the year before filming began.

After *Dracula*, Lugosi's vampyric sinematic oeuvre would prove less than consistent, appearing in everything from the utterly spook-ridden

sublime likes of Edgar Ulmer's *The Black Cat* to the lowest of the lowliest schlock such as, infamously, *Plan 9 from Outer Space*, Ed Wood's "Worst Film Ever Made." But regardless of the ultimate quality of the creature-feature in

question, Lugosi's performance in it, whether as "Dr.
Alex Zorka" or "'Murder'
Legendre," is *always* sure to
feed a horror ghoul's appetite
for the macabre and the
morbid, the terrible and the
terrifying.

When Lugosi died of a
heart attack in 1956 and was
buried here at Holy Cross, at
his meager service, attended by fellow creepy-crawlers Price, Lorre, and
Ackerman, the darkened halls of Horror lost one of its truest and most profoundly resonant spook-stars. To stand there before Lugosi's grave, where
his body long ago became so much worm-food, and look down upon his
simple plot-marker, embossed in black with his infamous stage name,
"Beloved Father," and the years of his life, all beside, ironically enough, a
rose-entwined cross, was to stand in remembrance, in reverence, in respect,
before a true, and truly godly, legend of the horror-fied screen. Were not
my black bride and I the luckiest of krypt-fiends, Creepy Reader, to be
thusly basking in Lugosi's deathlessly ghastly glory? Yes, indeed we were!

After rising from Lugosi's grave, we gruesome twosome returned to
our terror-touring hearse and bid an awfully appalled adieu to not only
Lugosi but *Creepy Crawls'* Hollywood Deathtrip. With the cremains of
Vincent Price and John Carradine
having been scattered at sea, Peter
Cushing's stowed away in some
unknown repository, and Boris
Karloff's interred at the Guilford
Crematorium across the cold
Atlantic in Surrey, England, our
humble horror-haunted hunt for
the remains of that Gold (and

Silver) Age of Celluloid Horror's most horrendous, hideous, and horrifying bone-chillers was doomed to be left grievously incomplete.

However, the posthumous mementos that we had indeed exhumed, and consumed, between Hollywood Forever, Forest Lawn, and Holy Cross, on our Deathtrip were by no means some paltry repast of the poorest of horror-ed peculiarities, now were they, Creepy Reader? But before our trusted, and gore-encrusted, butchermobile drops you at your vault's cobwebbed door so that it can return to the inexorable Charnel House of yours cruelly, please remember: if you should get caught, spade in hand, unearthing the grave of some other passed-on sinematic horror-monger, *don't* tell them that *Creepy Crawls* sent you!

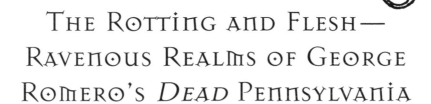

Chapter Eight

THE ROTTING AND FLESH—
RAVENOUS REALMS OF GEORGE
ROMERO'S *DEAD* PENNSYLVANIA

"Stumble in somnambulance so
Pre-dawn corpses come to life
Armies of the dead surviving
Armies of the hungry ones

Only-ones, lonely-ones
Ripped up like shredded-wheat
Only-ones, lonely-ones
Be a sort of human picnic"

—The Misfits
"Night of the Living Dead" (1979)

According to those time-honored traditions handed down by the advertising and greeting card industries, Yuletide is a season of peace and good will. But, Creepy Reader, it would seem, at least to yours cruelly, that the *true* spirit of Christmas is a thing defined by neither the harmoniously pseudo-socialist humanitarianism of Charles Dickens's *A Christmas Carol* nor the beloved "Auld Lang Syne" beneficence and brotherly love of 1946's *It's a Wonderful Life*.

No. The unfortunate fact of the "Merry Christmas!" matter is that it is during these joyous and jovial days of Yule that humanity's true nature is indeed unveiled—and, verily, it is a deeply disturbing thing, as I had the opportunity to witness with my very own bloodshot eyes some Christmastide not so very long ago whilst lurking so very loathsomely about the unquestionable Mecca of that mercantilism-mad season: the mall!

As I wormed my horror-wanton way about some ubiquitous Grue Jersey mall, hunting for holiday offerings for my kith and kin, yours cruelly espied the grotesquely gluttonous, gift-gobbling masses as they worshipped at that accursedly consumptive altar of popular culture.

The disquietingly dreadful behavior of the Christmas season's standard mall-shopper was distinctly erratic. Some of them shambled about unsettlingly, a septic drool dripping sickeningly from their slackened mouths as they stared about deadly. Others were as ravenous and rabid predators, repugnantly ripe to rip out some poor regardless patron's rank guts in order to possess some miserable "present" for their mewling progeny. With such a ghastly and gruesome display of that supposed "Season of Giving," yours cruelly could see no better way to herald the shockingly carnivorous spirit of the holiday than with a journey unto that zombie world that is George Romero's Pennysylvania!

Of all the zombie films I have gorged my ghoulish self on in all my years upon this graveyard Earth, Creepy Reader—from the ritualized low-budget resurrections of *Children Shouldn't Play with Dead Things* (1972) and the Hispanic undead eco-horrors of *Let Sleeping Corpses Lie* (1974) to the late maestro Lucio Fulci's eye-gouging masterpiece *Zombie* (1979) and the delirious sci-fi dead-doings of *Night of the Creeps* (1986)—George Romero's *Dead* trilogy of flesh-eating terror has always been yours cruelly's favorite of that moldering and maggot-ridden Horror celluloid subspecies. I can recall feasting my as yet not so very bloodshot eyes upon his black-and-white 1968 classick, *Night of the Living Dead,* on a local cable station late one All Hallow's Eve some strange eons ago. His film's stark horror noir aesthetics and suffocatingly shuddersome atmosphere truly struck some virgin chord in my so very young horror fiend's black heart.

Along with the early, and extremely transgressive and terroristic, work of Wes Craven, Tobe Hooper, John Carpenter, and those other post-"Peace and Love" directors who became carnage-kings within the unhallowed halls of Horror throughout the '70s and early '80s, Romero's *Night of the Living Dead* was the forefather of Modern Horror, a fierce and formidable departure from the Gothic horror of American International Pictures' Roger Corman-like Edgar Allan Poe adaptations and Hammer Studios' sumptuous Dracula and Frankenstein serials that were drive-in staples of the '60s. The film also established the deeply more morbid modern-day mythos of the zombie as a carnivorous re-animated corpse, something utterly different from its actual origins as a voodoo-shackled slave, known commonly from *White Zombie* (1932), *I Walked with a Zombie* (1943), and the like from that Golden Age of Horror.

Well, yours cruelly would finally have the opportunity, so very long after first being infected by the cruelly cadaverizing contagion of Romero's *Dead*, to explore that woe-begotten western Pennsylvania wilderness where the Zombie King's very own living dead had lurched and lumbered in his moribund triumverate of macabrely postmortem horrorshows: 1968's *Night of the Living Dead*, 1978's *Dawn of the Dead*, and 1985's *Day of the Dead*—all followed up, 20 years after that last installment of his living dead legacy, with *Land of the Dead*, his return to walking rotted meat.

After we gruesome twosome had torn through our sundry curio-shopped presents, my crepuscular bride and I interred our hideously Horror-fiending selves within our butchermobile and, taking our leave from the all-too-real dead who plagued mall-pocked Grue Jersey, began to journey, like that Hunnish biker gang from *Dawn of the Dead*, westward towards Pittsburgh. Won't you join us then, Creepy Reader, for our nauseatingly necrophilous terror-tour of George Romero's lovably loathsome *Dead* lands!

Our creeptastically worm-eaten campaign's directions were very, very simple: head our meatwagon west and motor thusly for 300 miles. As we gruesome twosome carved the bloodthirsty swath of our expedition deeper and deeper into the Keystone State, the countryside became more and more surreal. The roadway beneath our touring hearse's wheels kept rising, the land looming mountainously all about us. In places where the terrifically rocky terrain was too formidable for civil engineers to simply pave over, passages had been eaten through the hulking earth in order to fashion huge tunnels, some of which were almost a mile in length and of which we had to traverse at least five.

Although winter was indeed well underway back in Grue Jersey, it was nothing like what had that unforgivingly dead-frozen world by the throat that deliciously dismal December day. The ill-forboding clouds in the sunless sky were forbiddingly heavy and, about 20 miles from our journey's end, weak flurries became a true, and truly treacherous, snow. Confronted with such thusly weathered environs, yours cruelly was haunted by the affearing fancy that we were verily living out the final tableau of Michele Soavi's *Dellamorte Dellamore* (known more commonly in the U.S. as *Cemetery Man*), the 1994 Italian opus that is perhaps the most beautiful zombie film ever made.

To deepen such a dead-delirious unreality of our expedition's last legs, we began to play *Dawn of the Dead*'s score, begotten by Italian "horror-prog" gods, Goblin, whose tunes can only be relished in the film's Dario Argento-edited European cut, as Romero decided, in their stead, to use an oddball mixture of stock musick for his very own version of the 1978 zombie classick. With such a glorious gorehound-hexing album as our very own soundtrack, it was verily as if we gruesome twosome were lurking unto a *true* land of the dead.

An almost blinding snow was falling when our butchermobile finally—finally!—exited Interstate 76 and motored into the Pittsburgh suburb of Monroeville, our crypt-away-from-krypt whilst in Romero's severed neck of Pennsylvania. Having made reservations at a somewhat uninhabited Monroeville hotel—which bore no small resemblance to the haunted lodge in *The Shining* because of its putrid '70s carpeting—my black bride and I, after a simple late-night meal, adjourned to our room to rest our repulsive selves for the following day's unwholesome funereal undertakings and so, with nightmares of exploding zombie heads, slumbered . . . well, Creepy Reader . . . like the *dead!*

Early the following mourning, my unspeakable wife and yours cruelly, after gobbling down a hearty breakfast that would choke the most ferocious of undead fiends, began our day's unhallowedly horrific zombie hunt. And the first cadaverous curiosity of our disgustingly putrescence-dripping itinerary festered in Evans City, a sleepy little burgh all but hidden amidst the hulking Allegheny Mountains almost 40 miles from Monroeville. But what, you may ask, Creepy Reader, was there for we gruesome twosome to drag onto our dread-ridden *Dead*-exploration's chopping block? Well, it was, verily, in Evans City that *Night of the Living Dead* was made throughout the twilight months of 1967!

What had called George Romero and his Pittsburgh partners in the most macabre Horror-mongery, like drooling ghouls to a fresh grave, to this small town amidst the unspoiled wilderness of northwestern Pennsylvania—settled in 1800 as Boggs Mills but then, almost 80 years later, incorporated as Evans City, the Butler County borough named after distinguished miller, Thomas B. Evans—because it was here that those would-be filmmakers, after searching for some months throughout the suburbs of Pittsburgh for a house that they could plague with their undead plans, finally found the vacant farmhouse that would become that appallingly zombie-swarmed abode at *Night of the Living Dead's* black-and-white unbeating heart.

Five years later, Romero would also use Evans City as that little doomed town whose inhabitants become homicidally deranged after a chemical weapon-spill in *The Crazies*, one of a handful of low-budget and little known features—not all of them Horror!—that the director made between *Night* and 1978's *Dawn of the Dead*. But it is indeed for the Zombie King's 1968 horrorshow, his directorial debut, that Evans City is so very infamous within the verily vile vermicious annals of Horror history.

"Run Barbara—They're Coming for you
Graveside attack, Johnny's through
Panic takes hold as the ghouls pursue"

— Engorged
"Night of the Living Dead" (2002)

EVANS CITY CEMETERY
Franklin Road
Evans City

Our butchermobile had been motoring further and further west along Interstate 76 and then, for a short while, north along Interstate 79 until, almost an hour after we had begun our December day of detestable *Dead*-disinterring, we exited onto Route 528 towards Evans City. In comparison to the hustle and bustle of Monroeville's suburban Pittsburgh sprawl, these Romeroed parts of western Pennsylvania were deeply rural in all its sylvan simplicity.

Yours cruelly would have truly—*truly*, Creepy Reader!—loved to have feasted upon *Night* 's fiendishly flesh-eater-fallen farmhouse, but, alas, it was torn down not so very long after the film was finished, something we knew all too well before departing our Charnel House. That rusticatedly white-washed Evans City residence, owned by the Gass Family and known to the film's cast and crew as the Monster House, was actually already doomed for demolition before that summer and fall of 1967, its thusly cleared property to be used as, of all things, a sod farm.

But hearing of the place and its owner's plans for it, the *Night* crew lurked out from Pittsburgh to eyeball it and, eventually, arranged to rent it for but $300 per month. Romero and the rest of the film's macabre-makers were then free to wreak any sort of Horror-ific monstrous havoc upon that vacant farmhouse. After they verily no longer had any use for it, their Monster House met its inevitable end and was turned into so much lumber.

Knowing already that a sod farm had been planted upon the Horror-historic house's final rotting place and being unsure of not only the current existence of even that but, if it was indeed extant, of the spooksome thrills to be had from rolls upon green rolls of aspiring lawn, yours cruelly decided, in the end, not to unearth it. But, Creepy Reader, we gruesome twosome had motored to Evans City for some other horrifically ghoul-necrosed *Night of the Living Dead* unhallowed ground: the Evans City Cemetery!

Yours cruelly had dug very deep for the exact address of the Evans City Cemetery—where the terror-appalled events of that truly archetypal 1968 *Night* of undead horrors began to unfold with but the simplest of graveside memorials—but, so very unfortunately, with nothing to show for it. And so, our directions thusly ended with our arrival to Evans City. Because of this, we motored along Route 528 into what seemed like the middle of that small town and stopped at the first convenience shoppe we came upon to see if we could finally learn its address from some unzombified locals.

Despite some strange looks amongst some still sleep-slowed patrons buying their mourning's coffee, all of them knew very well what we were in search of—and why we gruesome twosome were in search of it! And so with that information of the Horror-loathsome cemetery's location, yours cruelly wheeled our touring hearse around and returned on Route 528 westwards from whence we came. Almost immediately after passing over a rusted line of railroad tracks, we turned left onto house-lined Pioneer Road, which, in but no time at all, became Franklin Road. And it was almost a quarter of a mile along Franklin before I brought our butchermobile to a dead stop, as yours cruelly espied, to our left, an oddly nameless narrow road worming its paved way up through the dense thickets and trees at the side of the road.

Motoring so very slowly up this very same side road and following it to the height of the hill, we gruesome twosome were met by a squat, gray marble slab, upon which was carved the name of that curiously cadaverous place we had been hunting for, because this was indeed the Evans City Cemetery! And that unnamed funeral drive my black bride and I had only now made our wretchedly fiendish way up was indeed—there was no mistaking it, Creepy Reader!—the very same road those shockingly ill-fated siblings, Russ Streiner's Johnny and Judith O'Dea's

Barbara, had taken to their dread-shrouded date with Romero's zombies at the very beginning of *Night of the Living Dead*!

As our butchermobile crawled into the Evans City Cemetery, we passed a small brown-bricked building off to the side of the boneyard's outer path. It was not very difficult for yours cruelly to recognize it as the very same graveyard edifice alongside which Johnny and Barbara had parked their simple tan sedan before their visit to their grandfather's forgotten grave. It was also here where, but a few minutes later, Barbara was attacked by *Night*'s first walking dead—or "# 1 Zombie," as Bill Hinzman, who played with gleefully growling relish that film's ghastly and gaunt first ghoul, signs his photographs—the undead thing having stalked the poor shrilly screaming girl here, to the seeming safety of her car.

While the two-floored structure was very possibly some sort of caretaker's shack, that December day we gruesome twosome found it festering there, it was in a sorry state of disrepair. Its windows had been battened with thick planks of plywood and its closed front doors had been further barred by some chain and a heavy lock. Because of this, whatever was to be found within it remained unknown to yours cruelly, although we did, whilst lurking about the back of the place, find a heap of the very same

sort of brown bricks from which it was fashioned, one of these specimens having since become a morbid *Night* memento mori within our Charnel House's curio cabinet!

After we had explored that thusly shuttered caretaker's shed—at least as exhaustively as we gruesome twosome could!—we pulled our meatwagon alongside one of the tombyard's burial-plot-hemmed paths and disinterred our gore-hounding selves so that we could shamble amidst the living dead-befouled belly of *Night*'s Evans City Cemetery.

As my unspeakable wife and I lurked about its grimly grave-plotted grounds, what we espied, aside from that seemingly abandoned shack, was not all that similar, at least not to yours cruelly's bloodshot eyes, to what we had witnessed, an unwholesome slew of times, as the forbodingly funereal background in *Night of the Living Dead*'s opening scenes. The boneyard not only looked much smaller than it had in the 1968 film but also much less populated with postmortem inhabitants, these disparities produced not only by the passage of almost 40 years, and the years of weathering therein, but, perhaps more profoundly, by Romero's camera work and editing.

Despite the latter, however, a good many of those looming trees that had shadow-shrouded *Night*'s cemeterial beginning so very shuddersomely had been, sadly, extirpated by a mammoth tornado some years ago, this natural disaster having actually stopped the producers of the film's redundantly repugnant and renownedly *Dead*-fiend-reviled 30th anniversary redux from using Evans City Cemetery for their new footage. Perhaps if those trees had not been uprooted, the cemetery would have resembled its late-'60s self in Romero's film.

Had we still found those trees there, perhaps, Creepy Reader, we gruesome two-some would have also found, under the veil of their thick boughs, the small and simple headstone that had stood in for that of the siblings' dearly departed grandfather, to which Barbara had brought her little cross-and-flowers memorial and before which Johnny had teased his already awfully affeared sister with what could very well be the morbid motto of horror history's modern zombie film: "They're com-

ing to get you, Barbara!", Russ Streiner's merrily mocking, Boris Karloff-mimicking delivery so very marvelously memorable. Although there were also a few other tombstones throughout Evans City Cemetery that were featured in that opening of *Night of the Living Dead*—such as the one that had split open poor Johnny's skull during his mortal struggle with Hinzman's repulsively re-animated #1 Zombie—but, alas, yours cruelly could not discern any of them.

Although our search for these *Night* headstones had been for naught, it was truly an extraordinary experience for we two devotedly dreadful *Dead*-disciples to simply walk upon the frozen charnel earth of the Evans City Cemetery, that otherwise ordinary backwoods boneyard that was ushered into Horror's unspeakably horrid halls almost 40 years ago because of the undead infamies of George Romero's *Night of the Living Dead!* And so, after doing our very best zombie impersonations while my black bride and I posed for photographs amongst the cemetery's tombstones, we returned to our butchermobile so that our fingers and toes didn't verily turn black from frostbite.

But before we gruesome twosome departed from the small cemetery, Creepy Reader, yours cruelly was urged by an unwholesome hunger for all that is Horror to exhume some stinking graveyard soil for yet another macabre memento of our visit. In fact, John Russo, *Night's* co-writer and producer, had done a similar thing himself some years before but sold his ghoulish toil's crop at horror conventions in vial-sized portions for $20 each! But it was not so very easy an act, as the cemetery's earth was frozen through and the only tool available to us was an ice scraper. But after some minutes of graveyard-digging, we gruesome twosome did indeed come away with a good haul of ghastly dirt, which indeed put a sickeningly ghoulish smile upon yours cruelly's face!

Bidding farewell to *Night of the Living Dead*'s Evans City Cemetery and, with it, all of Evans City, my noctiflorous wife and yours cruelly set our most shocking zombie-hunting sights upon that very hideous unbeating black heart of George Romero's rottedly ill-renowned *Dead* realm: Pittsburgh!

Putting Evans City behind us, our butchermobile motored southwards back towards Pittsburgh and, after almost an hour, we came upon that somewhat sprawling, spare "Steel City" but before dusk. Once there, we wormed our wretchedly necrosis-wanting way into what is known as the Golden Triangle: an 11-block-by-11-block quarter, at the very head of the city's East Side where the Monongahela and Allegheny Rivers meet to make the more massive and magnificent Ohio, that is Pittsburgh's financial and cultural precinct. And because of the wintry December winds blowing from off those thusly wed waters, we gruesome twosome were shrouded by a cruelly bitter cold as we lurked out amidst the loathsomely unliving luridness of Pittsburgh's utterly *Dead* underbelly.

MARKET SQUARE PRODUCTIONS
20 Market Square
Pittsburgh
(412) 471-1511

The very first contemptibly vermiceous curiosity of our terrible walking *Dead* tour of Pittsburgh was but a block from where yours cruelly had stowed our meatwagon amidst the seemingly modish surroundings of Market Square: the home of John Russo's aptly named Market Square Productions. We gruesome twosome found

20 Market Square between a pizzeria and an oyster bar, but the only thing that informed us that the somewhat desolate simple door was indeed that of Russo's production studio and—at least from what I had read—his very own shuddersome curiosity shoppe was a note, scrivened on Market Square Productions' very own stationary, taped to the deadbolted glass door instructing "Deliveries and Visitors" alike to ring the address's door bell, but if no answer should be had, to call from a payphone upon either of the neighboring premises. We tried both the payphone and the bell but, alas, Creepy Reader, neither method proved a fruitful means of partaking of Russo's Market Square Productions.

Regardless, somewhere behind that door was indeed where John Russo—as either writer, director, or producer—begot many, if not most, of his post-*Night of the Living Dead* productions, such as 1982's *Midnight* and 1986's *The Majorettes*, as well as, in 1998 and 2001, respectively, *Night*'s two severely sickening and shameless siblings: its repugnant 30th anniversary edition redux and, perhaps worse, its stiff and stale Tor Ramsey-directed and Karen Wolf-scripted "sequel," *Children of the Living Dead*, which, seemingly, attempted to use its über-zombie, Abbott Hayes, as the utter Freddy Krueger of the undead.

Both of these rottenly reviewed *Night*-related celluloid reprobates— as well as Russo's involvement with *Scream Queens Illustrated*, whose somewhat sleazy sundries, such as nipple print trading cards from your favourite straight-to-video starlets, yours cruelly supposed we would find him selling at 20 Market Square—have not done Russo's reputation amidst foully hardcore Horror-fiends any good, which is, in the end, a truly unfortunate thing, as he, along with his cohorts in creepiest cadaverous chaos, was indeed responsible for one of the most exquisite Horror exemplars ever filmed. 'Tis a shame, is it not, Creepy Reader?

THE LATENT IMAGE
(Former Location)
247 Fort Pitt Boulevard
Pittsburgh

Departing from the derelict deadness of John Russo's Market Square Productions, my crepuscular bride and yours cruelly lurked from Market Square towards the Golden Triangle's South Side. And after shambling for some minutes through a Pittsburgh December's sinking degrees, we gruesome twosome came upon our terror-tour's next decaying mouthful of *Dead* meat: 247 Fort Pitt Boulevard. And perchance you would ask, Creepy Reader, why we loitered in all our living dead-loving loathsomeness before this otherwise ordinary office building, especially in weather such as that in which we found ourselves that day? Well, this was, verily, the former location of The Latent Image!

Before that *Night of the Living Dead*, George Romero, John Russo, Russ Streiner, and a fiendish handful of other college friends came together to found their own commercial-production company here in Pittsburgh, which they begin in 1961 under the name The Latent Image. Through it, they produced an abundance of television advertisements and non-fictional industrial films for various Pittsburgh businesses. Through this sort of work, Romero and the rest of the increasingly more learned crew at The Latent Image were not only accruing an ample arsenal of professional filming paraphernalia but, perhaps more importantly, endless hours of educative technical experience. And so, with all of this at their deeply enterprising disposal, they decided to make themselves a little horror movie.

The Pittsburgh company's very first creature feature film was to be based upon a short story—inspired by Richard Matheson's *I Am Legend*, that seminally shuddersome 1954 story of an atrociously abhorrent vampire apocalypse—that Romero had himself written. The tale of undead terror was then fleshed out into a screenplay by Russo, who had been a teacher until he began working as a writer with his friends at their humble production house. The shooting title for The Latent Image's film had originally been *Monster Flick*, but, after its first 35 mm print was finished, this was changed to *Night of the Flesh Eaters*. However, when they were threatened with a lawsuit by some other filmmakers who already had a horror feature with that very same name, Romero and the rest of them finally called it—of corpse!—*Night of the Living Dead*.

It was, verily, on July 7, 1967, after finding all the necessary funding— in the end, a sum of about $114,000—that most ghastly, ghoul-glorifying gang of 10 fond Pittsburgh fiends, under the newly raised banner of Image Ten, lurked out unto the otherwise uncreepily charming countryside of Evans City and the rest, Creepy Reader, is the most horrendous of Horror history!

Romero and his morbidly creep-mongering cronies of Image Ten— perhaps the unacknowledged ghoulishly gangrenous godfathers of independent sinema—had begotten, throughout that summer of 1967, one of the most authoritative, awfully archetypal, and appalling films in the putrescently perverse annals of Horror. Not only was *Night of the Living Dead* a critical success—film critic Rex Reed declared that it stood as an example of what "turns a B-movie into a classic" and it was, indeed, the very first horror film to be shown at New York's Museum of Modern Art—the film was a financial success as well, becoming one of the very first midnight or cult movies, playing somewhere in the world—continuously!—for 10 years after its 1968 premiere. Simply put, Creepy Reader, without *Night of the Living Dead*, modern horror would not be the same.

As we gruesome twosome stood within the shockingly *Night* shadowed silhouette of 247 Fort Pitt Boulevard, it was not simply the fact that this had been the former home of both The Latent Image, and Image Ten—the eminent five-story modern Queen Anne style edifice, founded in 1910, is today owned by K. Goldsmith & Company, Inc., a "commercial and indus-

trial real estate" firm—that had us, we two most terribly *Dead*-thirsty of thanatologists, worshippingly so wretchedly before it but also because the premises were actually used in the film itself. Because that folksy Evans City farmhouse did not have a cellar of its own, Romero and his crew of would-be living dead connoisseurs turned the basement of the building into a makeshift set on which those scenes purportedly unfolded deep down within the stale darkness of the house's earthen subterranean space.

Thusly, it was at 247 Fort Pitt Boulevard, and not, verily, in Evans City where Kyra Schon's young Karen Cooper awoke from her "hurt"-ing to become but another woefully carnivorous walking corpse and where, with *Night*'s dreadfully nihilistic denouement, Duane Jones's hopelessly heroic Ben hid from the shocking swarm of zombies storming that formerly homey farmhouse.

When yours cruelly began our crime scene photography of that once odiously ghoul-occluded office space, two workers waiting before it for their bus asked if they could be of any help to me. Smirking our most sickeningly shuddersome smiles towards them, we shook our heads as we took our last photos. And so, that having come to an end, we worshipped amidst the gruesome *Dead* glory that once was George Romero's Latent Image here at 247 Fort Pitt Boulevard for a little while longer before putting a bullet in the head of our first day's creepiest *Night*-crawling.

Every Pittsburgher we met had declared utter disbelief when we told them that we were on a Horror-fiending holiday there, a reaction that did not shock us because, in the end, Pittsburgh did indeed seem rather . . . dead! This—of corpse, Creepy Reader!—made for an awesomely moribund atmosphere for our terribly *Dead*-terrored tour; however, it did not urge us to seek out Pittsburgh's other wholesomely less Horror-fied offerings, at least not on this journey. And so we returned to our crypt-away-from-krypt to rest our shockingly Romero rot-reveling selves for what our creepy carrion-craving *Dead* crusade would next drag upon our chopping block: the Monroeville Mall, that altar to the most atrocious commercial appetites at the hideous black heart of Romero's 1978 *Night* sequel, *Dawn of the Dead!*

"Steal a copter, flee the scene, make sure that nobody sees
Fly for hours, low on fuel, sanctuary filled with ghouls . . ."

— Engorged
"Dawn of the Dead" (2002)

THE MONROEVILLE MALL
Business Route 22
Monroeville
(412) 243-8511

The Monroeville Mall lay slumbering in all its cult Horror splendor but a few miles from our hotel and so, after our breakfast, we buried ourselves within our butchermobile and motored down Route 22, the main drag that, seemingly, split Monroeville in two. In *Dawn of the Dead*, the Monroeville Mall appeared, at least to yours cruelly's bloodshot eyes, as if it was amidst some truly isolated territory, cut off from the rest of the surrounding community—whatever type of community that may have been! However, the mall was, in fact, Creepy Reader, at the very heart of an especially unsightly stretch of suburban sprawl inhabited by monotonous strip malls, fast-food charnel pits, and other commonplace monuments to American consumerism.

When we came to some road signs for the mall, yours cruelly wheeled our meatwagon onto a service road that would usher us, after worming its winding way over Route 22 and then under some bulky nameless office building, unto it and we gruesome twosome did not espy the mall until we were nearly upon it. And then there it was: the Monroeville Mall!

This was indeed that very same skin-crawlingly zombie-stormed structure from *Dawn of the Dead*—yours cruelly's very favorite of George Romero's infamously decomposing foursome of *Dead* features—where the film's quartet of shrewd and stalwart zombie holocaust survivors—

Gaylen Ross's Francine, David Emge's Stephen, Scott Reiniger's Roger, and Ken Foree's Peter— settled their stolen television chopper in search of shelter. Yes, Creepy Reader: this was it!

Given a sweeping facelift sometime during the '80s, the Monroeville Mall looked very little like it did in *Dawn*—with the exception, however, of the weird lamp posts in the parking lot! But motoring about the side of the mall, our meatwagon pulled to a stop outside what is the mall's Southeast Entrance. To the less than bloodshot eye of your general mall-goer, it was, about the back of the squat building, but one of its less used entrances. But Creepy Reader, to the most grotesque of grisliness-glutting ghouls such as our shockingly ghastly selves, it was *the* gateway into the mall's immensely *Dead*-infected innards, as this Southeast

Entrance, before which we gruesome twosome lurked so very loathsomely, recurred rather regularly in Romero's most exquisite 1978 walking dead extravaganza.

The Southeast Entrance was first witnessed when that swaggering zombie-stomping twosome of S.W.A.T. troopers, Peter and Roger, put their strategy of securing the mall from the malodourously maggoty undead masses into action. It was indeed at this very same entrance, referred to by *Dawn's* steeled foursome of survivalists as the loading docks, that the delivery trucks they had hot-wired so very handily had been dumped, thusly preventing that hideous zombie horde from choking the mall's parking lot and entering their would-be home sweet home.

During *Dawn's* atrocious third act, it was also through these very same wide bay-windowed doors of the Southeast Entrance that the film's mayhem-mongering mob of motorcycle marauders—featuring Tom Savini himself as the ballsy machete-butchering Blade—so very savagely invaded the security of those survivors' stronghold, thus introducing *Dawn of the Dead's* fantastic bloodfeast of a finale, for which Savini's name, as the master of the most extremely splatter-tastic of special effects, was made.

Opposite the Southeast Entrance was the steep James Street, which ushered would-be shoppers down unto the Monroeville Mall, such as the troopers in their commandeered trucks and those iniquitous Hunnish interlopers on their choppers. It may interest you to know, Creepy Reader, that the dead-desolate depot where Roger and Peter had found those trucks they would use to block the mall's various entrances was some miles away and not, at least as *Dawn* would have had it, but atop this very same hill. It had been owned by a very real trucking ring known, simply, as B & P, but a huge Sam's Club wholesalers is found upon the location today.

Having undertaken our external exploratory examination of the Monroeville Mall, my black bride and yours cruelly ventured through those very same doors to dissect whatever decomposing *Dead* delicacies lay within! Although the mall was but a standard structure of concrete and steel not so very unlike the Grue Jersey like in which we had been, veritably, bred, I must confess, Creepy Reader, that, as we stepped within, my horrendously Horror-hungry black heart began to beat more hastily, for in this very same Pittsburgh suburban mall, the extremely ensanguined flesh-eating exploits of some dreadful 1,600 walking dead had unfolded, in all their gruesomely grisly glory, almost 30 years ago in one of the finest, fiercest, and simply most *fun* horror films of all time!

The very idea for *Dawn of the Dead* was, in fact, begotten from the mall itself. As the story goes, George Romero had been friends with one of the mall's main managers and had been given a tour of the then-new $50 million shopping centre, which was one of the very first monstrous indoor malls in those parts of Pennsylvania.

While walking through the business-bustling belly of that boxy building—in particular, several somewhat secluded office spaces therein—the seeds for a sequel to his shocking 1968 living dead spookshow were planted in his most morbidly gifted gray matter. And, thus, *Dawn of the Dead* was born. Romero would film it over the course of four months between late 1977 and early 1978. He and his distressingly committed *Dead* crew took over the mall after its daily business was done and there, within that space where shoppers had strolled but hours before, they would unleash some of the most consummately countercultural, gun-crazed chaos and gore-gargling cadaver-caused carnage ever captured on celluloid from about 10:00 at night until 7:00 the next mourning.

Because the mall's doors opened at 8:00 A.M. each day, Romero's crew had only an hour to clear out not only all of the film's equipment and props but—egads!—the seemingly endless swarm of flesh-starved zombies with which they had filled it by night, an endeavor that, without doubt, made for an utterly singularly riotous spectacle! Yours cruelly wondered, Creepy Reader, if some all-too-early shopper had unsuspectingly come upon that gruesomely gangrenous gang of blue-and-green-faced ghoul-extras walking out of the Monroeville Mall after a prolonged night's portrayal of the most dreadfully nauseating living dead and been shocked so severely into a *corpse* themselves!

The Monroeville Mall was not all that different from any of its now-ubiquitous suburban brethren. Perhaps large for its day—when the very first of its pestilential kind pocked the land like pustules upon the face of a pox victim—it would be considered only but average size today. On the shopping front, the mall offered all the usual suspects: Barnes & Noble, Bath & Body Works, Brookstone, and so on. At the Suncoast Video—now known as the Suncoast Motion Picture Company because of the veritable death of video!—we gruesome twosome were somewhat shocked to see that there was but three copies of *Dawn* in stock!

Although the mall did indeed appear to be a popular place for pubescent packs of purposeless teenagers, there was a conspicuously large company of security cops all about it, and it was they that would prove to be more of a nightmarishly pervasive nuisance than zombies who would gobble upon our guts.

Creepy Reader, let me explain. Before my unspeakable wife and yours cruelly embarked upon our excursion unto the most egregious Romerovian extremities, I had read the accounts of others who had made their very own morbid pilgrimages to the Monroeville Mall and each and every one of them stressed the fact that the mall's would-be constabulary did not allow photography of *any* kind upon the premises. There had even been some thusly found *Dawn* fiends who had been escorted out of the mall under the threat of arrest. Knowing this, yours cruelly tailored our tour of the terribly *Dead*-tainted Monroeville Mall with the utterly unsane utmost of covertness in mind, which, in the end, paid off so very perversely, as I did indeed take many photos of not only without but within, albeit—alas!—without the use of that foully incriminating flash.

It was with no small sum of shock, however, that we gruesome twosome learned, some years after our return from this very same expedition unto Romero's execrable Pittsburgh, that true *Dawn of the Dead*-themed tours were undertaken from time to time within the Monroeville Mall—not only with the management's blessing, not only with a small escort of security, but with some of the film's very own cast and crew (Ken Foree himself!) as its gruesomely expert guides—and all of it after the mall had closed for the day!

Despite the fact such a thing seems, at least to yours cruelly, like a profoundly patent cash-in on *Dawn*'s perpetual popularity on the part of the mall's powers that be, what an opportunity for the most unfetteredly fiendish *Dead*-feeding that must have made for! But nevertheless, Creepy Reader, let me horrify you with the dreadfully *Dead*-delectable delights that we disinterred on our very own tour of *Dawn*'s Monroeville Mall!

The ineffably foetid innards of the Monroeville Mall were, structurally, the same as they had been in *Dawn of the Dead*. The exclusive set of escalators which zombies had haltingly haunted to hilarious effect in *Dawn* were still there for the convenience of today's shoppers, as were the two squared-off staircases at either end of the mall. The two short and shrunken wooden bridges on the mall's lower level were also throwbacks to the dated living-dead-lousy days of the film.

After *Dawn*'s foursome of zombie-fighters go on their hunt to clean their future home of any and all walking dead, their revoltingly reeking, twice-deceased remains were seen stacked upon these very same bridges.

Also remnants from those deeply dreadful days of *Dawn* were the garden planters which decorated the mall's lower floor. It was in one of these that the wrapped corpse of a regrettably zombified Roger had been interred after he—it?!?—was put down by Peter's revolver.

Other features of the mall's first floor that were espied in *Dawn* were the wishing fountains, of which there were two: a large circular one in front of the department store known so very ironically as Lazarus—now a Macy's—and a smaller, squarish sort at the other end

of the mall. Unfortunately, however, neither of them was working its watery ways the day we were there. While the latter had been, seemingly, closed for repairs, the former, being that it was indeed but days after Christmas, was buried beneath a holiday photo booth the size of a small house! This very same fountain had been the location of one of *Dawn*'s most memorably humorous moments, in which a wondrously corpulent walking corpse wearing only shorts crashes screamingly into its waters. Alas, we could not revel in all its *Dawn* renown. Curse you, Santa Claus, curse you!

The most infamous of all the Monroeville Mall's shuddersomely *Dawn of the Dead*-loathsome structural locations, featured so very prominently in Romero's fearfully fabulous 1978 film, was indeed, Creepy Reader, the second floor's utility hallway. But as my black bride and yours cruelly began to shamble down it, it was not so very recognizable, at least not at first.

The hallway—which we gruesome twosome found standing upon the Macy's side of the mall—was indeed much longer than it had appeared in

Dawn, and accurately so, as Romero had actually had his crew build a fake wall about three-quarters of the way down it so that it would look shorter. Inhabiting this thusly truly *Dead*-transmogrified hallway were a row of payphones, some small lockers, and a photo booth that, from the hairstyles and fashions of the models from its preposterous sample pictures, could have been there since '78!

Further down the hallway, past the restrooms on either side of it, we found a duo of black doors set back into a small recess. It was, indeed, but past them that that film-found façade had been fashioned and it was through those very same doors that Peter and Roger had first lurked out into the mall after their copped news-copter had landed upon its roof.

Later in the film, these doors would be hidden behind a fake wall of the four-some's very own fabrication in order to keep their very own well-stocked upstairs safe house—the scenes were actually shot within some anonymous Pittsburgh apartment and not, in fact, at the mall itself—a secret from anyone, living or undead! This wily painted plywood wall would only find itself, with *Dawn*'s extremely chaotic and calamitous ending, torn down into nothing but timber by a horrifically hungry zombie horde.

Made paranoid by the sensible presence of security all about the mall, yours cruelly dared not try either of the doors' golden knobs to see what waited behind them. Pray tell, Creepy Reader, if you should find yourself in this very same *Dawn*-harrowed Monroeville Mall hallway, before these very doors, will you have the nerve to venture unto that unexplored beyond . . . ?

Despite these gloriously ghoulish and ghastly Romerovian remains amidst the Monroeville Mall, there were indeed a few places from *Dawn of the Dead* that were, so very sadly, no longer fragments of the place's fabric. The first of them was the two-story-tall clock tower, whose hourly ringing had toned so ominously in the film. Where it used to stand before "Kaufmann's" was a holiday train ride that would entrance any blubberingly bored toddler being borne about the mall.

But the one fixture of that macabrely *Dawn*-era mall whose absence was the most pronounced was the ice rink, where Gaylen Ross's Fran prac-ticed her shooting on some sorry storefront mannequins. This generously roomy ice rink had, in fact, been removed sometime after the film was fin-ished to make way for a full-sized food court. Shoppers at the mall today are called forth to feast not so very foully upon human flesh but "TREATS!" as the neon sign before it declared.

If yours cruelly abided in all my abhorrence anywhere near the Monroeville Mall, I would attempt to open my  very own sickening food stand serving dishes inspired by zombie flicks! Yes, there would be the "*Burial Ground* Breast of Chicken Sandwich," the "Lucio Fulci plate with Wormy Linguini," and—but of corpse, Creepy Reader!—the "Romerovian Barbecued Rack of Ribs"! I am truly shocked that no one has undertaken this very same sort of gruesomely gore-met gastronomic gimmick already!

As we two most horrendously Horror-hungry of *Dead*-hunters continued to walk the fiendishly unhallowed floors of the Monroeville Mall, there was but a terribly *Dawn*-bloodied twosome of businesses that had, almost 30 years ago, actually appeared in Romero's fantastically rot-reveling film. Although video game technology has indeed improved since 1978 when the likes of Pole Position and Gunfight humored *Dawn*'s heroic mall inhabitants, the plain but popular arcade that we gruesome twosome found upon the mall's second floor was still there to entertain the quarter-bearing crowd. Known so very simply as Tilt, the arcade, today, featured the grisliest of first-person shooter games, which were, perhaps, much more violent and vicious than that feature Romero himself had filmed here!

Just across the mall's wide mezzanine from the arcade was the second of the two *Dead*-depicted businesses, the only sizeable department store that was actually featured in *Dawn of the Dead*, mostly because, in the end, it was the only one that would allow Romero to pervert its profoundly proper premises with his pestiferous zombie plague: JCPenney! And it was indeed, Creepy Reader, a true treasure trove of terrifically *Dead*-terrored treats! Throughout the years since *Dawn* was filmed here at the mall, stores have come and gone, but JCPenney was, seemingly, as undying as the zombies that had once groped so ghastly against the dense glass of its security gates.

Entering through JCPenney's first-floor entrance, my crepuscular bride and yours cruelly made our wantonly *Dead*-wanting way past the women's department to the back of the store and the customer elevator therein. It was at these very same otherwise dull elevator doors that David Emge's Stephen attempted his escape from those iniquitous motorcycle invaders during *Dawn of the Dead*'s concluding mall combat, only to be shot and, later, scathed so very savagely by zombies, dooming him to become nothing but the dreadful walking dead himself!

But, alas, Creepy Reader, the insides of the film's elevator—through which *Dawn*'s plucky protagonists had entered, by way of its small trap door, and where they had found the dim air duct within the elevator shaft that would become their early means of evading the mall's zombies, as it lead, at least in *Dawn*, to the utility hallway we had explored but earlier—were actually those of an elevator from 247 Fort Pitt Boulevard. But despite this, as we stepped within Penney's elevator, we espied its very own diminutive would-be escape door with a most sickeningly Horror-fiending smile but the same.

After we gruesome twosome were lifted to JCPenney's second level, we lurked unto the badly *Dead*-blighted belly of the store and, therein, the

escalators that connected its two floors. In one of *Dawn of the Dead*'s many light-heartedly less-Horror-fied moments, Roger—pumped through with the pleasures of unimpeded plunder—slid down the middle of the two escalators before he and Peter made their escape from Penney's with a booty-burdened wheelbarrow.

Thereafter, we walked out of JCPenney and stood at the balcony but outside its second-floor entrance and looked out at the Monroeville Mall before us—at all of those assortedly vermicious *Dead*-vile adornments therein—the staircases, the elevators, the bridges, the planters, the fountains—and at all of those slothful and surly holiday-seasoned shoppers shuffling and stumbling and shambling all about them. Standing upon that very same spot, the deep-voice-distinguished Ken Foree had delivered some of *Dawn's* most dreadfully ominous dialogue, very possibly one of the most shudderingly infamous slogans in all of Horror history:

"When there's no more room in Hell, the dead shall walk the earth . . ."

As my unspeakable wife and yours cruelly gazed down upon the Monroeville Mall so very ghoulishly with our extremest bloodshot eyes, we were truly, Creepy Reader, at the very birthplace of one of Horror's most loathsomely undead legends.

After we gruesome twosome had inhaled all-too-unhealthily the abhorrently *Dead*-appalled atmosphere that, after all these many, many years, still hung so very horridly about the Monroeville Mall like the most morbid of miasmas, we returned to our butchermobile as happy as two ghouls with a grossly undug grave. And so we bid a foulest Horror-fiend's farewell to the Monroeville Mall and motored back to our temporarily rented tomb. The following day, we would be crawling back to our Krypt, our explicitly *Dead*-exhuming exploration of George Romero's putrefacted Pittsburgh parts having concluded—but not, Creepy Reader, before dissecting the contemptibly decaying corpse of his most exceedingly ferocious 1985 exercise in extinctest flesh-eating: *Day of the Dead*!

And so early the next mourning, my unspeakable wife and yours cruelly checked out of our makeshift Monroeville morgue and began motoring to the Ohio-bordering Pennsylvania burgh known as Wampum, almost 50 miles northwest of us, where, in 1984, George Romero would stillbirth his third dealing in dreadfullest living dead disgust, *Day of the Dead*, which many Horror-fiends saw with utter sorrow—until 2004's *Land of the Dead*, of corpse—as his very last zombie horrorshow. It was also been seen, in all those years since its then-renowned 1985 release as the *least* of his terrorizingly zombie-tainted trilogy—an unfortunately final failing feature from that morbid Pittsburgh master of macabrely modering mortality.

After 1968's *Night of the Living Dead* and, 10 years later, that new *Dawn* for Romero's walking dead, awfully Romerovian-rot-ravening aficionados of those mid-'80s had extremely exaggerated expectations for him that, simply, could not be fulfilled. It is indeed very true, Creepy Reader, that the hardcore zombie horror that Romero ultimately filmed was, in fact, a very different sort of *Dead* from what he wanted to film, at least as his original screenplay attests. But the cruelest budgetary constraints, as well as Romero's very own requirement that the film remain unrated, cut short the somewhat epic size, and even the subject matter, of what *Day of the Dead* could have been.

Despite the fact that such a revision of Romero's hitherto "epic"-regaled return to exquisitely *Dead* extremities was a very well-known thing to the fiercest fan-addicts of his films, the unenthusiastic reaction to *Day of the Dead*, by film critics and cult Horror-fiends alike, was an all-too-common response as that negative estimation seemed to be of *Day's* essential nature. Its absolutely cadaverous atmosphere was cruelly claustrophobic; all was utterly dismal, desolate, and doleful; nihilism was its excruciatingly inescapable ethos, despite the humanizing turn of its trio of heroes—Lori Cardille's Sarah, Terry Alexander's John, and Jarlath Conroy's William— and, through them, its sunny-island-sanctuary ending.

Yours cruelly must confess, Creepy Reader, that I, too, did not truly begin to appreciate Romero's third revoltingly *Dead* rotter until some years later because, very simply, it was not a lot of fun to watch! While it was not always the case, *Day of the Dead* has, indeed, become an abundantly adored celluloid atrocity within Horror's hideously sanguinolent halls.

Day of the Dead's dispiritingly suffocating demeanor was rooted not simply in the substance and style of George Romero's film but, verily, in its very setting as well: the Wampum Industrial Facility, a monstrously cavernous mine in the harsh northwest hinterlands of Pennsylvania. Some of Romero's 1985 zombie film was shot elsewhere. Its very beginning, with that mostly cynical helicopter crew's search for survivors amidst a loathsomely lost, living-dead-lumbering landscape, was filmed upon the otherwise serene streets of Fort Myers, Florida, not so very distant from where Romero, at least then, had a home. Also filmed in

Florida was the simple and spare surface—whereupon that helicopter would be set down—of that shudder-somely zombie-shrouded subterranean military stronghold, as was the delightfully walking dead-delivered ending of *Day.*

Of the former scene, the soldiers, civilians, and scientists inhabiting that "great big fourteen mile tombstone," as blithe-hearted Caribbean-born John called it, would descend down into the depths of their dreadful underground dwelling through an extraordinarily huge elevator. Both within and without, this elevator—upon which, during *Day's* fantastic foully flesh-fatal finale, an abhorrent army of re-animated atrocities is lowered into the human-bounteous bowels of that below-ground base to unleash one of Horror's most marvelously morbid gut-munching massacres—was found by Romero and his corpse-worshipping crew in the form of the Manor Nike Missile Base, known as PI-25.

It was only but north of Monroeville, Creepy Reader, amidst the somewhat less populated stretch of Pittsburgh suburbia known as Plum— although, variously, dread-devouring *Dead* disciples attribute its location to either Monroeville itself or Murrysville—that the decommissioned Cold War-era depot for distinctly homeland defense-designated NIKE surface-to-air missiles, but one of a dozen all about those parts of Pennsylvania, deteriorated in deepest disuse until, in 1984, Romero made it the stupendous entrance and exit of *Day of the Dead's* setting.

If you should be extremely curious to explore *Day's* very same elevator—if it should indeed be there still!—it can be found amidst the Plum properties about, approximately, either 713 New Texas Road or 428 Presque Isle Road: the first address being the former missile installation's command facility, which is, today, the home of—egads, Creepy Reader!— the University of Pittsburgh's Primate Research Laboratory, whilst the latter was its previous launching pad, where an elementary school and a junior high were founded since *Day.*

"Stronghold in a missile silo
Tensions and aggressions running high
A tourniquet and amputation to stop the infection
Hope you don't return once you die!

— Engorged
"Day of the Dead" (2002)

GATEWAY COMMERCE CENTER
(Meritex Enterprises)
State Route 18
Wampum
(724) 535-4300

But it was unto Wampum—and, therein, that massive former limestone mine where most of *Day of the Dead*'s infamously foul horrors
unfolded—that we gruesome twosome were motoring. After about an
hour, yours cruelly wheeled our meatwagon off the Pennsylvania
Turnpike and onto State Route 18. Wampum was a truly bucolic burgh
and it was but a little while longer through that conspicuously mountainous countryside before we espied, upon the left-hand side of that long
straight road, the simple red sign for the Gateway Commerce Center,
which was the Wampum Industrial Facility. And it was this that was transmogrified so very *Dead*-terroredly into an all-in-one, brazenly bellicose
military base, extraordinarily egregious living-dead-experiment laboratory,
and a terror-shrouded tomb-esque shelter for those severely tumultuous
survivors of Romero's profoundly portentous pestilence.

Our butchermobile motored down the Gateway Commerce Center's
drive and, in but a minute, we found our hideously Horror-hungering
selves before a small but widespread concrete awning set into the very rock-
face of the hill looming there behind it. To the side of those seemingly
would-be parking spaces, yours cruelly saw an unobtrusive squared-off
opening dug into the mountain itself. These were, verily, Creepy Reader,
the only evidence that this was indeed the entrance to *Day*'s former

Wampum Industrial Facility, as—of corpse!—the rest of it rotted in all its once-revoltingly zombie-ridden ill-renown but beneath us.

Medusa Cement Company had mined this very same lot of Wampum land for its limestone until sometime not so very long after World War II. Thereafter, it came under the ownership of Page Avjet and its thusly excavated extensive expanse was made into a wondrously mammoth warehouse, all 125 acres of it, all 2.5 million square feet of it, closed below the earth's crust.

Its constantly regulated temperature as well as its simple subterranean security made that former Wampum limestone mine a fitting storage facility for everything from non-commercial bulky vehicles and boats to canisters of motion picture celluloid, even flourishing crops of food-grade fungi. But in 1984, it would become the substantial, and substantially tenebrous and tortuous, set of George Romero's *Day of the Dead*, where—with the exceptions previously explained—the horrors of the film's macabrely human meat-mutilating mayhem happened. From that cruel living-dead corral overseen by that churlish cigar-chewing Private Steel (Gary Klar) to the loathsomely unspeakable laboratory of that dead-dismembering mad doctor, Doctor Logan (Richard Liberty), all of *Day*'s horridly hidden haunts were all filmed here beneath Wampum.

But, alas, Creepy Reader, we gruesome twosome would not be able to explore any of them, because, as yours cruelly was told by one of Gateway's telephone operators, the facility does not offer tours of its stretches of subsurface storage space to the general, and generally un-*Dead*-polluted, public. And without any sizeable commercial surplus to stow away within the majestic Pennsylvania mountainside, we had to settle for but standing before the mouth of George Romero's third monstrously morbid zombie-murderous masterpiece.

However, we could at least witness that badly *Dead*-brutalized belly of that bygone Wampum Industrial Facility by way of the Gateway Commerce Center's very own commercial included, as an extra, on *Day of the Dead*'s most recent DVD release. Therein, yours cruelly not only saw that the former mine, houses equipment as well as employees—computer operators, telemarketers, and so on—but that as a consequence for the facility's very permission to use that short promotional spot for the DVD, no on-site tours of the mine were allowed to be given. Yet, whilst the management does not give tours to dreadfully repugnant disciples of that terrible *Dead* trilogy such as we two most horrendously necrophilous of Horror-fiends, they do not seem to shun their past partnership with Pittsburgh's most shuddersome son, George Romero.

And so, after some crime scene photography of *Day of the Dead*'s Wampum Industrial Facility—at least of its extant Gateway Commerce Center exterior!—yours cruelly wheeled our touring hearse eastwards and we gruesome twosome began our laboriously long lurk back to our Charnel House. When we had returned, our profoundly Horror-possessed pilgrimage unto George Romero's putrescently *Dead*-plagued Pennsylvania was but the most macabrely vermicious memory. But our expedition had been, verily, the best Christmas gift of them all, wrapped up—but of corpse, Creepy Reader!—with an ensanguined ribbon of egregiously rotting entrails!

If you hunger so very horrendously for all that is *Dead*—be it *Day* or *Dawn* or even that *Night!*—then this same shocking sort of exploration will not disappoint, but I would suggest, however, undertaking it during a less cruelly colder clime such as that which froze our hot Horror-fiending blood whilst we lurked through those particular Pennsylvania parts.

But before I take my leave of you, Creepy Reader, I would tell you one last thing. Although yours cruelly was still extremely exhausted from those *Dead*-horrored Pennsylvania hinterlands, I decided all-too-unwisely to deposit myself amidst the mad swarms of mall-shoppers to exchange some undesired gifts. With more than usual bloodshot eyes did I look out upon those monstrously ravenous masses that mob the mall during those Days of the Unending Returns that follow the feast of Yule.

Had it not been for our communion with the living dead upon our carrion-campaign, I am affeared that it would have escaped me that something was horribly . . . wrong. For these shoppers, were they not more . . . repellent. . . than last I saw them? What of that sickeningly pungent stench that permeated amongst them, like that of a slab of raw meat blossoming with wormy putrescence under the sun? And was not their disposition more heinous—more inhuman—seemingly all-too-capable of seeking out human victims and committing unspeakable acts

of murder? Forbid it, I begged as I backed towards the exit, but—
egads!—it was true: the shoppers had become . . . ZOMBIES! The living
dead! The walking dead! The all-too-dreadfully hungry dead! Beware!
Whatever you do, beware the malls! The horrors, Creepy Reader! The
horrors . . . !

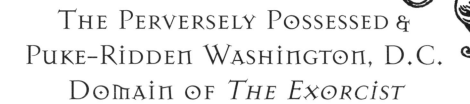

Chapter Nine

THE PERVERSELY POSSESSED & PUKE-RIDDEN WASHINGTON, D.C. DOMAIN OF *THE EXORCIST*

"Decapitated saints
Fall from the sky
God's chosen one burns
Sin gives birth to life
The command of darkness
And all that surrounds
Thorns of uncreation
Spit upon the kingdom of light"

— Necrophagia
"Deep Inside, I Plant the Devil's Seed" (1998)

The summer when yours cruelly was about 15 years old and hungering so very horridly for all that was gloriously grisly and gore-ridden, my fiendish cohorts and I rented just about every creepshow that our local video shoppe had on its modest shelves. As we passed those sweltering weeks deep down in the dark belly of the family basement drooling over some new video nasty, our options dwindled before our unwholesome appetites for Horror of the most horrendous order. We then decided to try the one film that had escaped our attentions.

Although its box cover was not as lurid or lascivious as all the others we had devoured thus far, like cemetery ghouls would gobble up dead guts, we rented it all the same and returned to my basement-tomb to feast upon this latest offering. Two hours later, the end credits began to crawl down the television's glaring screen and we self-respecting gore-adorers were truly speechless. More than that, however, if we were to confess to such a thing, we were scared: skin-crawlingly and stomach-churningly *scared*. What had unfolded before our gaping eyes was a nauseatingly shocking nightmare the likes of which none of us newly baptized bloodfreaks had witnessed before that summer. And exactly what film was it, Creepy Reader, that had choked us so with the basely bitter balm of utter Horror? Why, *The Exorcist*, of corpse.

When *The Exorcist* was unleashed in 1973—so very unnaturally on December 26th—upon an unsuspecting movie-going populace like a biblical plague, it shocked audiences across America with its terrorizingly horrid and vomitously hideous spectacle of an innocent preteen girl possessed by the blackest of evils, blasphemy made into nubile flesh. The controversy that followed the film's release is a thing of Hollyweird legend: unsuspecting audience members fleeing the theatre or fainting in the aisles; some others seeking out religious counseling or psychiatric treatment to cleanse their timorous hearts and troubled minds of the atrocious anti-Christian abominations they had espied.

Along with the lauded archetypal loathsomeness of 1968's *Night of the Living Dead* and 1974's *The Texas Chainsaw Massacre*, William Friedkin's monstrously unsettling masterwork, based upon William Peter Blatty's best-selling 1971 novel—which was itself inspired by an ill-rumoredly "true" late-1940s case of possession in suburban Maryland—and featuring the supremely chunkblowing special effects of Dick Smith, ushered in the modern age of celluloid horror in a vicious flood of daemonic violence and vilest obscenity that is still to this day very rarely, if ever, equaled. Put simply, Creepy Reader, *The Exorcist* remains verily *the* scariest horror film of all time.

And so during an otherwise serene vernal season not so very long ago, my necrobella bride and I lurked down to Washington, D.C., on an macabre expedition to those unassuming locales perverted so very pro-foundly by Friedkin's infamous 1973 horrorshow, that fiendishly fearful flick that had curdled my blood so inexorably all those years ago. Well then, Creepy Reader, won't you join us on our damnably diabolic dread-tour of that possessed domain of *The Exorcist.*

When our butchermobile motored into Washington, D.C., the city was amidst its annual National Cherry Blossom Festival. Thus, the whole town was crawling with tourists, picnic baskets, and kites. But profane purveyors of the putrefacted that we are, we ignored all such springtime revelry. After all, we had made this pilgrimage not to behold its vegetation but to exhume and exorcise some of the city's more unholy curiosities. And so, ignoring all that blossoming flora, we headed towards Georgetown, the city's oldest quarter and the setting for *The Exorcist*'s hideously sordid Satanic happenings.

"THE MACNEIL HOUSE"
3600 Prospect Street
(at the corner of 36th &
Prospect Streets)
Georgetown

Although the upscale and somewhat exclusive neighborhood was nightmarishly crowded with window-shopping tourists and suffocated by almost bumper-to-bumper traffic, we were able to finally find a good parking space along Wisconsin Avenue, inhabited by fashionable shoppes and restaurants where that swarm drawn out by the spring clime loitered. Our daemon hunt thus begun, we walked past blocks of aged Colonial-style houses that distinguished Georgetown's somewhat narrow, tree-shadowed streets. In but minutes, we came to those Georgetown parts that locals call the Hilltop and, therein, the corner of 36th and Prospect. And it was then that we saw it there before us: the MacNeil House.

It was here that dwelled famous actress Chris MacNeil (Ellen Burstyn) and her prepubescent Pazuzu-possessed daughter Regan, played by a 12-year-old Linda Blair, truly the most cherubic little girl in sinema ever to masturbate with a crucifix whilst puking forth such delightfully disquieting dialogue as "Let Jesus fuck you!" Any true horror-worshipper would undoubtedly recognize the two-floor, red-brick house that sits at 3600 Prospect Street, especially if they should find themselves lurking about it on a forsaken and foggy moonless night.

Although at first glance the house looked rather unchanged from the days when it stood as the backdrop for the unspeakably dreadful sinematic devilry witnessed in Friedkin's exercise in emetic extremity, there were some disparities that yours cruelly's bloodshot eyes did indeed espy. The boxy home appeared smaller than its '70s celluloid self, something that was not at all surprising because of the fact that the director had a whole addition built onto the left side of the edifice so that it would thusly abut the adjacent stairway, such a film-arisen fabrication's raison d'etre unforgettably cruel.

Because Regan's bedroom was placed in this faux wing of that MacNeil abode, it was through her bedroom's window that MacNeil's confidant, Father Damien Karras (Jason Miller), plunged to his dreadfully gruesome death in his ultimately suicidal efforts to save that young girl's soul after selflessly summoning her daemon into his very own devout flesh. This façade was also, Creepy Reader, the backdrop for what is perhaps *The Exorcist*'s most well-known tableau: the Magrite-inspired mise-en-scene of the fateful arrival of that hoary and heart-sick titular man of faith, Father Merrin (Max Von Sydow), to the accursed MacNeil home, his blackly silhouetted body standing before this corrupted place, eerily swathed in a stream of unnatural light spilling forth from Regan's bedroom windows.

As we gruesome twosome scrutinized that simple Georgetown dwelling, we wondered whether the residents who live there today truly appreciate the place of profoundly profane dishonor that their otherwise unassuming abode has in the most foetidly foul annals of horror history. Did its present-day owners open their home's Devil-darkened door for *Exorcist* aficionados such as we two dread-devouring demonomaniacs? Did they allow would-be Captain Howdy-possessees to toss and turn in mock daemon-torture upon an upstairs mattress for $13 a go? Or did they ladle out heapingly horrid helpings of unpalatably chunky pea soup for Pazuzu-worshippers each year on the 26th of December? The cautiously curtained windows and tall, black wooden fence that had been put up around the property since 1973 seemed to answer our questions.

THE EXORCIST STAIRS
Between Prospect &
M Streets
Georgetown

Having our fill of Friedkin's sinematic house of hellish horrors, we lurked around its less expansive side to welter in the wondrously gruesome and ghastly wickedness of the one Georgetown locale that has become truly synonymous with Friedkin's '70s tribute to Satanic terror: the iconic and infamous *Exorcist* Stairs! When William Peter Blatty was an undergraduate English student (class of 1950) at Georgetown University— in whose collegiate shadow 3600 Prospect, and this deeply steep descent of slate stairs, verily stood—they were known as the Hitchcock Steps because of their treacherous, and seemingly thriller-worthy, nature.

Despite such prophetic sinema-peril potential, the steps—which join Prospect Street up on the Hilltop with the end of M Street lying at their base—seem to have been, for untold years, a notably notorious place for "Hoya" athletes to burn out their muscle tissues after an already grueling workout, something they still do to this day. But after 1973 with the release of *The Exorcist*, the place was not only unblessed so very diabolically with that new name but a new, and profoundly more perversely profane, claim to infamy because of that film's bone-splintering climax.

Standing before those *Exorcist* Stairs, they were *truly* a macabrely menacing marvel to behold, Creepy Reader, as they, despite the presence of three landings, seemed to plummet *straight down* to M Street—a frightful fall that is said to be equivalent to *five stories*. We gruesome twosome could not help but be filled with a creepily unknown sense of bloodcurdling unease as we embarked on our descent down all of its 97 stone, and unforgivingly solid, steps.

As we hurled ourselves thusly, we espied many examples of graffiti that had been left upon either side of the stairway's rock-fashioned throat by outrageously overzealous *Exorcist* aficionados over the years. Those drippingly spray-painted pentagrams and inverted crosses were illicit yet truly fitting tributes to a horror film of such an unsavorily infernal sort as *The Exorcist* and, for torturously tenebrous terror-tourers such as we, such iniquity only added to the stairs' infamy.

As we continued, so very slowly and steadily, to make our way down, the place veiled us with a dreadfully disturbing atmosphere that made those 97 steps feel even *more* steep—even *more* fatal to the flesh—and yours cruelly was truly relieved when we gruesome twosome came to the bottom, stepping out upon the very spot where Father Karras, broken and battered from his suicidal plunge from poor possessed Regan MacNeil's bedroom window, died in a black pool of his own boldly self-sacrificing blood.

Looking all the way back up towards Prospect Street, yours cruelly was *truly* at a

loss as to how a flesh-and-blood stunt man, well before the time of digitally effected humans, verily took the priest's fall not once but *twice* for Friedkin's piety-offending opus. No matter how much foam rubber had been secretly affixed to each and every step, doing such a thing not once but twice would no doubt cause your sorry skull to twist about well more than Regan's did, would it not, Creepy Reader?

As we worshipped at the fiendishly befouled foot of that place of *The Exorcist's* last gasp, yours cruelly, the greedily gorging collector-ghoul that I am—and shall always be!—hungered to take some pieces of those slate steps back to our charnel house as a macabre memento mori of our communion with that loathsomely legendary location. But, alas, Creepy Reader, having failed to bring a hammer and chisel with us on this severed leg of our eerily egregious *Exorcist* exploration, I had to suffice with but my most grotesque memories of those nefariously notorious *Exorcist* Stairs. After a few minutes of celluloid crime scene photography, we gruesome twosome trudged back up to Prospect Street and returned to our meatwagon for the rest of our impiously profane and pestilent tour of the horror-haunts of *The Exorcist*.

Perhaps the thing about *The Exorcist* that frightened audiences so very ferociously upon its riskily untested release in 1973, Creepy Reader, was not the shockingly real and still-renowned special effects work of Dick Smith, the deeply disturbing and disquietingly diseased-throated utterances of the grievously uncredited Mercedes McCambridge, or even any of the truly unsettling editing and sound tools of the film-maker-as-terrorist trade of director William Friedkin but, rather, the film's "true" pedigree.

In 1949, when Blatty, who wrote the film's screenplay based upon his very own novel, was working towards his bachelor's degree at Georgetown University, the 20-year-old New Yorker came upon an article from *The Washington Post*, from the twentieth of August, that recounted the reportedly all-too-real story of a 14-year-old boy from a nearby Maryland neighborhood who had undergone the orthodox, yet seemingly obsolete, ritual of exorcism to purge his soul of an unspeakable impurity.

Throughout the three months during which the purportedly innocent youth was but a prisoner of that ungodly power, what was witnessed not only by the boy's family but also by the clergymen who ministered to him was said to have been the sordid and sinister stuff of nightmares: it was rumored that the teenaged boy made things about his bedroom shift and shudder violently; that he rabidly struck out at his horrified caretakers with unspeakably inhuman strength, screaming obscenities and speaking in tongues he could not have possibly known; that he snickeringly spat a vile spew at those piously praying priests from all the way across his bedroom; and, perhaps most unhallowedly horrifying of all, that the word "Hell" arose from the prepubescent pinkness of his possessed flesh.

Some decades later, Blatty, having found the sort of Hollywood comedy for which he had hitherto been employed as screenwriter since graduating from Georgetown a thing of a now-bygone age, began work on a novel woven about that unforgettable, and unforgettably terrifying, "true" tale of daemonic possession and exorcism he had heard all those long years before. And it was all said to have happened in Mount Rainier, the next stop of our cadaverously creep-ridden *Exorcist* campaign.

WILLIAM PETER BLATTY'S
***EXORCIST* HOUSE**
3210 Bunker Hill Road
(at the corner of Bunker Hill
Road & 33rd Street)
Mount Rainier

The somewhat simple and sleepy Washington, D.C. suburb of Mount Rainier was a little more than five miles from the terror-vomitting territory of 36th and Prospect in Georgetown and it was but a short while before we gruesome twosome found our horror-mongering selves prowling down the town's unassuming streets in search of the birthplace of *The Exorcist*'s deeply diabolic dread. In only minutes, we came upon Bunker Hill Road and parked our touring hearse. There was truly nothing either macabre or morbid about the town park and garden, with its gayly quaint gazebo and its beatific flower-blossoms, that we found at the corner of Bunker Hill and 33rd Street.

But such small-town serenity had not always characterized these Mount Rainier parts because it was on this very same plot of land that 3210 Bunker Hill Road had once stood: the home so very commonly held as that atrociously ill-omened abode at the black heart of that Washington Post-published case of possession.

It was here that the dreadfully infamous domicile is said to have stood, abandoned for some years after those bedeviled-doings of 1949 were rumored to have unfolded here. Sometime thereafter, it was burned down, either by accident or arson. In the late-'70s and early-'80s wake of *The Exorcist*'s nefariously horrific notoriety, the thusly vacated lot is said to have become a popular hangout for Mount Rainier's local teenaged burn-out population.

Believing that this was indeed the place where that poor boy once lived amongst such infamously Luciferian loathsomeness, these mischievous leather-and-denim-clad teenagers, looking to commune with the supremely profane spirit of the place, would haunt the property at all hours of the night, drinking cheap beer whilst dancing about inverted crosses they had erected in the charred earth to an impious cacophony of heavy metal chaos. Obviously in an attempt to put a very grateful end to such unwontedly unwholesome practices, the town had this very scenic park fashioned upon that corner of Bunker Hill Road and 33rd Street. So instead of the  ear-splitting sounds of Slayer and empty Schlitz cans, we gruesome twosome were greeted by flowers and park benches when conducting our autopsy of the cremated cadaver of 3210 Bunker Hill Road.

From Blatty and Friedkin to the BBC who produced 1998's phantastic *Fear of God* documentary—meant to celebrate the 25-year ban of the film in England—and the various other documentarians and authors who have delved into the "true" story behind *The Exorcist* over the years, all have further authenticated the widely accepted "fact" that those shuddersomely Satanic spooks of the late 1940s did indeed happen in the sober suburban sprawl of Mount Rainier, at that very corner where we two grisliest of grotesquerie gore-mets still stood.

However, more contemporary investigations into the real facts of that 1949 exorcism and its oft-reported, ill-reputed backstory have exposed that, verily, Mount Rainier's claim to Horror's most hideous infamies as the impiously profaned birthplace of *The Exorcist* is, simply, the persistent stuff of urban legend. But perchance, Creepy Reader, you would ask, if not Mount Rainier, then *where?* The tenebrously terror-tainted wellspring from which *The Exorcist*—the Blatty book and the Friedkin film both—and the "true" story behind them poured forth so very putrescently like so much daemonic puke lay no more than half a mile away in the small community known as Cottage City.

THE REAL *EXORCIST* HOUSE
3807 40th Avenue
Cottage City

We gruesome twosome were motoring yet again for but minutes before we came to the small, one-story house that resides at 3807 40th Avenue in the even smaller Washington, D.C. suburb of Cottage City. Identified by those *Exorcist* investigations to which yours cruelly had before only referenced, this—*not* 3210 Bunker Hill Road—was the *real* home of the ill-fated teenaged boy whose celebratedly terrifying and "true" tale of exorcism birthed one of the most fantastically fierce and frightening horror films ever made.

Although the nondescript brown house was smaller and perhaps somewhat more meager, it was no different from those that we passed earlier whilst driving through Mount Rainier. Why, then, do both local urban legend and the hideously rank annals of horror history allege, time and time again, that the birthplace of *The Exorcist*'s inspiration is Mount Rainier and not, in fact, the settlement of only 1,200 residents in which we gruesome twosome found ourselves? Well, it would seem, Creepy Reader, that the clergy who presided at that eldritch rite of exorcism and purged that infamous 14-year-old's soul of some unclean presence, in an attempt to assure his anonymity, attributed the creepy case of innocence's corruption to the neighboring burgh of Mount Rainier. And so a "fact" it became.

But once the actual location of those 1949 events behind *The Exorcist* had been sorted out, yet another question remains to be asked, Creepy Reader: was that 14-year-old boy, John Hoffman—a name as bogus as his Mount Rainier address—who lived at that simple Cottage City bungalow more than 50 years ago ever *truly* possessed to begin with? Such a thing has become yet another "fact" furthering *The Exorcist*'s fiendishly frightful ill-renown. Some sort of exorcism was indeed committed upon the teenager— by a pre-Merrin man of the Catholic cloth named Father Lawrence—

after his abominably antisocial aberrance harrowed and horrified his affeared single mother.

However, those post-*Exorcist* investigations of the circumstances of the seminal 1949 case have shed doubt upon whether any true possession tormented that Cottage City 14-year-old. Was the teenaged boy who dwelled within that modestly middle-classed abode which we espied that less than eerie spring day *truly* plagued by a fearfully infernal foulness not of this world? If the somewhat disreputable past of that now-notorious youth, John Hoffman, prior to those otherworldly 1949 occurrences is exhumed, it would seem that his deeply disturbing deeds and demeanor arose not from iniquitously daemonic influence but, rather, a disturbingly pseudo-sociopathologic strain of teenage disaffection.

Regardless of the thusly controversial truth of those momentously macabre exorcism matters, both the young boy's tortured family and the priests who heeded their desperate call—and, seemingly, the reporter from *The Washington Post* who chronicled their tale of wickedest underworldly woe—believed, *truly* believed, that the most profoundly primeval and pervertingly potent of evils had found an all-too-hapless home at that house on 40th Avenue. And the rest, Creepy Reader, is horror history.

Whether or not that teenaged boy was *truly* infernally defiled so despicably in 1949—and, ultimately, whether or not he lived in Mount Rainier or Cottage City—it was hard for yours cruelly to believe that such an ordinary home, in such an ordinary corner of Maryland, had begotten such a disturbing, and seemingly deranging, legacy of dreadfully extreme and inexorable horror as that which *The Exorcist* has vomited forth in its more than 30 years of exquisitely suppurated existence upon this graveyard Earth.

And so, Creepy Reader, after taking a few photos of this small Cottage City house, devil-possessed or not, from whose walls the horrendously ensanguined epoch of modern horror was heralded with a truly grotesque geyser of pea-soupy puke, we two horror-worshippers, awfully abhorrent adorers of celluloid atrocity, returned to our meatwagon and then, with morbid smiles upon our pallid faces, to our Charnel House, our journey into the Hollywood horror hell that is *The Exorcist*'s Washington, D.C. now complete.

Yours cruelly's very vilely vermiculosed expedition into the horrendous black heart of *The Exorcist* was well worth worming our way amidst the sometimes headache-breeding Washington, D.C. hustle and bustle, as I am certain it would be for any hell-born horror fiend who has ever been disturbed, dread-filled, and drained by Friedkin's 1973 macabre celluloid masterpiece. To descend down those steep, blood-drenched steps that have become so very infamous in the history of modern horror sinema was a deeply thrilling experience that neither my unspeakable wife nor I shall ever forget. Those sinister soul-hungry spirits of *The Exorcist* beckon, Creepy Reader: do you dare answer their call? But you would do *very* well not to play with any Ouija boards whilst you are there!

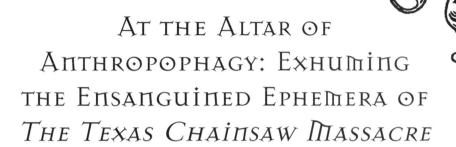

Chapter Ten

AT THE ALTAR OF ANTHROPOPHAGY: EXHUMING THE ENSANGUINED EPHEMERA OF *THE TEXAS CHAINSAW MASSACRE*

"Return to Texas
The grill is on
Meathook sharpened
And so is the saw . . . "

—Necrophagia
"Return to Texas" (2005)

C reepy Reader, the year was 1974. It was the year of my birth amidst the nuclear wastelands of Grue Jersey; it was also the very same year that a little film was shat out of the befouled, worm-ridden bowels of the collective American unconscious, a grueling exercise in sinematic terrorism that would not so much change the face of celluloid horror as peel its wrinkled flesh from the grinning skull beneath. This film—no, this *experience*, for that is what it *truly* is for those who worship at its eternally offal-adorned altar—that spilled out in a steaming sanguinolent surge from the slit throat of the rotting ruins of the American Dream was *The Texas Chainsaw Massacre*.

Even though I have seen *The Texas Chainsaw Massacre* more times than I can count since its horrors were first burned into the retina of my mind's eye 13 years after both it and yours cruelly were loosed into existence, Tobe Hooper's grisly buzzsaw opus, an excruciating homage to the gruesome regimen of man-eating, remains for me and coffinfuls of other like-minded fiends one of the utter epitomes of modern American horror.

Along with the likes of George Romero's zombified masterpiece *Night of the Living Dead* and Roger "Victor Janos" Watkins's Grand Guignol snuffie *Last House on Dead End Street, Chainsaw*—first called *Headcheese* and then *Leatherface*—ushered in this unrelenting epoch where visceral carnage was king. Gone was the horror of the days of yore, a safe sort of escapism found in the arms of the Wolfman or the Mummy where the horrors retreated back under the bed with the rolling of the credits and the comforting restoration of the status quo.

Chainsaw was cut from a far more tarnished and transgressive cloth. For this species of sinematic horror-beast left your world, like its victims, debauched, defiled, and desecrated—a quivering, gutted carcass stewing in its own piss. The savage misanthropy and ferocious nihilism of the Texas sun-scorched atrocity that is Hooper and company's *Chainsaw* was born out of the disillusioned idealism of the 1960s, the rape and ruin of its peace and love rhetoric.

The film's inverted fairy-tale nature represented its makers' bitter skepticism of the utopic safety promised by the American Dream; mirroring the horrors of the real world upon which they had been forced to feed since birth, *Chainsaw* stood as a seething "Fuck you!" in the face of this bankrupt illusion. To say it like it is, Creepy Reader, *The Texas Chainsaw Massacre* drove a howling, oil-spitting chainsaw up the ass of Americana. It not only served to define the gloriously depraved age of 1970s drive-in horror but to also set a standard for modern genre films that has rarely, if ever, been reached, let alone *challenged.*

With its pseudo-documentary feel and surreally nightmarish spirit, the inexorable terror of *Chainsaw*'s exquisite corpse had, *and has still,* the same skull-splintering impact as the horrendously holocaustic hammerblows of its burly Gunnar Hansen-portrayed überbutcher, the loathsome homicide-lusting lord of the charnel house, Leatherface. From the John Laroquette-narrated "true crime" introduction to the unforgettable final

tableau of Leatherface's macabre dance against the rising Texas sun, it is a death-train of mutilation hurtling deep down into the utter depths of human darkness. Not many things can be called godly, but is there *any* denying that *Chainsaw* is one of them?

So join me then, won't you, Creepy Reader, on my journey through the extricated entrails of that celluloid ode to human butchery and cannibalism, *The Texas Chainsaw Massacre!*

When my unspeakable wife and yours cruelly walked out of the air-conditioned confines of the Austin airport that weekday mourning and felt the dry heat already creeping across our tender flesh, we *knew* that we were in Texas. While it was thankfully devoid of the choking miasma of humidity that makes New Jersey summers so abominable, this simmering Texas clime let us know what it must feel like to be a raw slab of beef broiling within the guts of an oven—and summer had only just begun to work up a sweat. But, fearless explorers of the nethermost reaches of the macabre that we are, we let the June heat set the deliriously surreal atmosphere for our expedition through *Chainsaw*'s one-time sinematic abattoirs.

We gruesome twosome knew this carrion chainsaw-consecrated cruelty-campaign down the monstrous slavering maw of one of horrordom's most ravenous atrocities would be the proverbial be-all of our wealth of horrid journeys when we espied a freshly exterminated armadillo painting the side of the scorching Texas blacktop, its expelled viscera a deliciously putrescent shade of purple, which was a weirdly familiar sight as it was this same species of flattened Texas varmint that filled the screen seconds before the introduction of *Chainsaw*'s doomed vanful of teenaged prime meat. Basking in the gangrenous, gutted glory of this fly-swarmed omen, we knew that our execrable expedition of Texas extremity-exsection had truly been blessed by the gods of Horror!

BAGDAD CEMETERY
North Bagdad Road
and Route 2243
Leander
(512) 259-4855 (Bagdad
Cemetery Association)

Our first savory mouthful of *Chainsaw*'s vermiculated stew was the Bagdad Cemetery in the Austin suburb of Leander. We took Route 1431 out of Austin proper and west into Leander, passing the incessant succession of strip malls that seemed to have become indelible parts of Austin's corpus, until we came to North Bagdad Road (also known as Route 278) after about 10 miles. Turning up North Bagdad Road, we drove by an endless acreage of town house communities, the suburban sprawl made molded flesh.

It was at the very top of this sedate residential way that we came upon Bagdad Cemetery. It was *here*, at this wholly modest and well-kept boneyard dating back to 1857, nearly 30 years before Leander itself was incorporated, that Edwin Neal's deranged Hitchhiker performed his perverse graveside disservice, turning the exhumed bodies of the dead into the bizarre corpse-art witnessed in *Chainsaw*'s flash bulb-lit establishing shot.

Rounding the corner onto Broade Street (Route 2243), we motored slowly past the chainlink fence of the cemetery and then through the main entrance with its arching Bagdad Cemetery gate and posted historical marker (the graveyard is on Texas's registry of historic places).

We rolled down the dirt drive, coming around the dusty caretaker's shack, and then there it was! Although missing the carneous accoutrements with which they had been hung in *Chainsaw*'s grisly opening, it was not difficult to recognize the truncated column-topped gravemarker and casket-like above-ground tomb that had been the site of the Hitchhiker's ghastly necro-erotic artistry.

As we approached them through the arid stretches of the graveyard, our ears were met not by the noise of Austin's city limits but rather by the dull scraping of the gardening tools of the caretakers toiling harmoniously a few yards away. Covered in a skin of lichen, their common plot surrounded by a short stone wall, the funeral monuments, slumbering in the older, eastern portion of the cemetery, seemed like a place fitting not

the desecration that Hooper and company had visited upon them in 1973 but, rather, a decoration of flags and flowers, as the rest of the Bagdad Cemetery was. As we breathed in the solitude of the place, we pondered exactly how *Chainsaw*'s makers had been able to film such a ghoulish scene like *that* in a place like *this*.

After taking a few photos before these two monuments to grave-robbing, we decided to take our leave of the *Bagdad Cemetery*. Because we thought an actual recreation of the Hitchhiker's cadaverous ministrations in the name of gore might disturb the serenity of such a peaceful locale, we settled for a little morsel of its gritty charnel earth for the old curio cabinet back at the Krypt; however, because the soil was so very sun-baked, it was difficult to dig up even a meager sample without the proper implements. But my morbid bride, experienced as she is in the weird sciences, wet the parched earth with some water so as to expedite the memento-pillaging. Creepy Reader, what would a ghoul like me ever do without her?

RYAN'S HILLS PRAIRIE GROCERY
1073 Highway 304
Bastrop
(512) 321-2049

Bidding farewell to the despoiled haunts of the Bagdad Cemetery, we followed the very same journey unto a doom of dismemberment taken by that van-load of human steaks and so made our way east. Traveling in our rented meatwagon, we took the fireworks-stand-riddled Highway 71 for several miles, leaving the urban (and even suburban) wards of Austin behind for the more rural countryside of Bastrop County. Taking Highway 304 towards Gonzales, we found the roadside gas station where Sally Hardesty (Marilyn Burns, whose skin-tight hip-hugger bell bottoms still bring a tear to the eye) and her day-tripping companions stopped after their shocking introduction to *Chainsaw*'s cannibalistic clan in the form of the photo-taking, straight-razor-wielding Hitchhiker: Ryan's Hills Prairie Grocery.

A few miles down the left side of 304, the little market looked as if not a *day* had passed since it became a blood bedewed denizen of the black annals of horror after its prominent role in *Chainsaw* all those years ago. It was all still there: the rusted corrugated tin roof, the drooping porch awning, the wooden white walls with their peeling paint, and, ghoulest of all, the decades-old gas pumps that were just as dry as they were on that ill-fated summer afternoon when Sally and her chainsaw-fodder cohorts rolled up this same dusty drive. The *only* thing that could have made our visitation *more* nostalgic would have been the heady odour of thick cuts of succulently sauced human flesh being lovingly barbecued within.

After some photos of the time-damning exterior of this one-time human butcher shoppe, we two gore-mets stepped inside for a closer look at the place's shadow-drenched belly, where Jim Siedow's Cook dished out his gastronomic blights. The insides of the Cook's man-beef bistro were actually much larger and more modern than I had thought they would be. I must say, though, that I did not recognize any of the market's interior space from *Chainsaw*, Cook's specious rescue of the hysterical Sally to be specific; however, upon seeing an Employees Only sign on a door to the side, I supposed that it was in whatever room that lay behind this unassuming door where this expectations-confounding interior scene had transpired.

As my unspeakable wife and I wandered about the small offering of aisles, devouring every inch of the small market with our sanguinivorous eyes under the pretense of shopping, I truly wondered how many patrons who frequent Ryan's Hills know the role it played in the tribute to homicidal carnivorosity that is *The Texas Chainsaw Massacre*? Perhaps if they did they would rethink buying those salty strips of smoked meat.

Although I looked about for a rot-tisserie upon which some *sweet* young thing's torso was a-basting, I found only row upon row of the foodstuff found in any local convenience store. For while there was indeed much food to be found within, from soda and chips to more substantial fare like sandwiches and fried chicken, alas, there were *no* carneous victuals to sate the cannibal thirst I am sad to say, Creepy Reader. I thought of asking the teenaged girl behind the counter where yours cruelly could gorge upon a murderous delicacy such as this but decided to buy an iced tea instead.

QUICK HILL
Quick Hill Road &
Route 1325
Rocky Point

Departing from Ryan's Hills, that former recessed rustic locale of the Cook's charnel house brasserie, we headed back to Austin for the next course of our bloodily blightful buffet of *Chainsaw's* still-rotting remnants. As I had heard before we left on our excursion of ephemera exhumation, the Texas capital did not at all conform to the Wild West stereotype that northerners such as myself unfortunately hold of the Longhorn State. It was indeed a rather progressive town, offering an array of vegetarian eateries, organic food co-ops, little arty boutiques, and sundry "hip" establishments along Sixth Street, Austin's answer to Bourbon Street, and "The Drag" (Guadalupe Street). And driving about the hustle and bustle of the highways and byways that wormed through it, it was clearly evident that Austin was burgeoning, truly a city on the rise.

The telltale signs of this growth were everywhere. From the numerous sites of massive road construction meant to contend with a dilated flow of motoring commuters to the many indistinguishable housing communities that were in the midst of taking root, such a surge of development would be indeed difficult to miss. However, this prevalent commercialization of the city's identity and spirit seemed, to yours cruelly, to be not the least bit dubious.

As we drove through Austin and its surrounding burbs, we were treated to a tediously middle-class backdrop of strip malls, fast-food charnel pits, office complexes, and the unremarkable like. While there *was* a very distinctive flavor that rose out from beneath this truly expansive caul of "progress," it seemed sadly to be the exception rather than the rule. And nowhere was this unfortunate happening

more apparent than with our third taste of the rotten repast of *Chainsaw's* extant locales: Quick Hill.

Having returned to Austin from Bastrop, we took Interstate 35 to Route 1325 West, and it was here that we were introduced to La Frontera, a  mammoth development project that would, when all is said and done, consist of not only corporate complexes and housing units but, yes, for what would this world be without them, *strip malls*.

When we came down 1325, La Frontera was *everywhere*, roadside signs heralding its arrival like the coming of some sort of manna for the ailments of the unbrainwashed, unprocessed, and uncommercialized masses. And it was here, amidst all of this rising corporate indoctrination, that we found Quick Hill. But, Creepy Reader, you may be asking yourself, what part did this slowly devoured locale play in *Chainsaw's* nightmarish descent into depravity? Well, the wooded ridge on the outskirts of Austin that is known as Quick Hill was the home of *Chainsaw's* family slaughterhouse.

Exiting off 1325 and onto Quick Hill Road (also known as Route 172), it sat slumbering to our right. Or at least what was left of it did, as most of the hill had been utterly gutted to make way for more highway lanes, an enormous barren chasm marking the site of what will be State Highway 45. As we came around Quick Hill on 172, we did not see what remained of its northern face until we had already passed it, so we parked our borrowed touring hearse along the shoulder of the road for a closer examination.

Rather oddly, the wasted beginnings of Quick Hill resided at the entrance to what looked like the very heart of the La Frontera properties. It was also at this same spot that we had the opportunity to look out upon Old Country Road, which cut a path through the brush and trees that still covered Quick Hill. Gated off, the extinct roadway looked like it hadn't been used in years, at least not by the public; its surface worn away by years of wear and neglect and hard to distinguish from the stony soil that lay all about the gate. Despite its decrepit state, we knew that this was the *place!* Up this same aged road, hidden in the woods to the left atop Quick

Hill, had been the mysterious house where those witless Texas teens would find nothing but menace and mutilation at the malevolent hands of Leatherface and his freakish family of flesh-eaters.

The driveway to the actual house used in *Chainsaw* had led out to Old Country Road, and it was along this gravelly path that a handful of the flick's truly most violently vile scenes had been filmed, such as Leatherface's chainsaw-stifling of the ever-whining Franklin (Paul Partain) and Cook's silhouetted caning of the disobedient Hitchhiker. However, it was not until the film's final moments, with Sally's escape from the family madhouse, that Old Country Road and the house's driveway were most prominently featured.

When the gruesome twosome of Hitchhiker and Leatherface are chasing the terror-maddened Sally, it is first the driveway and then Old Country Road that she flees down; the latter can be best seen, from a northern perspective atop Quick Hill down towards where we now stood, when the pick-up truck driver aids her escape from out of the very mouth of madness. And it was also along Old Country Road that Leatherface later performed his lumbering, chainsaw-accented two-step before the ruddy backdrop of the red Texas dawn.

Alas, Creepy Reader, I had read the accounts and seen the photos of horror aficionados such as we who had made a similar pilgrimage to the altar of *Chainsaw* during which they had not only traversed Old Country Road, but had drooled upon both the driveway and the lot upon which the house had once festered. But because of the massive construction that was occurring just past the horizon of Quick Hill, we doubted if *any* of it still remained.

While we would indeed liked to have ventured up Quick Hill, as these others had before its dissec-

tion, to see if either the driveway to or the foundation of the family abattoir still remained, we thought it prudent *not* to test the validity of the stereotype of the severe bite of Texas justice by ignoring the No Trespassing signage that was posted all about the fences surrounding Quick Hill.

So it was from behind that gated fence at the toothless mouth of Old Country Road that we two gorehounds stood in devotion to the gruesome and grisly glory of what once was. It was oddly coincidental that we were standing there of all places, at this violence-tainted vestige of a bygone era, being erased by the encroachments of modernity, to pay tribute to the familial slaughterhouse of a cruelly carnivorous clan of Texas cannibals who were throwbacks themselves to an earlier age, isolated in their primitive brutality.

However, unlike Leatherface and his man-eating kith and kin, who hacked up for barbecue all who would trespass upon their den of mortal devourment and threaten their repugnant way of life, Quick Hill had no such antipersonnel capabilities, sadly defenseless in the path of progress. And so with it goes one of the *true* grue-adorned landmarks of American Horror.

★★★★★★★★★★★★★★★★★★★★★★★★★★★★★★★★★
KINGSLAND OLD
TOWN GRILL
"STEAKS ARE OUR SPECIALTY"

Celebrating
Aqua Boom 2000
1010 King · Kingsland, Texas 78639
Phone: 915-388-2681
Across From Antlers Hotel
(Closed Monday & Tuesday)
Open: Wed - Sun, 11-2 & 5-closed
★★★★★★★★★★★★★★★★★★★★★★★★★★★★★★★★★
47

THE KINGSLAND OLD TOWN GRILL
1010 King Court
Kingsland
(325) 388-2681

But what of the house itself, Creepy Reader? Well, before we had departed for our necrophilous campaign through *Chainsaw's* rank bowels, I had learned that the actual house, that anonymous backwoods abattoir drenched in the carneous cacophony of howling chainsaws and human screams, had been moved to the vacation town of Kingsland some years ago now. And so we left behind the slowly decomposing body of Quick Hill for an extant artifact from the heinously homovorous *Chainsaw* horrorshow.

Far out on Route 1431, Kingsland was about 60 or 70 miles west of Austin, past some rather remote, mountainous and cattle-crossed stretches. But once we made it to Kingsland, it was truly a bizarre feeling to be in such a picturesque locale as this only to feed upon a one-time human slaughterhouse! A serene retirement community as well as a seemingly popular vacation spot due to its adjacency to Lake LBJ, it seemed like the ideal spot to live out your twilight years rather than one to ruminate upon the mass celluloid mutilation of that so-called mortal coil. But indeed here it was, the *Chainsaw* house living out its own well-earned retirement after years of neglect during its inhabitance upon that now-highway-bound Quick Hill plot.

After *Chainsaw* was filmed there in 1973 and released the following year, the house apparently became a rather popular debauchery spot for Austin teenagers and thus suffered the abuse of various acts of drink-and-drug-induced vandalism. However, like the bruised and battered Sally at the end of the film, the late-nineteenth-century domicile received its own salvation in 1998 at the hands of Cheryl Brooks and her mother Noreta Genton, who bought the dilapidated dwelling and arranged its transport to Kingsland. After it was separated into seven pieces, it was moved, piece by piece over the course of five days, the same 70 or so miles that we had just traveled to the very location it now occupies along 1431 on the property of the The Antlers Inn on King Street.

As we pulled off 1431 and into the parking lot of what is now known as the Kingsland Old Town Grill, it was difficult at first to recognize that abhorrently atrocity-aroma-ed old abattoir. However, after deeper scrutiny, despite its masterfully renovated and pristinely white-painted façade, despite its porch full of cutesy, grandmotherly knick-knacks, and despite its flower-bed-bordered chlorophyllous lawn, the sanguinivorous spirit of that shuddersomest viscera-spattered abode of Texas anthropophagi began to show through such a ruse of refurbishment. And then there it was!

It was with a little hesitation that yours cruelly walked up the three steps that led up the house's porch and then rapped upon its wooden

door, as it was these same innocuous acts . . . mere moments before each of the two teenagers met their own execrably horrid hungry ends, the former by a savagely swung sledgehammer and the short-shorts-wearing latter upon torturous curve of a meathook.

But, deepest of red purveyor of the putrefacted that you know me to be, enter I did and it was as if I had stepped into the pages of my mother's old Lillian Vernon catalogs! The house's staircase, its banister wrapped in a glittering red-white-and-blue garland and its ascent populated with a few smiling animal welcomers, had been where Sally had fled the squealing wrath of Leatherface, scampering up these now-finely polished steps, only to later leap through the landing's window, and where Leatherface and the Hitchhiker had carried down their desiccated, corpse-like Grandpa (John Dugan) at the start of *Chainsaw*'s notoriously demented dinner scene.

Today, nary an inbred cannibal calls the house's second floor home sweet morgue but, instead, houses its current mother and daughter owners. And the curving main hallway beside the stairs, its white walls decorated with flowery wreaths and its ceiling hung with faux-antique brass lamps, was where the all-too-curious Kirk had shuffled down on his skull-crushing date with a seizure-wracked snuffing. As I said, despite the high sheen upon the wood and the saccharine cuteness of its decor, there could be *no* mistaking the *Chainsaw* house for just *any* ordinary homey restaurant!

After this initial examination, we were seated by the Flo-like waitress in the right-side dining room, this entire wing of the structure never used in the film because it was occupied by the home's then-owners during the duration of the shoot. After we had ordered our lunch, the options coming not from a menu but rather the scant list read to us by our waitress, we sat there with our wide bloodshot eyes in constant motion, our hunger to be slaked not by any of the down-home grub that would soon be served to us but by the  verminous traces of *Chainsaw*'s celluloid gutsfuck that had drawn us here like maggots to rot-blossoming carrion!

Creepy Reader, it was as surreal an experience as watching the film itself to sit there, surrounded by senior citizens chowing down upon the Grill's lunch special in a room whose creepiest decor was a huge cow's head with a toothpick in its mouth, discussing exactly *which* stomach-churning act of nastiness had happened *where*.

The front left dining room had been the family's living room in *Chainsaw*, its ghoulish adornments inspired by the Ed Gein school of interior design with furniture accented with and entirely fashioned from bones, skulls, and leather-made flaps of human skin, upon whose feather-strewn floor Pam had fallen just before her date with a meathook, perhaps the film's *most* violent scene, in what continues on today at the back of the house as the Grill's kitchen. The middle dining room behind it had been the family's own, where the bound and gagged Sally was made the terrified dinner guest at the disgusting banquet table of Horror-history's most hallowedly hideous horde of human-eaters.

This is *Chainsaw's most* notoriously disturbing and horrific scene, made even more so by by the all-too-real story behind its filming. Picture it, Creepy Reader: this very dining room, mere feet from where we sat that afternoon, its closed windows covered in black cloth to create the illusion of perpetual night-darkness, its stagnant, heat-choked air thick with the rank pungency of not only the formaldehyde-treated head cheese, sausage, and and other still-spoiling carneous shite spread out upon the long table as the family's supper (or at least its putrefying first course!) but also the actors' very own overworked sweat glands, most odiously so those of Gunnar Hansen, who, according to rumors, had only *one* suit to wear throughout the entire production! Taking some *26* hours to complete in the smothering heat of the Texas summer, this scene utterly *reeks* of the disquieting terror and disturbing torture that made *Chainsaw* such an archetypal study of the darkest foetid depths of human degradation and inhumane depravity. And no one, Creepy Reader, who has ever witnessed Hooper's film can forget it!

After our lunch, yours cruelly rose from the table to use the head and walked down that main hallway. As I got to the end and the doorway that led out into the corridor beyond, I must admit, Creepy Reader, that I looked about rather cautiously before stepping through it as it was at this one-time animal-skull-adorned entrance that Leatherface was unleashed upon the unsuspecting underworld of Horror, his tyrannous reign of terror heralded by the horridly holocaustic hammerings of his sledge and the sinister clanging slam of that steel slaughterhouse door.

Upon my return, we gruesome twosome took a few crime scene photos of the still-dripping insides of this former anthrophagous chophouse and then happily paid our bill, money well spent not so much for the home-cooked chow but, of corpse, the chance to sup within the walls of the house which made chainsaws and cannibalism sordid staples of the horror genre.

And as we stepped out upon that porch again, where the only teeth you will find these days being those fallen out of the mouth of some octogenarian after a gut-busting meal of chicken-fried-what-have-you, and looked out over the Kingsland Old Town Grill's picturesque digs, we two gleeful gore-mands of all that is ghastly thanked the horror gods below for the opportunity to visit a locale such as *this*, so deeply buried in the abominable grue-glutted annals of the macabre, a place known to ravening Horror-fiends the world over as the atrocious altar of unadulterated anthropophagy, that witnessed the shuddersome phantasma-gore-ic orgy of utter sickness that is *The Texas Chainsaw Massacre*.

And so, if you should perchance find yourself lurking through Austin and have an insatiable hankering for a truly foul taste of the mad and macabre, then you would do well to grab a shovel and exhume some of these same Texas locales forever besmeared in the blackest of blood by *The Texas Chainsaw Massacre*. You will *not* be disappointed! And, don't forget, Creepy Reader, if you should see a disheveled and drooling hitchhiker shambling down the side of the road ranting and raving to himself out under the blistering Texas sun, let him rot with the dead armadillos!

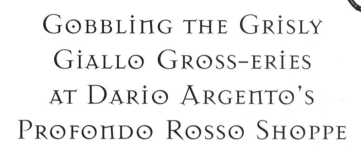

Chapter Eleven

GOBBLING THE GRISLY
GIALLO GROSS-ERIES
AT DARIO ARGENTO'S
PROFONDO ROSSO SHOPPE

A h, Roma! Risking being turned into a steaming pile of prosciutto by rampaging packs of Vespas, my unspeakable wife and I waded out amidst Rome's infamously trafficked streets to experience but a taste of the Eternal City's seemingly unending offering of wonders. We stood witness to the post-Passion of the Christ that is Michelangelo's masterfully chisel-conceived *Pietà* at the Vatican's Basilica of Street Peter. We savored the heady psychic residue of the orgiastic imperial bacchanalia of yore that smutted the very marble of the Palace of the Caesars. We pursued the spirit of Fellini's *La Dolce Vita* alongside Neptune and his Tritons in the penny-heavy waters of the almost six-century-old Trevi Fountain.

But no matter how many such artifacts and antiquities choked our Italy-tour's itinerary, alas, there was still something missing. Our less than wholesome appetites had been left sorely neglected by the City of Love's ubiquitous tourist fare, leaving us ravening for a perversely pleasing and profoundly blood-spattered plate of proverbial "Spaghetti Nightmares." Our hunger for the most sweetly twisted of gialli, for the most hotly carnivorous of celluloid bloodfeasts—for Italian Horror! And so our desire for the darkest of delicacies beckoned us to lurk beyond Rome's ordinary destinations to Dario Argento's Profondo Rosso, the unquestionable altar at which any Italian Horror sinemaphiliac must worship whilst in Rome!

PROFONDO ROSSO
260 Via dei Gracci
(06) 3211395

Festering mere blocks from Vatican City in a somewhat residential quarter of Rome that is populated by the likes of coffee houses, couture boutiques, and Catholic collectible kiosks, Profondo Rosso has its black roots in the obsessive depths of darkest Fandemonium, as it arose from the mutual horror devotion, concocting and collecting both, of that bloodcurdling "Italian Hitchcock" Dario Argento and his protégé in sinematic grue-gargling, Luigi Cozzi.

Argento bought the shoppe during his '80s reign as the Lord of Italian Terror with the intention of making it a place where he could sell horror memorabilia. But it was not until he rather literally handed the shoppe's keys over to Cozzi, that director of such Eurotrash as *Paganini Horror*, that Argento's intentions for the hitherto empty locale became more than mere unrealized aspirations.

Before he had been ordained by Argento as the high priest of his very own would-be Morbid Mecca of the Macabre, Cozzi had actually wanted to start his own store in the tradition of London's own Forbidden Planet, a place where Italian aficionados of the phantastic could commune and indulge their affinities—and addictions—for horror and sci-fi. Born from these shared entrepreneurial and curatorial urges, Profondo Rosso opened its doors on September 29, 1989, its raison d'etre seemingly embodied by Argento's statement to Cozzi that, "we'll fund a society, you and me, and create a temple of horror and sci-fi."

The shoppe was fashioned initially as a video renter, its shelves, appropriately enough, lined with thousands of horror and sci-fi titles. However, this earlier incarnation of Argento and Cozzi's mercantile monstrosity proved to be less than successful, at least monetarily speaking.

This all changed when Cozzi, his gray matter stretched by those early financial losses, decided not only to adorn Profondo Rosso's front windows

with a menagerie of monstrous miscellanea—a rubber and plastic bestiary of models, masks, and monsters, much of which was culled from Cozzi's own collection—but also, more significantly, to transmogrify the shoppe's stock from video rentals to horror and sci-fi collectibles and curios. This decision would seem to have been a thoroughly wise one, as Profondo Rosso has not only weathered those economic woes of its hideous infancy but has become the premiere attraction for horror devotees the world over who find their rotted selves creepy-crawling through Rome.

Thusly begotten by the gruesome twosome of Argento and Cozzi, owner and manager respectively, Profondo Rosso was rather unassuming, despite the gaggle of ghouls and goblins gladdening its front windows and its deep red-painted façade, looking as if the places had been bathed in the very same arterial spray from *Tenebrae*'s hatchet-amputated-stump-cum-blood-geyser.

The shoppe itself was comprised of a main floor—the store proper—and a basement, which has become Profondo Rosso's horror museum. With the former, almost everything was veiled with an authentic coating of dust, which left us sneezing rather than spooked out as we browsed through Profondo Rosso's splendid selection of shuddersome sundries. Of

these, there was a slew, there being *very* little empty space in the shoppe. The middle of Profondo Rosso's main floor was filled with boxes of horror magazines and comics, both old and new, in a babble of different tongues. The back wall was inhabited by row upon

row of rubber Halloween-esque masks, from the Universal Monsters and *Scream*'s Father Death, to those of a generally gruesomely ghoulish nature. Gorged into every cloying nook and noisome cranny were horror, sci-fi, and fantasy action figures and model kits.

Amidst all this, Argento's horrid oeuvre, as well as that of his dread-mongering kith and kin, was displayed in the form of a fine catalogue of video cassettes and DVDs. Further Argento worship could be had with t-shirts bearing infamous tableaux from his many sinematic opuses, such as the outrageous three-story-lynching from *Suspiria*. Also on the apparel front were both shirts and hats silk-screened with Profondo Rosso's logo, the former also featuring the place's mascot: the noosed, cleaver-holding baby doll from the promotional advertisements of the shoppe's namesake.

As we lurched with our coffinful of spook-ridden souvenirs towards Profondo Rosso's register (which Cozzi oversees himself more often than not, ready to not only ring up your ghastly goodies but parcel them in the shoppe's very own signature wrapping paper and shopping bags), we found many a possibility for a suitable soundtrack for our reminiscences of our time (and money) spent at the shoppe amidst the selection of albums from the likes of Goblin and Demonia (Claudio Simonetti's post-Goblin musickal endeavor) as well as some interesting horror score compendiums. And before we left, yours cruelly made sure to buy a copy of Cozzi's very

own book, *Giallo Argento* (a retrospective, published by Profondo Rosso's very own press, about his morbid-mentor's work, from 1969's *The Bird with the Crystal Plumage* to 2001's *Sleepless* and all the gory details in between), and had him sign it for me.

But such material-makings for wholesale consumptive gluttony aside, Profondo Rosso's real treat, the part about it that truly held the potential for provoking an utter "geek out," was what lay beneath: Il Museo degli Orrori di Dario Argento—Dario Argento's Museum of Horror, Profondo Rosso's celluloid atrocity exhibition dedicated to the director's mauled, maimed, and mutilated celluloid body of horror-works. Although the store itself opened in 1989, the Museum of Horror could not open until 1992, forestalled by what Cozzi refers to as "bureaucratic problems." Since then, it is here where Profondo Rosso holds all of its annual shocking Halloween sabbats and other Grand Guignolian galas, all attended by Argento himself.

For a mere three Euros, we gruesome twosome were given a ticket stamped "*Ingresso*" and a red velvet rope was let down (again, most likely by Cozzi's very own oft-gore-encrusted hand) to allow us to descend the tenebrous stairway that lead down into the bowels of Profondo Rosso and that den of Argento-nian iniquities therein. As we made our woefully wretched way down that flight of steps to the museum, on either side of us hung original posters, lobby cards, and other collectible ephemera from such Argento classicks as *Four Flies on Grey Velvet* and *Inferno*.

The basement-museum consisted of a long, brick-walled corridor with a number of cells branching off from it, the former painted the same Technicolor shade of sanguinolent red as the shoppe's outer façade and the latter cordoned off by black iron gates, imbuing the Museo with an utterly dungeon-like aesthetic and atmosphere, this no doubt also owing to the basement's inhabitance by an unhealthy number of cobwebbed skeletons and disembodied limbs chained to the walls.

Making a tour of the Museo all the more harrowing was the fact that its lighting was operated by motion detectors, which meant that standing in one place for too long whilst gazing all about us at its charnel house curiosities left us in the dark with only the cacophonous soundtrack of shrieks, moans, and creaking doors to keep us company down there in the pitch blackness beneath the shoppe!

The guts of Profondo Rosso's Argento museum were made up of veritable life-size dioramas (or, as Cozzi refers to them, "scenografic reproductions") paying tribute to Argento's infamous features from within the darkness of those cells on either side of the basement's corridor. Within the shadows of one such cell, the freakishly mutated monster-boy from

Phenomena lay in wait, spear in hand, to harpoon me like he tried to do to a pubescent (and pre-macromastic) Jennifer Connelly.

Standing beside this terror-faced tike was a tuxedoed puppet that could have been the cousin of that chill-inducing automaton from *Profondo Rosso*. In another cell, a daemoniacal head jutted out through a claw-shredded faux movie screen emblazoned with "Demoni" ("Demons") in homage to said extremely popular Lamberto Bava-directed, delirious, monstermoshing grotesquerie, produced and cowritten by the Maestro himself.

Amidst cells such as these, there were some non-Argento holdings to behold as well, such as likenesses of horrordom's favorite child-slaughterer Freddy Krueger and a sadly emasculated, light-saber-less Sith Lord Vader, both villains lurking within a cell seemingly meant to glorify the *giallo* grizzliness of Argento's *Opera* (both of them standing in for the noticeably absent effigy of a torture-plagued opera starlet, its eyes propped open by rows of straight pins and everything).

Cozzi's own work was not forgotten in all this Argento-philia, as yours cruelly risked being infected by some of the extraterrestrial spawn from the Profondo Rosso manager's own post-*Alien* gorefest, *Contamination*. Moving deeper into the shoppe's museum, the basement corridor widened into a semicircular chamber where even more morbid (in number and nature both) offerings could be found. The bare-breasted torso of a helpless damsel

stood chained behind an unfinished brick wall that will entomb her alive à la Edgar Allan Poe while, not far away, another somewhat nude female victim lay limply upon a slab.

While the former was no doubt inspired by Argento's absolutely vicious adaptation from *Two Evil Eyes* of his literary idol's "The Black Cat," the latter's source in celluloid was less certain. Perhaps Michele Soavi's sinisterly sublime *The Church*, cowritten and coproduced by Argento? Perhaps his own painful take on Gaston Leroux's *Phantom of the Opera*?

Unknown. Debauched, defiled, and done away with in the name of Italian Horror? Indeed!

Aside from such "scenografic reproductions" as these, the museum, naturally, boasted an assortment of props actually used in  Argento's fearful flicks. The most exquisite of these was without a doubt the butcher's assortment of human-carving knives that sat locked in a glass cabinet (next to what looks to be the face of *Profondo Rosso*'s wind-up puppet and the plaster cast of some Argento alum's mug—perhaps Anthony Franciosa's from *Tenebrae*?) upon one of the basement's red walls.

Not only was it awfully possible that these very blades had been made for some of the most memorable, and memorably stomach-churning, moments in the Maestro's homicide-mad oeuvre, but that some of them, perhaps all of them, had been wielded by his very own infamous, black-gloved hands, as he has the wonderfully morbid reputation of doing. Knowing this possibility made basking in the razor-whetted,

blood-weltered wonder of these woe-wrecking weapons an almost religious experience. But although Profondo Rosso was so very close to the Vatican, this brush with divinity was blessed by no other gods than those of Horror!

Whether you make the pilgrimage there for the horror-shopping or the macabre-museum-going, Profondo Rosso will not disappoint, particularly if you are an Argento-holic such as yours cruelly. Perhaps because of the "New Wave" flavor of the shoppe's white logo stenciled upon its crimson frontage, Profondo Rosso seems to stand as a terrifically terrible terror-born testimonial to Dario Argento's late '70s and '80s über-horror-splattered slay-day when his name, more so than that of his Italian blood brothers D'Amato, Deodato, and Lenzi (whether or not more so than the Gore-Lord Fulci's is another story!), was synonymous with not only Italian horror sinema, but Eurohorror as a whole and the gloriously notorious chunkblowing extremities and excesses therein. A visit to Profondo Rosso is a worthy excursion for any true worshipper of that iconic Italian Master of the Macabre, Dario Argento, when in Rome. Until next time then, *lettore di* Creepy Crawls—*Continui a decomporrsi!*

Chapter Twelve

EXHUMING THE MURDEROUSLY MORBID MYSTERIES OF THE HOME OF MICHAEL MYERS: A HORRID TOUR THROUGH THE HOMICIDAL SOUTHERN CALIFORNIA HAUNTS OF *HALLOWEEN*'S "HADDONFIELD"

"Bonfires burning bright
Pumpkin faces in the night
I remember Halloween

Dead cats hanging from poles
Little dead are out in droves
I remember Halloween

Brown leafed vertigo
Where skeletal life is known
I remember Halloween. . . "

—The Misfits
"Halloween" (1981)

n the spring of 1978, a 30-year-old USC film school graduate by the name of John Carpenter directed his third feature film. It had its roots in the horror-mongering of independent distributor Irwin

Yablans. Inspired by the seminal likes of *The Exorcist* and, in particular, *Psycho*, Yablans wanted to make a little, low-budget horror feature and wanted to make it with Carpenter, having worked with him two years before on the young director's gangbangered *Night of the Living Dead* exploitation redux, *Assault on Precinct 13*. What the would-be horror mogul had in mind for the burgeoning auteur was something Yablans called "The Babysitter Murders."

To give celluloid flesh to these plans for babysitter-predation, which suckled at the teat of carnage and carnality both, Yablans put his money (rather, the money of financier and producer Moustapha Akkad) on the partnership of Carpenter and Debra Hill, the latter not only the film's cowriter and producer but Carpenter's then-girlfriend. Carpenter agreed to not only write and direct the feature but also compose and perform its score for a paltry $10,000, this sum sweetened not only by the appending of "John Carpenter's" before the film's title but by some unknown cut of its box-office take.

Over the course of 20 days, the gruesome twosome of Carpenter and Hill made their little film. It was released but months later—mere days before October 31st. Having cost only $300,000 to make, it would eventually gross almost 200 times that in theatres, making it for many, many years the most successful "independent" film ever made. This movie, Carpenter's third and, even though he would make some 17 after it, the one he would be the most infamous for, was *Halloween*.

Its financial harvest aside, the truer crop sown by *Halloween*, the real reason why it and Carpenter both would go on to become household names, names spoken in whispers by the easily goose-fleshed and worshipped by the ghastliest of horror-ghouls throughout this graveyard Earth, was because it is an almost flawless exercise in celluloid terror.

With its holiday setting, its "Final Girl" finale, its predatorily subjective Panaglide photography, and, perhaps most arterially critical of all, its unapologetically gratuitous teenaged body count, *Halloween* exists as the archetype for a hitherto unknown sinematic sub-genre: the slasher film. It thusly begot the "stalk-and-slash" paradigm that would be gobbled and regurgitated umpteen times throughout the '80s and even into the very early '90s, making way for the birth of such similarly epochal, and profitable, horror franchises as those founded upon the original *Friday the 13th* and *A Nightmare on Elm Street*.

Of the Four Celluloid Horsemen of this 1980s Slasher Holocaust, Michael Myers was furnished with the most simple, stark, and spooksome of accoutrements. He had no daintily crafted human-hide-hood like that buzzsaw-masturbating Texas man-eater, no gaily coloured knit sweater like that garrulous child-killing Springwood burn victim, and no collectible phantastic goalie's mask like that brutalian Camp Blood-born genocidroid. No. All "The Shape" had were blue coveralls, black boots, a resplendently polished butcher's knife, and, most infamous of all, the now-iconic weird and wraithen, bluishly white-faced trick-or-treater's mask molded from William Shatner's very own mugging mug. And such outwardly grim austerity is perhaps apropos for the midnight murder maniac stalking and slashing a sinister swath through the film that slasher connoisseur Adam Rockoff called "a prime example of an anti-cerebral horror film": "Well-made and technically proficient" yet "not psychologically deep."

Despite this, throughout the years, many a film critic and cultural theorist have sought to manifest Michael Myers as an atrocity-wrecking avatar of sexual repression, his hewing and hacking as the declarations of some unconscious psycho-sexual manifesto, its neoconservative "rules" catalogued and burlesqued most explicitly by the winking self-conscious-ness of Wes Craven's 1996 post-slasher, *Scream.*

Even throughout the many, and inevitably lesser, sequels that would shamble in *Halloween's* blood-weltered footsteps, the sundry writers and directors therein tried to root the slash dementia of Michael Myers in heathenish blood rites, such pagan unholy passions kindled by the morbid Samhain fires flickering within the series's only "Shape"-less chapter, *Halloween III: Season of the Witch,* and culminating in the fanciful yet now-forgotten Thorn mythos of *Halloween 666: The Curse of Michael Myers.* Such maneuvers would seek to analyze and explain what, as Donald Pleasance's Dr. Loomis, Michael Myers's psychiatrist and nemesis, called "purely and simply evil." But for what is veritably the boogeyman, there is no "Why?" Only darkness—and *death.*

While Michael Myers was supposed to have hunted and hacked his torturously tenebrous trail of tyrannical terror through 'Haddonfield, Illinois,' this beguilingly banal deathbed of babysitter butchery named after the suburban sprawl where Debra Hill was reared amidst the nuclear wasteland that is New Jersey, Carpenter's *Halloween* was, in truth, born in sunny and serene South Pasadena and Hollywood.

And so, during a summer not so very long ago, a horrendously unwholesome hunger for the most horrifying of homicide called my crepuscular bride and yours cruelly to the West Coast so that we two most monstrously morbid mass-movie-murder-musers might be possessed by the black spirits of *Halloween*'s atrociously macabre, autumnal moribundity amidst that Southwest swelter. So join us then, won't you, Creepy Reader, on our journey throughout the man-slaughterous Southern Californian haunts that were *Halloween*'s "Haddonfield"!

During the 1978 production of *Halloween*, it was the job of Tommy Lee Wallace, the film's production designer, to not only turn a dime-store rubber Captain Kirk mask into the very face of unspeakable horror but, harder still, to transmogrify the sunny and hot environs of a vernal Southern California into those of an October-embraced Illinois. But Wallace's skillful masquerade is definitely worthy of praise, as any *Halloween*-ophiliac who undertakes an expedition to the film's "Haddonfield" will have some difficulty finding anything distinguishing, at least upon initial appearances, it as Wallace's filmic simulacrum of Midwest suburbia.

However, the fiendishly autopsical attentions of the true devotee of Michael Myers and his diabolical dread-dripping doings, can dissect out some telltale locales that are evidence that these seemingly innocuous locales in South Pasadena and Hollywood were indeed where Carpenter's celluloid season of the dead had once reigned. Such an unrelenting postmortem of *Halloween*'s Haddonfield begins in the former of these: South Pasadena.

"HADDONFIELD": OPENING SHOT
Oxley Street & Montrose Avenue
South Pasadena

Located on historic Route 66, South Pasadena is only six miles from Downtown Los Angeles. Carpenter and his crew were drawn to South

Pasadena's modest parts because, with its hushed, tree-lined streets, its historic Craftsman-styled bungalows, and, all throughout its almost four square miles, its easy-going atmosphere, it embodied Smalltown, U.S.A., its classic Americana exactly what *Halloween's* very own small town called for. And in the more than 25 years that have passed since Carpenter's film was made here, very little has changed. It is perhaps appropriate, then, to begin our tour of this neck of Haddonfield with *Halloween's* very own beginning, or, to be more exact, the beginning of the film's then-contemporaneous (by way of 1978) events.

Following Michael Myers's storm-sung and endlessly ominous escape from Smith's Grove Sanitarium on Devil's Night, *Halloween's* mourning unfolds upon an empty street that is as lively as the dead leaves scattered about its gray asphalt: welcome to Haddonfield. This first glimpse of that ill-fated little Illinois town was filmed at the intersection of Oxley Street and Montrose Avenue, Carpenter's camera looking west down Oxley and aimed at the very heart of the sleepy town, perhaps like the steely tip of the butcher's knife that Michael Myers will be using to carve up Haddonfield's teenaged populace in a matter of hours.

"THE STRODE HOUSE"
The corner of Oxley &
Fairview Streets
South Pasadena

Following the path of that opening shot, *Halloween*'s next funereal taste of Haddonfield can be found less than a mile away at the intersection of Oxley and Fairview Streets. For at this corner, across from the South Pasadena Public Library, was the Strode House, from which Carpenter offered audiences his introduction to Laurie Strode (the character named after one of Carpenter's ex-girlfriends). Jamie Lee Curtis was cast in the role of the young, naïve, and, most crucial of all, virginal high-school student primarily because of her horror pedigree: the mother of the as-yet-unknown actress was none other than Janet Leigh, star of Hitchcock's *Psycho*, which was, again, one of Yablans's deepest influences for this horror endeavor of his.

While the somewhat boxy, two-floor house is no longer as white as Laurie's chastity but a subdued beige and the car parked before its double garage is not a gas-guzzling Cadillac but a Scion as boxy and beige as the house, it looks just as it did when Curtis's Laurie, books in hand and dress down to her knee socks, stepped out into the nightmare-doomed world of film.

HALLOWEEN'S "AFTER SCHOOL WALK"
The corner of Fairview & Highland Streets and Highland Street approaching Meridian Avenue
South Pasadena

This Haddonfield Horror tour's itinerary ordered not by screenplay chronology but macabre resonance, we will turn, for now, Creepy Reader, not to Laurie's walk *to* school that seemingly unremarkable Halloween mourning but, in its stead, to her walk *from* school a few scenes later. When the 3:00 P.M. bell rings, Laurie and the all-American coquette Lynda, played by P. J. Soles, begin their walk home.

After Lynda complains about her Halloween night's profusion of teenage distractions, Laurie complains that, "as usual," she herself has nothing to do. As she speaks, they turn a corner distinguished by a cobblestone pillar a few feet tall and a knee-high cobblestone wall to the side of it. (Perhaps a testimonial to Southern Californian masonry, both can still be found today at the corner of Fairview and Highland Streets in South Pasadena.) Laurie's self-bemoanings made, the two continue to walk further along that cobblestone wall down what is tree-shadowed Highland towards Meridian Avenue, an exasperated Annie, played by Nancy Kyes (formerly "Loomis") rushing after them, asking them why they hadn't waited for her.

Now a threesome, the schoolgirls cross to the other side of Highland and keep walking homewards until Laurie suddenly stops, realizing that she has forgotten her chemistry book. As the other two try to convince her not to worry about it, Laurie looks back down the street and, Carpenter's minimalistic yet utterly chill-evoking synthesizers rising, sees a drab brown station wagon turning the very same corner about which they themselves had just come. It creeps ever so slowly past the three friends, Lynda asking whether or not the driver is Devon Graham. "I don't think so . . ." Laurie answers forebodingly as she stares, with no small hint of inexplicable fear, at the mysterious station wagon, looking as if its passing is as that of Death itself.

After the station wagon's driver turns to look at the three girls, the car speeds off down Highland, inciting Annie to yell, "Hey, jerk! Speed kills!" Framed by an ivy-swum, split-trunk tree and a plot of ivied lawn, the car menacingly screeches to a halt. This makeshift frame can be

easily found about halfway down the north side of Highland by a *Halloween*-iac with a vulture's eye for carrion detail. Stopped in the middle of Highland Street for a handful of skipped heartbeats, the station wagon then motors away, all three girls sadly ignorant of the fact that the car's shadow-shrouded driver, the "jerk," the "guy with a car and no sense of humor," is none other than Michael Myers, returned to his boyhood home of Haddonfield after 15 years of maximum institutionalization and hell-bent on having a killer reunion. This leaves Laurie's scolding of the now-sheepish Annie—"You know . . . someday you're going to get us all into deep trouble"—murderously portentous.

HALLOWEEN'S "HIDE & SEEK"
1017/1019 Montrose Avenue
(Montrose Avenue between Oxley & Mission)
South Pasadena

The next hacked-off leg of the three friends' walk home in *Halloween* was actually filmed back where Haddonfield was introduced but a few scenes earlier: upon Montrose Avenue between Oxley and Mission Streets. After Lynda takes her leave of Laurie and Annie, the two have only just continued on their way when it is again Laurie, Carpenter's creep-inducing score again knelling, who sees a tall, white-masked stranger lurking in the sidewalk before them, silently staring down at them as a meat-hungry wolf would two unsuspecting does. Before Annie can see him with her own eyes, he slowly lurches behind a leafy, red-tinged hedge several feet tall and is seen no more. Frightened, Laurie tells Annie what she has seen and even though the latter does not see anything herself, she stalks down the sidewalk towards that hedge to confront the "creep" but finds nothing, The Shape having very spookily disappeared and leaving Laurie visibly disturbed.

Unless you are a Michael Myers-ite with more than a cursory knowledge of botany, it will be difficult to determine exactly which hedge along this block of Montrose Avenue he had used for his phantastic disappearing act. But a very good possibility, after a process of firsthand investigation, is the somewhat ruddy hedge at 1019 Montrose Avenue. If not this, then the greener-leafed specimen one house further down, 1017 Montrose Avenue.

The fact that both of these have been considerably pruned in the two-and-a-half decades since Carpenter celebrated *Halloween* here, again, makes an exact identification of Michael Myers's foliaged camouflage a none too easy thing. Whichever of them it is (if indeed either), they would both make for horrendous, albeit far more humorous, additions to the mise en scene of any *Halloween*-atic's very own forensick photography.

"THE MYERS HOUSE":
FORMER LOCATION
(formerly 707 Meridian Avenue)
Meridian Avenue between
Magnolia & Mission Streets
South Pasadena

With such fearful features of Laurie and her friends' walk from school now sliced off this terror-tour of *Halloween*'s Haddonfield haunts, the film's clock will now be turned back to, again, that Halloween mourning and Laurie's walk to school. After saying goodbye to her father, Laurie starts on her way and is next seen turning the corner of what is the eastern half of Magnolia Street onto Meridian Avenue, almost a mile from that location of her house and only a matter of blocks from Highland Street. Laurie then crosses to the other side of Meridian, passing in front of 637 Meridian Avenue, whose hedged lawn and tree-lined sidewalk can be recognized with little difficulty. She then comes to the intersection of Meridian and what is the western half of Magnolia Street, where she is met by Tommy Doyle (Brian Andrews), Laurie's boogieman-affeared babysittee.

Walking down Meridian towards what is Mission Street, Tommy asks her why she has taken this particular route to school that Halloween mourning. As she tells him that she has to drop off some keys for her real-estate-salesman-father, they come to it: the Myers House, where, 15 years ago, a little Michael Myers shockingly stabbed his post-coitused older sister to death—his diminutive, knife-wielding hands played by those of Debra Hill—in what is perhaps one of the most sublimely horrific opening scenes in the black, bloody bowels of Horror.

However, any *Halloween* horror-adorer who would like to visit that very same location of this spook house that had witnessed the woeful birth of Michael Myers will be sorely disappointed. While the Myers House, that dwelling that represented all of Tommy Doyle's boyhood fears, had once stood at 707 Meridian Avenue, only two houses from Magnolia Street, it stands there no longer. In fact, whatever else had stood on the 700 block of Meridian Avenue along with it has since been removed to make way for the construction of what looks to be some townhouses.

Alas, although you can see a whole crew of contractors and day laborers pounding nails along that stretch of Meridian, you will espy nary an emotionless, clown-dressed six-year-old with "the Devil's eyes" committing sororicide there today, as sad as that may be.

"THE MYERS HOUSE":
PRESENT LOCATION
(South Pasadena's "Century House")
1000 Mission Street
(the corner of Mission Street &
Meridian Avenue)
South Pasadena

But no tears, Creepy Reader, for while *Halloween*'s Myers House no longer festers with an almost supernatural malevolence at 707 Meridian, it does still exist. This sister-slaughterhouse of Michael Myers is in fact known as the Century House and is one of the oldest standing residences in South Pasadena. Declared a cultural landmark by the town some years ago, it was saved from destruction and moved to the corner of Mission Street and Meridian Avenue, only a 100 or so yards away from its former location.

Curiously enough, it was actually moved across from what was Nichols Hardware in *Halloween*, which Annie's father, Sheriff Brackett (Charles Cyphers), tells her and Laurie, on their way to an evening date with slasher infamy, was robbed by some "kids" who "only took a couple of Halloween masks, some rope, and some knives." Located at 964 Mission Street, it is today part of the Mission Meridian Village Information Office (whatever that is).

Since the move of the Century House, though, that olde Myers House has undergone massive renovation. Gone are its dingy and peeling white-painted façade, hanging gutters, and broken and boarded-up windows. Painted a coat of light blue with lovely red and white trim, given a fresh set of redbrick front steps, and adorned with healthy green plants, the house that sits, somewhat askew, at 1000 Mission Street looks much different than it had in *Halloween* back in 1978. However, it is the structure's singularly carved porch roof-posts that testify to the Century House's place in the sanguinolent, worm-lousy annals of Horror.

While the house has since been separated into leasable office space (some of which is occupied today by a design studio, a chiropractor, and a financier) and while the house's made-over appearance has dissipated some of its former haunted house ambience, standing before it or upon its shadowed porch can still call forth the macabrely black spirit of *Halloween* from the very place's wooden skeleton. No matter how genteelly it has been restored since Carpenter and his crew filmed there, it is still the perverted blood-unblessed birthplace of one of celluloid horror's most black-presenced boogeymen: Michael Myers.

With not only the Myers House but also South Pasadena hacked from the itinerary of our repugnant grave-robbing of *Halloween*'s Haddonfield Horror-Haunts, we gruesome twosome creepy-crawled next some 13 miles west to the glitz and glamour of Tinseltown—Hollywood! Although South Pasadena hosts the vast majority of unsavory *Halloween* stalking stuffers, there are two locations from Carpenter's film in Hollywood that make up for this scarcity with sheer and utter grue-gargling ghastliness: the Wallace House and the Doyle House. And my unspeakable wife and yours cruelly found both of these otherwise anonymous smalltown abattoirs upon the very same street about a mile and a half from the skidrow-throned tourist Mecca that is the Hollywood Walk of Fame.

"THE WALLACE HOUSE"
1537 North Orange Grove Avenue
West Hollywood

Practically in West Hollywood, we came upon the Wallace House can be found at 1537 North Orange Grove Avenue and is indeed the more diffi-cult of the two Haddonfield dread-domiciles to recognize. Since Carpenter and crew filmed their little experiment in babysitter-murder here in 1978, the home has undergone sizeable renovation and expansion. Not simply has a white fence been erected about the front of the property but, more substantially, a two-floor addition, comprised of a garage below and what looks to be living space above, has been built upon that home of little Lyndsey Wallace (Kyle Richards).

This construction has almost doubled the width of the now-yellow Wallace House, as a result getting rid of not only the left-hand side of the home around which an utterly terrified Tommy Doyle had witnessed Michael Myers carry Annie's limp corpse but also, yours cruelly can only suppose, the backyard garage where her brutal strangulation had happened.

Regardless, it is the house's two railings, the first about the front porch, upon which a flickering jack-o-lantern had sat, and the other atop the second-floor porch, that stand as wood-hard evidence that this was indeed where most of Michael Myers's savage spooks-shadowed Halloween of '78 snuffery had come down: again, the foggy-windowed-car-throttling of Annie in the garage around the back; the gravity-defying butcher's knife impalement of Bob (John Michael Graham); and, lastly, Lynda's garroting by telephone chord while talking with a thoroughly creeped-out Laurie. Try as they might, the present-day owners of the made-over 1537 North Orange Grove Avenue cannot exorcise the thusly-seeded spirits of horror from *Halloween*'s Wallace House.

"THE DOYLE HOUSE"
1530 North Orange
Grove Avenue
West Hollywood

As in Carpenter's film, cater-cornered across the street from the Wallace House is indeed the Doyle House, where Laurie babysat Tommy, and eventually Lindsey too,

on that ill-omened Halloween night. Standing at 1530 North Orange Grove Avenue, the Doyle House looks much as it did in 1978, with the exception of some relatively minor cosmetic alterations: a glass-paned front door; taller and fatter hedges between the stout brick pillars about the home's front lawn;

and an iron gate closing off the driveway from *Halloween* trick-or-treaters with an unhealthy penchant for trespassing. But the streetward façade of the house looks relatively unchanged from how it did when Michael Myers had stalked Laurie there in the dead-darkness of Halloween night.

The most recognizable things about the house are indeed found at the front: the small roof over the front steps, supported by two Roman-esque columns, and, built upon this, its bannistered second-floor landing. In *Halloween*'s bloodcurdling finale, with Loomis emptying his revolver's slugs into the already knitting-needled and coat-hangered bulk of Michael Myers, it had always seemed as if the obsessive headshrinker had blown The Shape out of the house's front windows and, thus, into its front yard. But not so, as, upon a closer investigation of that very same railing-decored face of 1530 North Orange Grove Avenue, Michael Myers's fall and feigned death must have actually occurred at the back of the Doyle House.

This home, Hollywood's 1530 North Orange Grove Avenue, was indeed the Doyle House of *Halloween*'s Haddonfield, where not only little Tommy Doyle but Laurie Strode and Dr. Loomis too learned that the boogeyman was real—and that his name was Michael Myers. This was where The Shape arose from his own death, to the bone-chilling tune of Carpenter's theme, in doing so, becoming the primeval slasher, endlessly imitated but very rarely duplicated in terms of his utter dreadfulness, seemingly existing as the very embodiment, like an apple full of razor blades, of all that is dark and dangerous about Halloween. As Carpenter has said, "There's something really creepy about the fact that evil never dies." Indeed.

With this eerie and execrable exploration of John Carpenter's *Halloween*'s Haddonfield now gutted and flayed upon the writerly butcher's block of yours cruelly, there is time enough for one more stop before I bid you a homicide-lusting adieu. In the late summer of 2003, rabid aficionados of the slasher were finally given what they had been anxiously awaiting for well over a decade: *Freddy Vs. Jason*. More "slasher action eek-stravaganza" than the "ultimate hack-and-slash apocalypse" that so many worshippers of Jason Vorhees and Freddy Krueger had been asking for, reviews from within and without the world of horror fiendom were mixed.

Despite this, the film's lucrative box-office take inspired Hollywood production houses to devise celluloid monster-man match-ups of their own making. First, from Dimension Films, there was the proposed "Michael Myers Vs. Pinhead" concept that was itself mutilated into so much headcheese by fanboy back-slash. Then, from *Freddy Vs. Jason's* very own sleepaway camp, came the possibility of a "Freddy Vs. Jason Vs. Ash" triple threat, a stillborn abomination that has come and gone (and come and gone again) like a very, very bad dream.

However, what if the difference, so to speak, between these two bastardized blood-bathed bouts was split like so much nubile, teenaged flesh? What if there was a hellish, hellacious, and horror-choked head-on collision between John Carpenter's Michael Myers, "The Haddonfield Shape," and Wes Craven's Freddy Krueger, "The Springwood Slasher"? What would a match-up between these two morbidly murderous madmen *really* be like?

"THE THOMPSON HOUSE: 1428 ELM STREET"
1428 North Genesee Avenue
Los Angeles

Well, Creepy Reader, after worshipping before the altar of Carpenter's All Hallow's Evil at those two houses on Hollywood's North Orange Grove Avenue, we gruesome twosome had to do but two minutes more Hollyweird lurching to approximate such a potential match-up. For only two or so blocks east of the Wallace and Doyle Houses is yet another utterly notorious slasher-hell-house: 1428 North Genesee Avenue, better known to devoted followers of the Razor-Fingered Glove and the Red-and-Green-Striped Sweater as *A Nightmare On Elm Street's* 1428 Elm Street.

In Wes Craven's 1984 oneiric slasher, this quaint house was that of Nancy Thompson (Heather Langenkamp) and her alcoholic divorcée-mother (Ronee Blakley). It was here that the child-killing fiend of a

1,000 bad dreams, Freddy Krueger (Robert Englund), terrorized young Nancy while she slept, lusting like the über-pervert that he was for her sweet, young soul.

Besides the fact that, today, the house at 1428 North Genesee has not a red but a green front door (even though, curiously, the first floor windows do indeed have red shutters), it looks no different than it did when, two decades ago, Craven filmed his own archetypal entry in the "slasher" phenomenon here. What makes it most recognizable as the Thompsons' home on nightmare-cursed Elm Street are its rounded, column-supported portion of the roof over the front door, replete with hanging light fixture, and its oddly green-shingled and sloping roof. Alas, the lack of bars upon the dozen front windows is evidence that, sadly, none of the present-day residents of what was 1428 Elm Street have been plagued by sleep-daemons of the Krueger-ian sort.

But in *A Nightmare On Elm Street*, even though Nancy would make one big anti-Freddy booby trap out of this house and seemingly defeat the nightmarishly returned Springwood Slasher in the film's finale, as happened with Michael Myers only two streets away, again "evil never dies." And so Freddy, like Michael, kept slicing and slashing casts full of victims feature after feature. Six sequels, a television series, and one *Freddy Vs. Jason* later, there is still no end in sight. So, again, what if Elm Street's grotesque phantasma-gore-ist did indeed find his immolated self charred-face-to-white-masked-face with Haddonfield's very own brutish Samhain-iacal butcher? Pray we never know, Creepy Reader. Pray we never know. Leave it to your own sick and twisted fancies to hack out this story of super-slasher-slaughtering.

To some horror-fiends and gore-adorers, *Halloween* is the definitive slasher film—not simply the first, but the *best*. But such ranking estimation aside, there is truly no debating that John Carpenter's taught low-budget terror-feast is one of the most important horror films ever made. And for any bloodthirsty disciple of the slaughter-cult of Michael Myers, whether you worship him by way of the Thorn or simply as the boogeyman, an expedition amongst his Haddonfield haunts spread all about South

Pasadena and on Hollywood's North Orange Grove Avenue will be a profoundly putrefacted pilgrimage to the harrowingly horrid black-heart of *Halloween* itself and, needless to say, will not disappoint. So grab your Halloween mask and your trick-or-treat bag full of butcher's knives, Creepy Reader, because the babysitters are waiting!

Chapter Thirteen

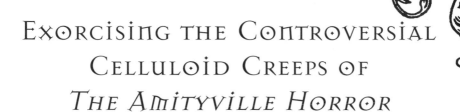

EXORCISING THE CONTROVERSIAL CELLULOID CREEPS OF *THE AMITYVILLE HORROR*

"I accept the pain
A vow unto contagion
Take my soul
Putrid sacrifice ordained
Defiled in demonic fluids
Showered in eternal bliss
Annointed with new life
Baptized by demon's piss"

—The Ravenous
"Baptized By Demon's Piss" (2003)

ot so very long ago, Creepy Reader, my unspeakable wife and yours cruelly bid a sorrowful farewell to our beloved home in Grue Jersey for the eeriest eastern extents of Rot Island so that she could further her minor medical malpractice and I could pursue my doctorate in the dreadfullest esoteric disciplines (also known as composition and literature to the layman). As we gruesome twosome were transplanting our Charnel House thusly, our butchermobile motored past something that seized my abhorrently unwholesome attentions: an exit sign along the Rot Island Depressedway for the scandalously shuddersome South

Shore suburb known to paranormal investigators and Horror-worshippers alike as . . . *Amityville!*

But 20 miles from New York City, Amityville is whispered with the same teeth-chattering tone as H. P. Lovecraft's Arkham, Stephen King's Salem's Lot, or John Carpenter's Antonio Bay, but the difference between them and Amityville is that it wasn't born out of the foully fertile fear-fiending fancies of writers and directors.

Although this Nassau County village, but two-and-a-half square miles in size, and its almost 10,000 inhabitants, are indeed *very* real, Amityville has verily *become* a fiction, at least amidst the collective gray matter of a morbidly infamy-mongering popular culture. Its repute and renown—both utterly *ill*—have become stained so very sinisterly by the suspect spook-seeping shadow thrown by the 1977 Jay Anson book and the Stuart Rosenberg-directed adaptation that declared the notoriously nefarious Horror of this otherwise simple and sleepy Rot Island town to a bloodcurdled and bone-chilled American populace.

Both of these creations were based not only upon the hideously horrid late 1975 hauntings at the Lutz family's 112 Ocean Avenue house, but also the revoltingly all-too-real multiple DeFeo murders that defiled that very same Amityville abode but a year before, a creep-ridden and still-controversial case—professed to be not only "A True Story" but "the non-fiction *Exorcist*" by Anson's publishers, Prentice Hall.

The resulting combination is a delectably delirious example of what happens when "true crime" fact is mixed with "haunted house" fiction to beget a macabre Horror icon of truly monstrous magnitude that spits forth a sickening swarm of Satan-unblessed black blowflies into the very face of those hair-raisingly paranormal "horrors." And, in so doing, fostering both the *continuity* of its infamous causes and egregiously excruciating effects, and, in the end, the *quality* of its heritage of celluloid horrorshows.

Simply put, Creepy Reader, regardless whether that "true story" of the Lutzes' harrowing 1975 hauntings is indeed evinced as less than true or whether its olde 1979 sinematic testament is indeed nothing but "remarkably unscary, conventional stuff" as cult gorehounding critic Chas. Balun deemed it, Amityville's "horrors," whatever medium tells its sensational and sordid tale of unnaturalest terror, would seem to know no end.

And so some time after my black bride and yours cruelly had interred our loathsome selves into our new Rot Island Krypt, we had all but forgotten about Amityville. But happening upon *The Amityville Horror* on some cable television station on an evening not so very long ago, we recollected how very close indeed we were to where those dreadfully diabolic 112 Ocean Avenue doings had unfolded 30 years ago. With such an ill-omened reminder of ill-famed Amityville's foulestly supernatural frights, we gruesome twosome concluded that we would finally pay this nefariously noisome Nassau County neighbor of ours a visit—in the viciously vitiable *Creepy Crawls* jugular vein! So join us then, Creepy Reader, on our journey into the black belly of the haunted house beast that is the Amityville Horror!

After our meatwagon had motored along what seemed like a ridiculous slew of Rot Island roadways—the Northern State Parkway, then the Sunken Meadow Parkway, then the Sagtikos Parkway, and then the Southern State Parkway—we gruesome twosome finally—finally!—came upon what we had crawled from the carrion-comforts of our Krypt for: *Amityville*! Or, at the very least, the exit sign for it onto NY-110 South.

Putting the Southern State Parkway behind us thusly, we made our woe-begetting way further southwards towards Rot Island's South Shore until yours cruelly wheeled our touring hearse eastwards upon Merrick Road, or Montauk Highway, which skirted the South Oyster Bay and then, once across the Suffolk County border, the Great South Bay.

As we lurked deeper and deeper into Amityville, what we found was a simple and somewhat modestly sized middle-class New York suburb that utterly belied its profoundly perverse popular-cultured portrait: a dreadfully decadent and decrepit brine-weltered wasteland plagued still by its abominably accursed past. No, yours cruelly espied nothing about that "Friendly Village"—settled sometime in the mid-seventeenth century by colonists from Huntington and, thus, called Huntington West Neck South until 1846 when, as local legend would have it, the village was given the name Amityville after a thoroughly discordant town meeting that was dulcified by a desperate plea for "amity"—that attested to the terrifying eldritch taint of wicked Satan-worshipping witches or diabolically degenerate Indian tribes. But we two horrid haunted-house hunters resolved to resist making any final judgments until we had explored the hideous black heart of Amityville's Horrors: 112 Ocean Avenue!

THE DEFEOS' & THE LUTZES'
112 OCEAN AVENUE
(Now 108 Ocean Avenue)
Amityville

In the very early hours of November 13, 1974—3:15 A.M. to be exact, at least according to the strivingly shocking paranormal mythos of *The Amityville Horror*, the book and the film both—23-year-old Ronnie DeFeo, Jr., commonly known as "Butch" to his family as well as the locals of that very same simple and rather sleepy village of Amityville my black bride and yours cruelly were lurking amidst that very day, stalked through his family's humble abode with a .35-caliber Marlin rifle and, as if they were no different than the deer he was very familiar with hunting, slaughtered all six members of his sleeping family: Ronald "Big Ronnie" DeFeo, Sr., aged 43; Louise, aged 42; Dawn, aged 18; Allison, aged 13; Marc, aged 11; and, lastly, John Matthew, aged 9.

With the very same disquieting cold-blooded deliberation with which Butch had walked from room to room, discharging his rifle into each of their blindly slumbering bodies—only one shot for each of them—he slunk through that Amityville home retrieving spent shell casings and anything else that he believed would incriminate him. Stuffing all of such crime scene evidence into a simple pillow case, he fled the DeFeo house under a pall of mourning darkness, dumping that rifle into the cold waters of the Great South Bay but blocks away and that swollen make-shift sack into a Brooklyn sewer. Returning to Amityville some hours later, a horrified and hysterical Butch burst into a local tavern, Henry's Bar, and declared to his beer-sipping cronies that he had returned from work only to find his mother and father dead in their beds.

After his friends from Henry's Bar helped Butch search through the home, indeed finding not only his parents' corpses but those of his four younger siblings, the police were called to investigate those most nauseatingly nasty murders. Almost twenty-four hours later, Butch DeFeo was the homicide detectives' prime suspect, their suspicions based upon finding his rifle's empty box hidden in his bedroom. According to police accounts, it was that very same night that Butch had confessed to the killing spree after his desperate and desultory attempt to make a "mob hit" of the murders—feeding into allegations of his maternal grandfather's involvements with the Columbo crime family's infamous iniquities—had failed to withstand his skeptical interrogator's scrutiny.

On October 14, 1975—almost a year after the six reports of that Marlin rifle had rung out like the death knell of Amityville's former anonymity— was Butch DeFeo's trial for that shockingly heinous sextuplet of homicides, which had utterly horrified that hitherto so very tranquil South Shore town. And it was during his trial that his defense-planned plea of insanity was first professed and, seemingly for naught, as, but a little more than a month later, he was found unanimously guilty on all six counts of second-degree murder, each of them carrying a 25-year-to-life prison sentence.

However, it was during his subsequent appeal of these convictions that his alleged murderously mental aberration was metamorphosed into something deeply more macabrely diabolic. Butch told a tenebrously terrifying tale of daemonic possession: the vilest of impious voices whispering the dreadfullest of deeds into his all-too-defenseless ears, telling him, at least as the 2005 remake of that celluloid *Horror* would have it, to "Katch 'Em & Kill 'Em"; "a pair of black hands" bringing him that .35-caliber rifle; sinisterly wraithen shadows bringing him, like some bedeviled slave, from one bedroom to another in his family's house so that he could slay his sleeping loved ones in the name of Satan.

But Butch's scandalous spookshow stories were sneered at as the simple possessed-play-acting of a sociopath, at least until December 18 of 1975, only 13 months after those mass DeFeo murders, when the newly married George and Kathy Lutz and her three children moved into that fiendishly exterminated family's eerily empty Amityville home. And verily, Creepy Reader, it was this infamously paranormally-terrorized 28-day-long inhabitance of the Lutz family that would not only make that Rot Island village of Amityville utterly synonymous with fearful haunted house frights, but the DeFeos' abominably atrocity-apalled abode at 112 Ocean Avenue into a now-definitive disgustingly death-disgraced domicile of darkest diabolic desecration. And it was before that very same home of *The Amityville Horror* we gruesome twosome finally found our loathsome selves!

Having motored along Merrick Road for little more than three miles, yours cruelly saw the street sign for Ocean Avenue to the right of us and so wheeled our butchermobile down it. After but two blocks, we turned right again, this time upon South Ireland Place, and there pulled to a dead halt along that so very scenically tree-adorned street. Disembarking from our touring hearse into what looked, to yours cruelly's bloodshot eyes, as a somewhat affluent stretch of Amityville—what with the big and beauteous yards and the driveways parked with luxury automobiles and boats—my unspeakable wife and I lurked to that corner of South Ireland, as, only opposite from us, Creepy Reader, was indeed 112 Ocean Avenue, the three-story Dutch Colonial dwelling, built in 1925, that had bore a wickedly woeful witness to the savage slaughter of the DeFeos and, a little more than a year later, the terrifyingly unhallowed torment of the Lutzes almost 30 years ago now.

But Horror-hungry ghost-hunters such as we would have none too easy a time actually finding a house along Ocean Avenue numbered 112, as, sometime ago, exactly when unbeknownst to yours cruelly, the property upon which it had festered so very infamously was reapportioned as 108 Ocean Avenue, this done in an attempt, by its then-present owners, to avoid the annoyingly unwanted attention of the all-too-curious, something which, by our putrefactedly perverse presence across Ocean Avenue from it, would seem to have been less than effective! But this was the least of the differences about that otherwise normal Amityville home that was indeed *Amityville Horror*'s notoriously real-life haunted house of hellish horrors.

For the very same reasons as its address change, 112 Ocean Avenue has also undergone some heavy remodeling since those maleficent days of murder and daemonic mayhem of the mid-'70s. Whereas then it was a deeply dark brown with white trim, the house has since been painted a less somber shade of tan, something much more similar, curiously enough, to the colour of that ill-omened "dream house" witnessed in Amityville's 1979 spookshow simulacrum. Also gone were the latticed adornments that had, before, ornamented its first-floor windows as well as its front lawn's former religious statuary.

However, Creepy Reader, the most notable difference about Amityville's *Horror* house was that one fanciful architectural feature that would seem to have symbolized so very sinisterly the shockingly Satanic stygian soul of 112 Ocean Avenue: its windows—those eerily eye-like windows that had testified to the extremity of this Amityville abode's evil upon the cover of Anson's 1977 book and, later, the promotional advertisements of posters for its 1979 celluloid adaptation. However, since those two "true story" works and the unseemly notoriety that both of them heaped upon the head of this sleepy South Shore village, the quarter-moon windows that had looked out upon Ocean Avenue from the home's third floor have been replaced with shuttered square frames.

It may interest you to know, Creepy Reader that those "eyes" of that former No. 112—one of which, verily, had peered out from what had been Butch DeFeo's very own bedroom—were not located upon the front of the house but actually, so very appropriately, its left-hand side. Because the lot of land on which this *Amityville Horror* house festers is narrow yet very long, extending from Ocean Avenue to the Amityville Creek that the property abuts, the somewhat sizeable home sits sideways upon it. But despite the absence of those weird woe-foreboding windows as well as those other, more subtle, differenes, Amityville's 108 Ocean Avenue looked extremely similar, at least to yours cruelly's bloodshot eyes, to its heinously infamous *1970s Amityville Horror* self.

While we gruesome twosome lurked across from what had been *The Amityville Horror*'s 112 Ocean Avenue, that distressingly ill-famed den of dreadfully devil-disgraced iniquities, for some time, neither of us espied any phenomena—natural, unnatural, or supernatural—that was sinisterly spooky or shuddersome in the very least about it . . . and neither did, at least according to their would-be "exposers," the Lutzes during their notorious, and notoriously horrific, 28-day habitation there.

Regardless of the fact that the Lutzes, in particular George Lutz, have been commonly accused of using that late-1975 tale of "haunted" terror as, to quote Amityville's very own official statement on their village's "tragedy," "a profit-making scheme"—and, by some detractors, as a contemptible attempt to give credence to Butch's claims of diabolic possession—the home that we found before our shockingly hideous selves was indeed the foully profane root of Amityville's profound infamy.

It was indeed here, between December 18, 1975, and January 14, 1976, that the Lutzes, experienced their hauntings, "true" or not: the whole family experiencing an eerily inexplicable coldness and foul odour about the house; George Lutz awaking with nameless terror each night at 3:15 A.M., unbeknownst to him—supposedly!—that hour when Butch is said to have slaughtered his family; Kathy Lutz uncovering a very strangely painted crawl space—"the red room"—hidden behind some shelves in the home's basement, at which the family's dog, Harry, would mysteriously bark; Missy Lutz, the family's youngest daughter, playing with a foul new friend whom she named Jody, who would appear to her as either a little boy—ostensibly, that youngest DeFeo, John Matthew, who was, in the 2005 remake of *The Amityville Horror*, made a little girl named Jodie DeFeo—or, far more fiendishly infamous, some supernatural species of hell-born hog, whose ghastly red-glowing eyes George Lutz said that he saw glowering at him from out of Missy's bedroom window. And after 28 days of such horrendously horrid *Horrors*, the ill-famedly affeared Lutzes fled 112 Ocean Avenue, it is said, leaving all of their belongings behind.

Different explanations have been offered as the unnatural cause of the house's horrifically haunted nature. In Anson's 1977 book, the foul, ocean-fogged land on which 112 Ocean Avenue festered was, in Amityville's perversely pagan precolonial past, an unspeakable place where the demented, decrepit, and dying were abandoned to suffer so very egregiously from exposure to the elements.

In Rosenberg's 1979 film, the home had been inhabited by a wickedly wretched witch by the name of John Ketcham, who had escaped the Salem Witch Trials of 1692 only to return to his pervertedly diabolic practices once he had hidden himself away in Amityville. Then with 2005's Scott Kosar-scripted remake, the former and the latter histories of 112 Ocean Avenue were commingled so very creepily, at least for yours cruelly: John Ketcham became the repulsively irreverent Reverend Jeremiah Ketcham and that eldritch Indian burying ground on which the home was founded became the torture chamber beneath the home where he committed his accursedly abominable atrocities upon Amityville's indigenous population.

As fabulously frightful as such explanations for 112 Ocean Avenue's foulness may be, research into Amityville's *true* past has proved it all to be simply very fanciful Hollyweird fabrications. While there were indeed Indian burial grounds around Amityville—since having become, so very unfortunately, Rot Island garbage dumps—there were none in Amityville itself. And while there was indeed a John Ketchum who came to Rot

Island from Ipswich, Massachusetts, he was a prominent public official—in Huntington—not some devil-worshipping witch, *Amityville*'s portrait of him forgetting the fact that, verily, Creepy Reader, there were *no* real "witches" burned in those late-seventeenth-century witch trials!

It is with a dread-devourer's utter disappointment, Creepy Reader, that we gruesome twosome festered so very Horror-fiendingly opposite that thusly *Amityville Horror*-historied 112 Ocean Avenue but without any goosebumps, any churned stomachs, any curdled blood to show for it—nothing but the patently disapproving glances of passers-by. With nary the simplest of shuddersome Satan-hailing squeals from that horrifically hideous hell-pig Jodie, yours cruelly knew that, even should we explore the black Great South Bay-dampened bowels of Amityville's 108 Ocean Avenue, we wouldn't experience any extremely eerie egregiousness either, just as the home's present-day owners have attested for some years now.

And so, after returning to our butchermobile and motoring around Amityville Creek to Riverside Avenue so that we could espy not the rear but the right-hand side of that former 112 Ocean Avenue and, therein, its *Horror*-infamied boathouse, my noctiflorous bride and I bid an unfortunately unsatisfied farewell to that horridly ill-rumored house of revoltingly haunted horrors and, with it, all of Amityville. With this South Shore Rot Island home of the "true story" now investigated,

Creepy Reader, we then resolved to lurk down to the Grue Jersey Shore where that 1979 celluloid *Amityville Horror*-show was filmed!

Like Amityville, Toms River is also a shore community sodden with the cold waters of the Atlantic. While it is a neighborhood and, because of that, does not have any exact boundaries, Toms River—said to have been named after eighteenth-century pirate, Captain William Toms—is spread throughout most of Dover County's almost 450 square miles and, thus, is the saltwater-taffy-clogged heart of the Grue Jersey Shore, an extremely popular tourist destination during the summer months.

But we gruesome twosome did not motor almost a 100 miles from Rot Island's South Shore simply to frolic so very unfiendishly upon some brine-stinking Toms River beach like two "bennies." No, Creepy Reader. Our butchermobile had lurked all the way down the Garden State Parkway unto Toms River because, in 1979, but two years after the bal-lyhooed publication of Jay Anson's blockbuster tale of "true" terror, it became the "Amityville" of that Stuart Rosenberg-directed and Sandor Stern-written . . . *Horror* that would even further deepen the still-dreaded infamy of that very real "Friendly Village."

***THE AMITYVILLE HORROR*'S "112 OCEAN AVENUE"**
18 Brooks Road
Toms River, NJ

According to Hollywood legend, Rosenberg's adaptation of Anson's novel was not filmed in Amityville itself because of some appallingly unexplainable "accidents" that plagued the production when filming was initially attempted there. However, if such profoundly pre-posterous publicity for *The Amityville Horror*, as promulgated by the film's production company, American International Pictures—which made

Roger Corman's gloriously Gothic Edgar Allan Poe adaptations but also a monstrous slew of other horror and exploitation features throughout the '60s and '70s, such as *Blacula*, *The Glory Stompers*, *Squirm*, and many, many other sinema classicks—is stripped away, the truth beneath those curse-purporting promotions is truly very simple: Amityville's town-fathers did not want to associate their peaceful little Rot Island village any further with either the hideous . . . *Horror*s of Anson's best-seller or the horrendous Lutz "hauntings" on which it was based, something they took to be, again, wholly a detestable hoax.

Because of this, A.I.P. was refused all the required permits it needed to make their adaptation there, which meant that another "Amityville" had to be found. And, in time, the film's producers would not only find it with Toms River but, therein, *The Amityville Horror*'s "112 Ocean Avenue" with 18 Brooks Road, unto which, Creepy Reader, our meat-wagon was hurtling!

Having exited the Garden State Parkway onto Route 527, we gruesome twosome motored eastwards into the basely *Horror*-befouled belly of Toms River. As our touring hearse lurked along Route 527 towards that adaptation's "112 Ocean Avenue," what we espied was, in fact, very similar to Rot Island's real Amityville: somewhat affluent shore homes skirting the wide mouth of the Toms River, whose waters emptied into the Barnegat Bay and then the Atlantic.

We followed Route 527 about those picturesquely bayside parts of Toms River until it became East Water Street. When East Water became Dock Street, yours cruelly wheeled our butchermobile right onto Brooks Road. And it was there on the right side of Brooks Road, at No. 18, that we two perverse purveyors of all that is horror-possessed espied the rather august blue-and-white Colonial abode which abutted the Toms River and knew that this was indeed what we had crawled down from Rot Island for: Horror-history's very own house of Amityville haunts!

More so than that real 112 Ocean Avenue—108 Ocean Avenue that we had investigated earlier in Amityville—18 Brooks Road was not so very similar to its *Horror*-ed 1979 self. Verily, much had been done to this three-story Toms River home by the film's production designers to make it the shuddersome celluloid simulacrum of that atrocious genuine Amityville article. The edifice's roof line had been utterly altered so that the roof would

be distinguished by an additional angle, and into the movie-house's new "barn" roof were fashioned gables and, into these, dormers, all of this perhaps an attempt to make their "112 Ocean Avenue" appear more eldritch—after all, Creepy Reader, it *was* the dreadedly daemonic dwelling of some shockingly sinister seventeenth-century ex-Salem Satanist!

But indelibly infamous to almost 30 years of horror-fiends is that monstrously eerie pair of quarter-moon "eye"-shaped windows that had been installed into 18 Brooks Road's third-floor façade—the home's chimney-seamed right side to be exact. Dressed thusly for *The Amityville Horror* in 1979, the Toms River house we gruesome twosome stood before was indeed the "dream house"—at least the outside of it, as the inside shots were filmed elsewhere, somewhere unbeknownst to yours cruelly—of James Brolin and Margot Kidder's George and Kathy Lutz and their three children, this happy and hopeful new family unknowing of the horrors awaiting them within their ill-historied home.

When the film's production was done, the house's appearance was returned to normal. And some years thereafter, the whole house moved to another location on the property. When it had been "112 Ocean Avenue" before Stuart Rosenberg's cameras, it had actually festered closer to Dock Street but was moved one lot over in order to make room for another home. It would also seem, at least to yours cruelly's bloodshot eyes, that it had been turned sideways during the process of this relocation, as, in *The Amityville Horror*, those execrable "eyes" glowered so very evilly out over what was supposed to be Amityville Creek (Toms River), while, today, had they still been rooted in the "head" of 18 Brooks Road, they would have looked towards Dock Street. A very small discrepancy, I will admit, Creepy Reader!

Despite the removal of its definitively *Horror*-fied accoutrements and its post-1979 repositioning, the utterly unassuming abode at 18 Brooks Road will always be—to not only long-time Toms River locals but also to the ghastliest of terror-touring gorehounds such as my black bride and yours cruelly—"*The Amityville Horror* House" and, despite the fact that there are indeed other lesser filming locations from the 1979 haunted house horrorshow elsewhere in Toms River as well as in neighboring Point Pleasant, it is the abhorrently maim attraction for any fiendishly hungry *Amityville Horror* aficionado.

From this otherwise ordinary Toms River house seeped forth—like the loathsomely unnatural luminescence spilling from the quarter-moon windows of that shockingly sinister-spirited "112 Ocean Avenue"—the celluloid *Amityville Horror* legacy, a disreputable and self-demeaned saga spread throughout a slew of successively degenerative sequels: 1982's *Amityville II: The Possession*, 1983's *Amityville 3-D*, 1989's *Amityville: The Evil Escapes*, 1990's *The Amityville Curse*, 1992's *Amityville 1992: It's About Time*, 1993's *Amityville: A New Generation*, 1996's *Amityville: Dollhouse*. Because of them, both "official" and "unofficial" sequels, *The Amityville Horror*'s is very well the worst franchise in all of Horror history, although yours cruelly does indeed relish the post-*Exorcist* shocks and repulsive sleaziness of that very first sequel, *Amityville II: The Possession*: a veritable "prequel" written, uncredited, by Dardano Sachetti, the writer behind such morbid Italian chunkblowers as *Cannibal Apocalypse*, *City of the Living Dead*, *The New York Ripper*, and many others.

But although their A.I.P.-produced 1979 progenitor is in the end—at least in yours cruelly's estimation!—but a tepid and somewhat trite little spookshow, *The Amityville Horror* was an undeniable box-office success that made "112 Ocean Avenue" and all of Amityville atrocious haunted-house archetypes, perhaps the most infamous in all of Horror history. And it was for that very reason alone, Creepy Reader, that my wretched wife and yours cruelly were exploring that Toms River house at 18 Brooks Road that day.

After whiling away some time taking celluloid crime scene photographs of that former "112 Ocean Avenue," we gruesome twosome, as if heeding a call to "GET OUT!" howling from 18 Brooks Road's perverted *Amityville Horror*-fied past, returned to our meatwagon and made our less than wholesome way out of Toms River and north towards our Rot Island Krypt.

While yours cruelly does not truly worship at the altar of *The Amityville Horror* as some other horror fiends verily do, our expedition amidst the film's Rot Island and Grue Jersey haunts was indeed worth all the motoring to and fro. But should you undertake such a tenebrous terror-tour yourself, Creepy Reader, know that the only hellish swine you will meet upon your investigation of fact or film's "112 Ocean Avenue" will be the repellently rank and rotten ham sandwich you buy along the way!

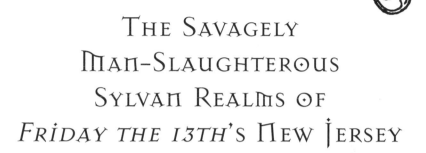

Chapter Fourteen

THE SAVAGELY MAN-SLAUGHTEROUS SYLVAN REALMS OF *FRIDAY THE 13TH*'S NEW JERSEY

"Killed a girl on lovers lane
I kept her toes and teeth
Every night I stalk around until I find my keep
I'll bring back a souvenir
For it's my mommy's dream

Can I go out and kill tonight?"

—The Misfits
"Mommy, Can I Go Out and Kill Tonight?" (1983)

Creepy Reader, if there was but one name that was utterly synonymous with "Horror!" back when the deplorably disgusting annals of sinematic dread were freshly foul to yours cruelly, it was Jason Vorhees. Although my dear olde mother's unrelenting stranglehold over the family VCR kept his woe-begettingly body count-wracked woodland mass-murder sprees from being played out before my hideously all-too-hungry young—not yet so very bloodshot!—eyes, the deathless celluloid documents of Jason Vorhees's deliriously deranged carnage-drowned doings—1980's *Friday the 13th* and its successive, and successively more slaughterous, stock of sequels—were *infamous* for me then.

I used to have my fiends who had actually eyeballed some of these sordid hack-and-slash horrorshows dredge, in the gloriously grisliest and goriest of details, all of Jason's ill-rumoredly repulsive iniquities, in particular relishing not simply the "Who?" but the "How?!?", the "What?!?": *how* did he exterminate, with such pathologically extreme prejudice, those ill-fated Camp Crystal Lake fun-fanciers and exactly *what* farm or forestry implements—axe, pitchfork, machete, etc.—did he use to do it?

Yours cruelly had even accoutered my shuddersome young self as the hockey-masked human-slaughterhouse one All Hallow's Eve without yet having seen *any* of those slasher flicks which bore witness to his insatiable hunger for human butchery. No matter that all-too-few of them—with perhaps the exception of Parts I, II, IV, and VII, yours cruelly's fearfully fiendish favorites of the now-10-chapter serialized slasher-saga—would, in the end, hardly *approximate* what my oddly grue-obsessed young brain had yearned for them to be, that profoundly revengeful, perversely murder-ravenous, and perpetually rotting Jason Vorhees and his unending Fridays the 13th do indeed still hold a horrid place in my hideous black heart.

And so, Creepy Reader, during the twilight of a not so distant December, when my unspeakable wife and I were picking our morbidly distempered gray matter for a suitable post-Yuletide day-trip destination, we gruesome twosome could not conceive of a better place to sate so very shockingly our hunger not simply for the road but, wholly more unwholesome, the gloriously ghastliest of the macabre than those actual locations in our very own Grue Jersey—that toxic wasteland called krypt sweet krypt by The Misfits—where the original *Friday the 13th* was filmed in the fall of 1979.

With a little midnight grave-digging, yours cruelly unearthed all the elementary crime scene evidence and, early the next mourning, we gruesome twosome departed in our blood-born butchermobile to explore the raucously atrocious roots of that loathsomely disreputable legacy of dreadfullest dismemberment that had thrilled my awfully repugnant adolescent ruminations all those years ago: the despicably doomed abode of that morbidly brutal behemythic master of slashers *Jason Vorhees*!

A woe-warning December wind met we two purveyors of the most perverse postmortem profanities as we motored towards our journey's atrocious destination within the extreme northwestern extent of our befrosted state, the slumberingly bucolic sylvan burgh of Blairstown. Finally exiting a seemingly unending Route 80 but 10  miles from the Pennsylvania border, we made our wickedest of ways down Route 94, which would usher us deeper and deeper into that so basely butchery-befouled belly of Jason Vorhees's most dreadful domain of death.

As we gruesome twosome lurked through those particularly rural parts, what my bloodshot eyes espied was a particularly intriguing mixture of the old and the new: a backwoods world of the rustified remnants of a bygone, and less bustling, age woven in with a burgeoningly bourgeois unurbanized retreat.

Motoring through these thusly metamorphosing hinterlands, yours cruelly thought it very odd indeed that, when it came time to make his would-be dread-ridden directorial debut in 1979, Sean Cunningham, whose last dabblings in celluloid horror's depravities, as producer, were two years earlier with *The Hills Have Eyes*—directed by Cunningham's partner in sinematic crimes, Wes Craven, these two dear fiends having already assured the most abominable of infamies in the shock-choked annals of Horror with the piss-your-pants perversions of 1972's *Last House on the Left*—chose *here*, these humble and hurtless northernest New Jersey hinterlands amidst which Blairstown was so very snug, of all places to do it.

While verily picturesque in a Rockwellian sort of way, these wintered woodlands made for a deeply less than grim setting, let alone one to be splattered and smeared with the burbling hot blood of lustfully teenaged camp-goers! But it was indeed here that *Friday the 13th* was filmed over the course of three months of an appallingly aberrant annihilation-scented autumn almost 30 years ago, and we gruesome twosome began to see the tell-slasher-tale signs of this frightening factoid as we made our way along Route 94 towards Blairstown.

MORAVIAN CEMETERY
Delaware Road (Rte. 609) at Route 655
Hope

As we two midnight-movie murder-mongers bore down upon Blairstown like a buck knife upon the shivering throat of a skinny-dipped teenaged schoolgirl, we came upon Cedar Ridge Cemetery and, at first, believed that this was indeed the eldritch country boneyard before which Annie, the ill-fatedly free-spirited would-be camp counselor, was dropped off by a local trucker, Enos, in *Friday the 13th*'s then-contemporaneous opening.

However, despite some superficial similarities—in particular its arched and autographed wrought iron front gate—upon deeper examination, yours cruelly savvied that this graveyard, but a mile from Blairstown on Route 94 in neighboring Jacksonburg, was, verily, *not* that cemeterial celluloid specimen. To espy it, we gruesome twosome had to hack short, at least for a little while, our hurtle into the horridly "Horror!"-fied heart of Blairstown's "Camp Blood"-y parts with a departure to Hope.

The similarly slumbering township of Hope was but seven or so miles from Blairstown and it was there, at the intersection of Routes 655 and 609 (also known as Delaware Road) where we finally found the Moravian Cemetery, that actual tombyard from *Friday the 13th* which we had reckoned, all too wrongly, we had found in Blairstown. While it was somewhat similar to that former Route 94-fringing graveyard, Hope's Moravian Cemetery, with its distinctively grassy main drive, was not simply smaller than Cedar Ridge but less grave-swamped as well.

Alongside the late-nineteenth-century-founded Street John United Methodist Church, the Moravian Cemetery is, verily, at least a 100 years older, its first plot marker dating from 1768. These most aged of the cemetery's gravestones—almost three rows of them, all so very matter-of-factly flat and figured—are, in fact, the boneyard's namesake, as they denote the interments of, as yours cruelly unearthed from a commemorative marker, "sixty-two persons who died in the early Moravian settlement of Hope, NJ."

Named thusly for these mid-eighteenth-century-expired Pennsylvania emigrants, the Moravian Cemetery, while bestowing the backdrop for but that solitary scene so very early in the 1980 film, not only swore to the separateness of Camp Crystal Lake's backwoods setting but also soothsaid the blood-chillingly moribund beginning of the end of poor Annie's proverbial "road." Perhaps it is for this reason then, Creepy Reader, why this otherwise quiet and quaint Hope boneyard is so very well-known to *Friday the 13th* worshippers—at least those who don't find themselves lurking amongst Blairstown-bound Cedar Ridge Cemetery's headstones instead!

BLAIRSTOWN DINER
186 Route 94
(908) 362-6070
Blairstown

Something that has truly come to *define* our belovedly weirdness befouled New Jersey for my unspeakable wife and yours cruelly is not so much its shopping malls—which verily deface the Garden State like the profoundly repulsive pustules upon the face of a pox victim—but its diners. While the horse-drawn progenitor of the classic prefabricated diners of popular culture prominence are said to have begun in Rhode Island, it is New Jersey that has the most diners in America, as a result reaping the ambiguously esteemed appellation of "The Diner Capital of the World."

In fact, it was a very real diner in Little Ferry, New Jersey—but miles from where yours cruelly de-evolved into the filthy horror fiend that you know and love—where Nancy Walker's Rosie the Waitress used to push her "quicker picker upper" in television commercials throughout the '70s.

Perhaps it will not come as a shock then, Creepy Reader, that one of the cruelly cadaver-cropping curiosities amongst those hideous New Jersey hinterlands of *Friday the 13th* was, yes, a diner, as it was at Blairstown's very own Blairstown Diner where Camp Crystal Lake's foolhardily death curse-damning head honcho, the spectacled and mustachioed Steve Christie, stopped for what would be—unbeknownst to him!—his last meal during that shuddersomely storm-racked night of *Friday the 13th*'s summer camp slayings.

Leaving the Moravian Cemetery and Hope's coffined Germanic forefathers therein, yours cruelly motored our meatwagon back towards Blairstown, and it was along Route 94, almost a mile-and-a-half from Main Street, that we gruesome twosome espied the Blairstown Diner. As we pulled into the diner's somewhat mobbed parking lot, what we found before us was not the endearingly enormous eyesores on whose savorily fried slop my black bride and I were well-nigh reared but, in their comparatively contemporary place, something of the traditional "tin box" species.

Made by the Paramount Dining Car Company in 1948, the Blairstown Diner was indeed smaller than most of the sort that can be witnessed about New Jersey today. However, we were there to neither appraise its size nor sup upon its sundry gut-bursting gastronomic grotesqueries, such as a Reuben or Monte Cristo sandwich. No. We hungered for something profoundly more putrefactedly unpalatable . . . *Horror!* And so we parked our touring hearse so that we could begin our austerely atrocious autopsy of the place.

Although the still-squat and squarish Blairstown Diner looked very much as it had in *Friday the 13th*, yours cruelly's bloodshot eyes did indeed, however, espy some differences about that ill-historied fast food institution, which came as no surprise as we knew that, since Cunningham filmed here all those years ago, it had been not simply refurbished but remodeled, to allow space for more tables and booths.

While it would be none too easy for even the most obsessive of horror fiends to discern exactly what colour the eatery was, other than the steeliness of its sheeny diner-defining siding, amidst those doom-riddenly dark and dreary scenes, it was, at least in 1979 and who knows for how long thereafter, a somewhat drab green. That late December day, however, the Blairstown Diner was adorned with a truly apropos blood-red trimming.

Furthermore, that favorable post-*Friday the 13th* face-lift had not only relocated, and awning-adorned, the diner's front door but, perhaps more conspicuously, had removed its former simple "DINER" sign, which had glowed so very luridly amidst the night's gloom of that infamous Friday the 13th. Within the belly of that Blairstown Diner, the establishment was both bigger and better kept than yours cruelly had believed the 1948-fashioned restaurant would be, but this was, again, the result of those renovations—

whose raison d'etre, you can rest assured, Creepy Reader, was to solicit and serve *more* creep-craving "Camp Blood" cavorters than before!

All in all, the Blairstown Diner, while not utterly indistinguishable from its slaughter-swamped *Friday the 13th* sinematic self, is different enough that vilely vicious and fandom-voracious Vorhees votaries may not recognize it, at least not at first. But this was indeed where ill-omened Steve Christie gobbled his "two-and-a-quarter" dollars worth of grub before becoming but another notch in that slasher classick's swelling body count.

We two spook-swallowing slasher-stalkers, however, could not while away our time stool-roosted along the diner's counter as he did and so, forgoing gorging our gruesome selves with the meat-gluttony of a Monte Cristo or Reuben sandwich, returned to our butchermobile to feast instead upon the uncoiled celluloid-abased bowels of Blairstown's Main Street.

My unspeakable wife and I had to motor east along Route 94, further into Blairstown, for but minutes before we veered down the left-hand path that was Main Street. Pulling our meatwagon to a dead stop along one of its tall, olde-style curbs, we disembarked for our necropsy of this notoriously terrorized New Jersey township. Lurking amongst the Small

Town, U.S.A. feel of Main Street, yours cruelly espied a Martha Stewart-esque woodland-buried wonderland in which the countrified became blended so very oddly with the cosmopolitan.

Amidst a backwoodsily rustic backdrop of hunting supply depots and that everywhere-rural essential that is Walmart, Main Street was home—a home ornamented by the finely porched and balconied-façades of Victorian-aged edifices—to an utterly alien species of mercantile enterprise: among others, a health food grocers, a crafting store, a fashionably provincial anti-quarian, and a gourmet book and coffee shoppe. All of these dwelling amidst that thusly architectured avenue, it was not verily a step back in time, as Blairstown's Main Street is seemingly so often portrayed, but a historical return that is unmistakably suffused with the most urbane modernity.

OLD MILL
Main Street
(at Carhart Street)
Blairstown

But it was Main Street, to yours cruelly's bloodshot eyes one of the oldest parts in all of

Blairstown, that told we two ghastliest of ghouls that we were indeed truly walking upon charnel earth deconsecrated so very dread-riddenly by the hideous gods of Horror, as it was this very same road—in particular, that less-than-a-quarter-mile-long Main Street sweep between Academy and Carhart—that was so very prominently displayed during *Friday the 13th's* unboundedly ill-omened beginning that witnessed the hideously deceptive arrival of Annie, that bloomingly beautiful, bouncing brunette fated so foully to become nothing but celluloid wormfood, and the very first flesh-and-blood offerings (not counting that couple of '50s-era copulators) into the slasher classick's murder-works.

And, Creepy Reader, it was to the eastern stretch of Main Street that called to us like stinking rot-black charnel does flies, as it was there, at the intersection of Carhart Street where Main became Blair Place, that we gruesome twosome found the Old Mill, perhaps *the* most architecturally recognizable artifact from Blairstown's bygone days of *Friday the 13th's* gory-drenched yore. Aside from its place in horror history, though, the Old Mill is also one of the most historic places in Blairstown.

While Blairstown was incorporated in 1845—and named, in 1839, after the township's most renowned resident and the day's most wealthy "Jerseyman," the Scottish-ancestored John I. Blair—its roots are more than a 100 years older. These parts, on either side of the Paulins Kill River, were settled by John Hyndshaw in 1729. Others followed Hyndshaw to those northwestern New Jersey hinterlands and, until the early nineteenth century, it was known as Smith's Mill because of a grist mill and a saw mill that had been built there sometime well before the Revolutionary War.

While the mill we gruesome twosome were investigating that day

was, verily, neither of these—whether it is a "grist" or "saw" mill is unknown to yours cruelly—as it actually dates from 1825, yet, like them, the Old Mill utilized Blair Lake, like those ancestral others, to manipulate its works. The awe-inspiring, five-acre-wide lake was stoppered by a stately

dam 17 feet in height and 45 feet in width in order to produce the mill's power supply in the form of the thunderous Blair Falls.

With this as the Old Mill's history, yours cruelly would bring you, Creepy Reader, almost 150 years forward in time to that appallingly atrocity-arousing autumn of 1979 and, therein, the historic celluloid horrorshow that would—finally!—steep the eldritch place in the most shuddersome of infamies: *Friday the 13th.* Any *true* horror fiend who has spent an unhealthy slew of nights slogging through the gruesome and grisly happenings of Cunningham's 1980 slasher film would no doubt immediately recognize that singular early-nineteenth-century structure.

With its hulking sundry-stoned façade and archway-punctuated tunnel walkway, the Old Mill—which, as a posted informational placard attested, has been placed on the American Register of Historic Places— was truly an awesome architectural achievement and yours cruelly did not wonder why Cunningham wanted it for the mise-en-scene of his masterpiece of sinematic macabre.

In the film, it was down Blair Place—coming upon the Old Mill from the east, on the way passing over, for but a few seconds, the bridge that passes atop the Blair Falls—and through that very same shadow-palled stretch of Main Street sidewalk beneath the aged mill that Annie strolled so very carelessly into the slavering maw of Horror's most slaughter-ravenous slasher franchises. It very well may satisfy your loathsomely unwholesome curiosities, Creepy Reader, to know that, Annie, after passing the Old Mill, is next seen walking down what is the opposite—western end—of Main Street, stopping then for help at a coffee shoppe that is, today, the all-purpose stationery store we gruesome twosome found at No. 26.

Having thusly explored that eeriest *Friday the 13th* crime scene evidence here upon Blairstown's Main Street, my crepuscular wife and I wormed our way around the Old Mill and beheld the Blair Falls and, beyond it, Blair Lake. As we climbed some olde stairs to have a better look at the frozen face of the latter, we espied an eldritch cemetery upon a hill behind Main Street. Not ones to let a boneyard lay unplundered, we made our way over to it and, once there, found ourselves lurking amidst some truly decrepit tombstones, all within the strange shadow of New Jersey's tallest funerary obelisk.

It was perhaps very fitting for such deeply dreary death-tributes to reign above a road so verily drowned in the disquietingly dreadful annals of celluloid horror as Blairstown's Main Street. While not one vermilion drop of *Friday the 13th*'s horrendously heavy blood harvest was spilt here, that otherwise unassuming street has nonetheless hacked out a hideous place of dishonor in Horror history, as it was here all those years ago now, Creepy Reader, that the terrifyingly homicide-mad Vorhees tale began to unfold.

"CAMP CRYSTAL LAKE"
(Camp No-Be-Bo-Sco)
11 Sand Pond Road
Blairstown
(908) 362-6088

But if not there, amidst that oddly charming setting of Blairstown's Main Street, then exactly where did *Friday the 13th*'s shuddersomely savage streak of serialized slayings stain the shadowed sylvan soil of these harrowed New Jersey hinterlands with red teenaged blood? Well, "Camp Crystal Lake," of corpse! To get there, my unspeakable wife and I would actually have to reverse the route taken in the film by poor doomed Annie on her terrible one-way trip to that irresponsible reopening of that ill-renownedly cursed summer camp, this journey of hers ending in a date with a slit throat.

Returning to our butchermobile, we motored up through Millbrook Road and left behind Blairstown's homely wholesome Main Street bosom for that macabrely murderous realm that is the shockingly infamous forest-shrouded acreage of "Camp Blood"!

Sometime in 1979, Sean Cunningham made a little "feel-good" feature about, of all things, a Catholic orphanage's soccer team. It was called *Manny's Orphans* and was, in Hollyweird parlance, "optioned" as the pilot for a television series. While he was left with some potentially lucrative possibilities with his post-*Bad News Bears* sports flick—from which, in fact, nothing ever did come—such "potential" was not going to pay his bills. Because of this, in that *Manny's Orphans* meantime, Cunningham needed a film project that would take very little money and very little time to make but would, very possibly, bring in a tidy profit. What he had in mind was a horror film.

The year before, a little independent creepshow, which had been made for the even then-small sum of $300,000, brought in almost *$50 million* at American box offices alone. This film was John Carpenter's *Halloween* and Cunningham, seemingly, studied its atrocious and appallingly archetypal slasher tropes so that he could bring them—particularly the symbolic "past event" title—to his very own horror film. From his scrupulous *Halloween*-scrutiny, in a most macabre history-making moment inspired by the grotesque Horror-gods themselves, he conceived of a strong title: *Friday the 13th*.

With but that provocatively ominous title—and an advertising campaign that was deeply more so—Cunningham, along with producer Steve Miner, who would go on to direct the franchise's first two sequels, was able to solicit $500,000 from financiers from all around the world, and this for a film that not only did not yet have either a cast or a crew, but was not even *written* yet. After a screenplay for the film was finally written—under the working title, *A Long Night at Camp Blood*—by Victor Miller, who had also written *Manny's Orphans*, Cunningham was prepared to begin production on *Friday the 13th*.

All that Cunningham needed, however, was someplace to film it—someplace that would not only serve as a somber and spooky atmospheric setting for the screenplay's "Camp Blood" but, perhaps more importantly for his particular budgetary purposes, someplace where both the cast and crew—mostly non-professional, mostly non-union—could be put up when filming was done for the day (or night). And that is what brought Cunningham, that would-be slasher-maven, to Blairstown, New Jersey, and, there, Camp No-Be-Bo-Sco.

During *Friday the 13th*'s production that autumn of 1979, he made his cruelly carnage-cursed Camp Crystal Lake out of this real-life Blairstown summer camp, whose name is not derived from some local Indian war chief but is, rather, an acronym standing for North Bergen Boy Scouts, although the campe is more commonly known as, simply, Camp No-Be.

As it was not only cut off from the rest of the already-backwoods Blairstown but was also open only throughout the summer, when young scouts were not in school, the camp, founded in 1927, could not have been more perfect for the director's perversely sadistic camper-slashing purposes. Cunningham had it all to himself that fall and transformed it, utterly, into a sinisterly sylvan-shadowed slaughterhouse of shocking proportions.

When yours cruelly learned this, that Camp No-Be was, verily, *Friday the 13th*'s Camp Blood, it was, truly, not so very surprising, as I had heard about the camp for years from my older brothers and boyhood fiends. Having been regaled with their tales of summers spent wreaking almost criminal acts of adolescent chaos amongst those New Jersey hinterlands, it did indeed seem like a very horridly proper home for *Friday the 13th*'s brutally bloodthirsty butchery. And it was towards this very same celluloid accursed Camp No-Be that our butchermobile was hurtling after we gruesome twosome left Main Street.

We motored north along Millbrook Road for a few miles, passing some rather palatial residences adjacent to some truly creepy shacks not unlike that foul Vorhees family spread seen in 1981's *Friday the 13th Part II*. After some wrong turns, we found our way onto Birch Ridge Road, then Shannon Road, and then finally—*finally*, Creepy Reader!—Sand Pond Road. And it was but another mile before our touring hearse pulled up to Camp No-Be's subdued entrance.

What with the utter lack of signs to show us the way to the camp, something yours cruelly attributed to it being December and, thus, the off-season, we'd had a somewhat difficult time finding it. However, this somewhat tortuous journey was all but forgotten when we espied the simple brown sign that told us that we had indeed come upon the repulsively rank and rotted remains of that abominably horrific 1979 archetype of sinematic sleepaway camps, "Camp Crystal Lake"!

As Camp No-Be's front gate was wide open and there were no signs warning the all-too-curious against trespassing—at least not to yours cruelly's bloodshot eyes—we two inveterate stalk-and-slash-aholics lurked down the camp's dead-tree-decored main drag to see what awaited us deeper within the dread-dripping bowels of doomed "Camp Blood."

As our butchermobile crawled so very slowly down that dilapidated asphalt drive, passing a fallen Welcome sign fashioned out of twigs and twine, we peered through the trees and thickets that bore down upon us on each side to see if we could behold with our very own bloodlusting eyesballs any of the camp's charmingly rustified cabins or the green-roofed archery range within and without which Kevin Bacon's Jack and his other lewd and lascivious teenaged counselor-cohorts had been slaughtered with such skill in the name of the garish gods of '80s slasher gore.

Friday the 13th's most morbidly murderous celluloid machinations were unofficially—and unadmittedly—inspired by the gloriously gruesome and grisly tableaux featured almost 10 years before in Mario Bava's *Twitch of the Death Nerve* (also known, in the U.S., as *Bay of Blood*), and this debt to the maestro of the macabre's giallo grotesqueries actually deepened with that 1981 sequel.

So who was it exactly that put those horridly extravagant homicides upon *Friday the 13th's* butcher's block? Victor Miller was a veritable horror neophyte, having been responsible, mostly, for scheming the film's "potboiler" nature and Cunningham has denied having even seen Bava's *Twitch* before 1979. Yours cruelly esteems them to nothing but expert, and bloodcurdlingly exquisite, homages on the part of that wizard of gore himself, Tom Savini, who was hired by Cunningham and the film's producers based upon his epoch-defining special effects in George Romero's *Dawn of the Dead* the year before. Following his infamous work on Cunningham's horrorshow, Savini would become, through such post-*Friday the 13th* drive-in mass-murder-fests as *Maniac, The Prowler,* and *The Burning,* the undisputed king of '80s slasher atrocity-artistry.

But as we gruesome twosome motored further into the thusly blood-weltered belly of Camp No-Be, we, so very sadly, saw *none* of those very same camp locations which had been turned into one big celluloid abattoir by that dreadful duo of Cunningham and Savini.

But yours cruelly did not despair, Creepy Reader, as, according to the map of the camp's limits that Camp No-Be's management had so very kind-heartedly made available on their webpage, many of those places that had indeed seen filming all those years ago, such as the Van Dusen lodge—which, in the film, had been Camp Crystal Lake's main cabin, where those ill-fated fornicating counselors were spooked by doom-heralding Crazy Ralph, where they played their all-too-friendly game of Strip Monopoly, and where, during the film's final reel, Adrienne King's scared and screaming Alice finally met the camp's unknown terrorizer—were all on the eastern side of Camp No-Be. And so deeper into Camp Blood we lurked!

But it was not until we gruesome twosome had motored along the camp's twisting main road for some minutes before we came upon that one location that seemed to utterly symbolize the vengeful spirit stalking these woefully dreadful North Jersey woods: Sand Pond. Never heard of it, Creepy Reader? Well, perhaps you and a host of other hideous late-night-horror ghouls would know it better as Crystal Lake! Parking our touring hearse along the shoulder of the road, we disembarked so that we could so very worshipfully plunge ourselves in its deep, dark waters—at least figuratively, as it was, after all, only but a few degrees above freezing out in those Northwestern Jersey woods!

A footpath of wooden steps led us down through the trees and then, when we stepped out upon the rocky shore, there it was! Sand Pond was the forest-hugged scenic heart of Camp No-Be's summertime events and activities, such as swimming or canoeing! With its woods-beautified

mountain backdrop, the 26-acre pond—not, in fact, a lake at all, the difference being a question of size—was, truly, a breathtaking sight to behold, utterly serene in its wintry sublimity. It seemed like the ideal subject for a landscape portrait—but one rendered with paints and a canvas, *not* arterial spray and death knells!

But it was indeed from out of these very same December-choked waters of Camp No-Be's Sand Pond, *Friday the 13th*'s Crystal Lake, where terror-shocked yet surviving Alice had hacked off the head of Mommy Vorhees (played by former late-'50s *Today Show* newscaster Betsy Palmer, who took the now-infamous role only because, by her own confession, she needed "a new car"). And, in Alice's post-nightmare delirium, she set herself adrift in one of the camps canoes, from which arose—in one of the most effectively unexpected endings in all of horror history—the 1958-drowned, deformed, and brain-defective Jason Vorhees (a 13-year-old Ari Lehman beneath Savini's prosthetics and effected detritus), who would become, throughout 10 sequels and through nine different actors, the monstrously moldering and morbidly misanthropic mass-murder-machine upon Horror's throne of bones as the King of Celluloid Carnage, the stalking-and-slashing slaughter-lord who would forever make a simple goalie's mask a sinisterly symbolic staple of Halloween regalia!

It was with memories of my earliest musings upon this very same Jason Vorhees and his as-yet-unseen extremely ensanguined exploits churning through my brain that yours cruelly stood upon the slasher-infamied shore of Sand Pond's "Crystal Lake." With its bare-bones plot, its cutthroat pacing, and its still-chilling Harvey Manfredini score, 1980's *Friday the 13th* was, and still is, the godfather of the stalk-and-slash scheme, systematizing what John Carpenter had done in *Halloween* only the year before.

It could be said that the greatest fault of Cunningham's film is that it set the standard for a substandard slew of straight-to-video slash-a-thons that were birthed in the home video boom of the early '80s. And it was this plague of mundane video stillbirths that would, eventually, bring about the subgenre's decline. Regardless, such offensive steaming offal as 1984's *Movie House Massacre* or 1985's *The Ripper* (which stars none other than Tom Savini as the ghost of Jack the Ripper!) could never, at least for yours cruelly, take away from the glorious goriness of that Camp Blood teenager genocide that started it all.

But such reverently memorializing ruminations were interrupted by the telltale sound of a vehicle driving down the very same road we had taken into Camp No-Be. Returning to our butchermobile, we gruesome twosome were greeted—and I use the word *very* hesitantly, Creepy Reader!—by the camp boss and his son on their way home from picking up some burgers, most likely somewhere along Route 94.

Although the gate had indeed been open and there had indeed not been any signs warning against trespassing, he told us, so very matter of factly, that only employees and members of the Boy Scouts of America were allowed on the premises and, thus, questioned what we were doing there. When I told him that we were there to see where *Friday the 13th* had been made he replied, shaking his head, with what must be the B.S.A.'s "official" position on Camp No-Be's horrific past, telling me that "it" had been filmed there a long time ago and that the camp would rather *not* be known for that reason.

While the reaction of the camp boss and his organization's towards Cunningham's film was not all that surprising—as parents would no doubt rather young scouts spent their summers tying knots and whittling sticks instead of whispering about Jason Vorhees's skills with yard tools—someone *was* paid so that Cunningham and his crew could make their film here, even if it was way back in 1979.

Nonetheless, yours cruelly apologized and my black bride and I returned to our meatwagon, pleased not only that he had been, somewhat, "nice," about it all, undoubtedly neither the first nor the last time that he has had to deal with violently voracious Vorhees worshippers such as us, but that he had not arrived but a minute earlier and, thus, interrupted our des-canctified pond-stood communion with that hockey-masked exemplar of extremest woodland extermination, the brutal bitch-born behemoth of butchery, the one and only . . . Jason!

Like a machete hacking through the throat of a teenaged camp counselor, that untimely arrival of Camp No-Be-Bo-Sco's woods-bound wintertime watcher had killed our exploration of *Friday the 13th*'s Camp Blood. What else was left there from its 1979 production, aside from Sand

Pond itself, that "Crystal Lake" for which Cunningham's summer camp was named, yours cruelly, unfortunately, cannot say. Regardless, our trip to Blairstown, that appallingly accursed birthplace of one of Horror's most infamous sons, Jason Vorhees, had been, truly, a trip to remember.

And so with snow beginning to fall upon this backwoods slaughter-house and the sun already setting, we gruesome twosome bid farewell to Blairstown and made our way back to our charnel house. If you, Creepy Reader, are an abhorrently gluttonous Vorhees gore-adorer and you should find yourself creeping through this very northwestern corner of New Jersey, this very same sickening sojourn into eldritch slasher country is for you. And I would suggest embarking on such an expedition during the vernal months when the woods of "Camp Blood" are stocked with plump camp-going pubescent game. Happy hunting!

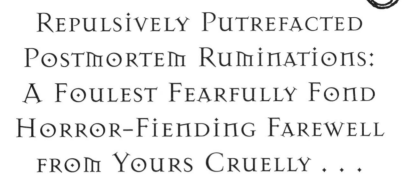

REPULSIVELY PUTREFACTED POSTMORTEM RUMINATIONS: A FOULEST FEARFULLY FOND HORROR-FIENDING FAREWELL FROM YOURS CRUELLY . . .

Alas, Creepy Reader, *Creepy Crawls* and, with it, your terrifically tenebrous terror-tour amongst some of Horror's most legendarily loathsome locales has concluded. From the hellish bottom of my hideous black heart, I offer you a greatly ghoulish and ghastly grateful "Fangs!" for joining my unspeakable wife and yours cruelly on our creepy crawls throughout the basest black bowels of culture and society, literature, and film and the horrors—*the Horrors!*—that fester so very foully therein!

I do hope that you have not only enjoyed your shuddersome sojourn amidst all that is sordid and shocking but have been inspired to undertake your own creepy crawls unto these very same prodigiously Horror-palled places. Should you do so, please send me an eek-mail at <u>charnellord@yahoo.com</u> and tell me of the cryptic coffins-full of creeps-coloured curiosities that you find.

But before yours cruelly returns to the cruel carrion comforts of our Charnel House krypt, know, Creepy Reader, that although *Creepy Crawls* has come to an end, the creepy crawls never will, because, in Horror, there is no such thing as "The End"! And so, as John Milton wrote in *Paradise Lost*, "Hail, horrors!" Indeed!

Bibliography

The Revoltingly Rotted Resources of *Creepy Crawls'* Rapacious Research

Balun, Chas. *The Deep Red Horror Handbook*. Albany: Fantaco, 1989.

——. *The Gore Score*. Albany: Fantaco, 1987.

——. *Gore Score 2001: The Splatter Years*. Seattle: Michael Matthews Publishing, 2000.

——. *More Gore Score: Brave New Horrors*. Florida: Fantasma Books, 1992.

Beahm, George W. *Stephen King Country: The Illustrated Guide to the Sites and Sights That Inspired the Modern Master of Horror*. Philadelphia: Running Press, 1999.

Brooks, J. A. *Ghosts of London*. England: Jarrold Publishing, 1991.

Cozzi, Luigi. *Giallo Argento*. Rome: Profondo Rosso, 2001.

De Camp, L. Sprague. *H. P. Lovecraft: A Biography*. New York: Barnes & Noble, 1996.

Duncan, Andrew. *Walking Notorious London : From Gunpowder Plot to Gangland: Walks Through London's Dark History.* New York: McGraw-Hill, 2001.

Eckhardt, Jason C. *Off the Ancient Track: A Lovecraftian Guide to New England and Adjacent New York.* Rhode Island: Necronomicon Press, 1994.

Flude, Kevin, and Paul Herbert. *The Old Operating Theatre, Museum and Herb Garret Museum Guide.* London: The Old Operating Theatre, Museum and Herb Garret, 1995.

Friday the 13th: The Website. http://www.fridaythe13thfilms.com/home.html

Friends of the Old Dutch Burying Ground. *Tales of the Old Dutch Burying Ground: A Walking Tour.* Tarrytown: Friends of the Old Dutch Burying Ground, 2001.

Gaiman, Neil, and Michael Zulli. *Taboo 6: The Sweeney Todd Penny Dreadful.* Vermont: SpiderBaby Grafix & Publications, 1992.

Haining, Peter. *Sweeney Todd: The Real Story of the Demon Barber of Fleet Street.* New York: Barnes & Noble Books, 1997.

Hand, Richard J., and Michael Wilson. *Grand-Guignol: The French Theatre of Horror.* England: University of Exeter Press, 2002.

Harden, Tim, webmaster. *Texas Chainsaw Massacre: A Visit to the Film Locations.* http://www.texaschainsawmassacre.net/

Harms, Daniel. *The Encyclopedia Cthulhiana: A Guide to Lovecraftian Horror.* Hayward: Chaosium, 1998.

Joshi, S. T. *H. P. Lovecraft: A Life.* Rhode Island: Necronomicon Press, 1996.

Kaplan, Stephen, and Roxanne Salch Kaplan. *The Amityville Horror Conspiracy*. Pennsylvania: Toad Hall, 1995.

LeVey, Benedict. *Eccentric London*. Connecticut: Globe Pequot, 2002.

Loucks, Donovan K., webmaster. *The H. P. Lovecraft Archive*. http://www.hplovecraft.com/

Lovett, Anthony, and Matt Maranian. *L. A. Bizzaro! The Insider's Guide to the Obscure, the Absurd and the Perverse in Los Angeles*. New York: Street Martin's, 1997.

Luther-Smith, Adrian. *Blood & Black Lace: The Definitive Guide to Italian Sex and Horror Movies*. England: Stray Cat Publishing, 1999.

Opsasnick, Mark. "The Haunted Boy of Cottage City: The Cold Hard Facts Behind the Story that Inspired *The Exorcist*." *Strange Magazine*, Issue 20, 2000. http://www.strangemag.com/exorcistcasenews.html

Pearsall, Anthony. *The Lovecraft Lexicon*. Tempe: New Falcon, 2005.

The Edgar Allan Poe Society of Baltimore, Inc. The Edgar Allan Poe Society of Baltimore. http://www.eapoe.org/

Ramseur, Michael. *Danvers State Hospital: The Castle on the Hill*. http://ramseursdanversstatehosp.com/

Rockoff, Adam. *Going to Pieces: The Rise and Fall of the Slasher Film, 1978–1986*. North Carolina: McFarland, 2002.

Rumbelow, Donald. *The Complete Jack the Ripper*. London: Penguin, 2004.

Russo, John. *The Complete* Night of the Living Dead *Filmbook*. Pittsburgh: Imagine, Inc., 1985.

Silverman, Kenneth. *Edgar A. Poe: Mournful and Never-Ending Remembrance*. New York: Harper Collins, 1991.

Stone, Colleen. "From Away: Stephen King's Bangor." *Maine Today*. Apr. 2004 http://travel.mainetoday.com/fromaway/040401.shtml

Wayne, Gary. "*Halloween* Filming Locations." *Seeing Stars in Hollywood*. http://www.seeing-stars.com/Locations/Halloween/index.shtml

BOOKS AVAILABLE FROM SANTA MONICA PRESS

American Hydrant
by Sean Crane
176 pages $24.95

**Atomic Wedgies, Wet Willies &
Other Acts of Roguery**
by Greg Tananbaum and
Dan Martin
128 pages $11.95

The Bad Driver's Handbook
*Hundreds of Simple Maneuvers to
Frustrate, Annoy, and Endanger
Those Around You*
by Zack Arnstein and
Larry Arnstein
192 pages $12.95

The Butt Hello
and other ways my cats drive me crazy
by Ted Meyer
96 pages $9.95

Calculated Risk
*The Extraordinary Life of
Jimmy Doolittle*
by Jonna Doolittle Hoppes
360 pages $24.95

Can a Dead Man Strike Out?
*Offbeat Baseball Questions and
Their Improbable Answers*
by Mark S. Halfon
192 pages $11.95

Captured!
Inside the World of Celebrity Trials
by Mona Shafer Edwards
176 pages $24.95

Childish Things
by Davis & Davis
96 pages $19.95

Creepy Crawls
A Horror Fiend's Travel Guide
by Leon Marcelo
384 pages $16.95

The Dog Ate My Resume
by Zack Arnstein and
Larry Arnstein
192 pages $11.95

Elvis Presley Passed Here
*Even More Locations of America's
Pop Culture Landmarks*
by Chris Epting
336 pages $16.95

**Exotic Travel Destinations
for Families**
by Jennifer M. Nichols and
Bill Nichols
360 pages $16.95

Footsteps in the Fog
Alfred Hitchcock's San Francisco
by Jeff Kraft and Aaron Leventhal
240 pages $24.95

French for Le Snob
*Adding Panache to Your Everyday
Conversations*
by Yvette Reche
400 pages $16.95

Haunted Hikes
*Spine-Tingling Tales and Trails from
North America's National Parks*
by Andrea Lankford
376 pages $16.95

How to Speak Shakespeare
by Cal Pritner and
Louis Colaianni
144 pages $16.95

Jackson Pollock:
Memories Arrested in Space
by Martin Gray
216 pages $14.95

James Dean Died Here
*The Locations of America's
Pop Culture Landmarks*
by Chris Epting
312 pages $16.95

The Keystone Kid
Tales of Early Hollywood
by Coy Watson, Jr.
312 pages $24.95

L.A. Noir
The City as Character
by Alain Silver and James Ursini
176 pages $19.95

Loving Through Bars
Children with Parents in Prison
by Cynthia Martone
216 pages $21.95

Marilyn Monroe Dyed Here
*More Locations of America's
Pop Culture Landmarks*
by Chris Epting
312 pages $16.95

Movie Star Homes
by Judy Artunian and
Mike Oldham
312 pages $16.95

My So-Called Digital Life
*2,000 Teenagers, 300 Cameras, and
30 Days to Document Their World*
by Bob Pletka
176 pages $24.95

Offbeat Museums
*The Collections and Curators of
America's Most Unusual Museums*
by Saul Rubin
240 pages $19.95

Quack!
*Tales of Medical Fraud from
the Museum of Questionable
Medical Devices*
by Bob McCoy
240 pages $19.95

Redneck Haiku
Double-Wide Edition
by Mary K. Witte
240 pages $11.95

Route 66 Adventure Handbook
by Drew Knowles
312 pages $16.95

**The Ruby Slippers, Madonna's
Bra, and Einstein's Brain**
*The Locations of America's Pop
Culture Artifacts*
by Chris Epting
312 pages $16.95

**School Sense: How to Help
Your Child Succeed in
Elementary School**
by Tiffani Chin, Ph.D.
408 pages $16.95

Silent Echoes
*Discovering Early Hollywood
Through the Films of Buster Keaton*
by John Bengtson
240 pages $24.95

Tiki Road Trip
*A Guide to Tiki Culture in
North America*
by James Teitelbaum
288 pages $16.95

ORDER FORM 1-800-784-9553

	Quantity	Amount
American Hydrant ($24.95)	_____	_____
Atomic Wedgies, Wet Willies & Other Acts of Roguery ($11.95)	_____	_____
The Bad Driver's Handbook ($12.95)	_____	_____
The Butt Hello . . . and Other Ways My Cats Drive Me Crazy ($9.95)	_____	_____
Calculated Risk ($24.95)	_____	_____
Can a Dead Man Strike Out? ($11.95)	_____	_____
Captured! ($24.95)	_____	_____
Childish Things ($19.95)	_____	_____
Creepy Crawls ($16.95)	_____	_____
The Dog Ate My Resumé ($11.95)	_____	_____
Elvis Presley Passed Here ($16.95)	_____	_____
Exotic Travel Destinations for Families ($16.95)	_____	_____
Footsteps in the Fog: Alfred Hitchcock's San Francisco ($24.95)	_____	_____
French for Le Snob ($16.95)	_____	_____
Haunted Hikes ($16.95)	_____	_____
How to Speak Shakespeare ($16.95)	_____	_____
Jackson Pollock: Memories Arrested in Space ($14.95)	_____	_____
James Dean Died Here: America's Pop Culture Landmarks ($16.95)	_____	_____
The Keystone Kid: Tales of Early Hollywood ($24.95)	_____	_____
L.A. Noir: The City as Character ($19.95)	_____	_____
Loving Through Bars ($21.95)	_____	_____
Marilyn Monroe Dyed Here ($16.95)	_____	_____
Movie Star Homes ($16.95)	_____	_____
My So-Called Digital Life ($24.95)	_____	_____
Offbeat Museums ($19.95)	_____	_____
Quack! Tales of Medical Fraud ($19.95)	_____	_____
Redneck Haiku ($9.95)	_____	_____
Route 66 Adventure Handbook ($16.95)	_____	_____
The Ruby Slippers, Madonna's Bra, and Einstein's Brain ($16.95)	_____	_____
School Sense ($16.95)	_____	_____
Silent Echoes: Early Hollywood Through Buster Keaton ($24.95)	_____	_____
Tiki Road Trip ($16.95)	_____	_____

	Subtotal	_____
Shipping & Handling:	CA residents add 8.25% sales tax	_____
1 book $4.00	Shipping and Handling (see left)	_____
Each additional book is $1.00	TOTAL	_____

Name _____

Address _____

City _____ State _____ Zip _____

☐ Visa ☐ MasterCard   Card No.: _____

Exp. Date _____ Signature _____

☐ Enclosed is my check or money order payable to:

Santa Monica Press LLC
P.O. Box 1076
Santa Monica, CA 90406

www.santamonicapress.com   1-800-784-9553